Indigenous Language Education in Critical Times

LANGUAGE, EDUCATION AND DIVERSITY

Series Editors: **Stephen May**, *University of Auckland, New Zealand*, **Teresa L. McCarty**, *University of California, USA*, **Constant Leung**, *King's College London, UK* and **Serafín M. Coronel-Molina**, *Indiana University Bloomington, USA*

The Language, Education and Diversity series aims to publish work at the intersections of language policy, language teaching and bilingualism/multilingualism, with a particular focus on critical, socially-just alternatives for minoritised students and communities. The series is interdisciplinary, drawing on scholarship from language policy, language education, sociolinguistics, applied linguistics, linguistic anthropology and the sociology of language, including work in raciolinguistics and translingualism. We welcome a variety of methodological approaches, although critical ethnographic accounts are of particular interest.

Topics covered by the series include:

- Bilingual and Multilingual Models of Education
- Indigenous Language Education
- Multicultural Education
- Community-based Education

All books in this series are externally peer-reviewed.

Full details of all the books in this series and of all our other publications can be found on http://www.multilingual-matters.com, or by writing to Multilingual Matters, St Nicholas House, 31-34 High Street, Bristol, BS1 2AW, UK.

LANGUAGE, EDUCATION AND DIVERSITY: 6

Indigenous Language Education in Critical Times

Voices of Community Reclamation in the Americas

Edited by
Julieta Briseño-Roa, Paulina Griñó, Vanessa Anthony-Stevens and José Antonio Flores Farfán

MULTILINGUAL MATTERS
Bristol • Jackson

DOI https://doi.org/10.21832/BRISEN8394
Library of Congress Cataloging in Publication Data
A catalog record for this book is available from the Library of Congress.
Names: Briseño-Roa, Julieta, editor. | Griñó, Paulina, editor. | Anthony-Stevens, Vanessa, editor. | Flores Farfán, José Antonio, editor.
Title: Indigenous Language Education in Critical Times: Voices of Community Reclamation in the Americas /Edited by Julieta Briseño-Roa, Paulina Griñó, Vanessa Anthony-Stevens and José Antonio Flores Farfán.
Description: Bristol; Jackson: Multilingual Matters, 2025. | Series: Language, Education and Diversity: 6 | Includes bibliographical references and index. | Summary: 'This book builds a space in which a diversity of voices – Indigenous teachers, activists and committed academics – are foregrounded in the processes of Indigenous education and language reclamation. It decenters state systems of education, thereby emphasizing diverse processes of language reclamation in complex and varied settings' – Provided by publisher.
Identifiers: LCCN 2025002416 (print) | LCCN 2025002417 (ebook) | ISBN 9781800418387 (paperback) | ISBN 9781800418394 (hardback) | ISBN 9781800418400 (pdf) | ISBN 9781800418417 (epub)
Subjects: LCSH: Indigenous peoples – America – Languages – Revival. | Indigenous peoples – America – Languages – Study and teaching. | Indigenous peoples – Languages – Social aspects – America. | Indigenous peoples – Education – America. | LCGFT: Essays.
Classification: LCC P40.5.L3572 A448 2025 (print) | LCC P40.5.L3572 (ebook) | DDC 497 – dc23/eng/20250220
LC record available at https://lccn.loc.gov/2025002416
LC ebook record available at https://lccn.loc.gov/2025002417

British Library Cataloguing in Publication Data
A catalogue entry for this book is available from the British Library.

ISBN-13: 978-1-80041-839-4 (hbk)
ISBN-13: 978-1-80041-838-7 (pbk)

Multilingual Matters
UK: St Nicholas House, 31-34 High Street, Bristol, BS1 2AW, UK.
USA: Ingram, Jackson, TN, USA.
Authorised Representative: Easy Access System Europe - Mustamäe tee 50, 10621 Tallinn, Estonia, gpsr.requests@easproject.com.

Website: https://www.multilingual-matters.com
Bluesky: @multi-ling-mat.bsky.social
X: Multi_Ling_Mat
Facebook: https://www.facebook.com/multilingualmatters
Blog: https://www.channelviewpublications.wordpress.com

Copyright © 2025 Julieta Briseño-Roa, Paulina Griñó, Vanessa Anthony-Stevens, José Antonio Flores Farfán and the authors of individual chapters.

All rights reserved. No part of this work may be reproduced in any form or by any means without permission in writing from the publisher.

The policy of Multilingual Matters/Channel View Publications is to use papers that are natural, renewable and recyclable products, made from wood grown in sustainable forests. In the manufacturing process of our books, and to further support our policy, preference is given to printers that have FSC and PEFC Chain of Custody certification. The FSC and/or PEFC logos will appear on those books where full certification has been granted to the printer concerned.

Typeset by Riverside Publishing Solutions.

Contents

Contributors	vii
Map	xv
Foreword: Weaving Indigenous Words and Worlds and the Work of Everyday Hope *Elizabeth Alva Sumida Huaman*	xvii
Introduction *Julieta Briseño-Roa, Paulina Griñó, Vanessa Anthony-Stevens and José Antonio Flores Farfán*	1

Part 1: Narratives of Reclamation: Lifework and Learning in Dialogue

1	'We Are Not Going to Be Who We Were Meant to Be if We Don't Speak Our Language': A Dialogue with Language Educators *Julee Dehose, Jennie Burns and Vanessa Anthony-Stevens*	23
2	Nunayaaġviŋmi itut Uvlumini in Anchorage: A Conversation about Language Revitalization and Reciprocal Research Practices *David E.K. Smith and Richard Atuk*	38
3	Reclamation of Language, Stories, Relationship to the Land: Niimíipuu Female as a Storyteller *Angel Sobotta Talaltlílpt*	50
	Poem: Nchií NaáKuú/¿Quién soy?/Who am I? *Celerina Patricia Sánchez Santiago*	68

Part 2: Pedagogies and Practices of Indigenous Language Reclamation in and around Schools

4	Communal Education, Existence of Shared Autonomy *Erika Candelaria Hernández Aragón and Haydée Morales Flores*	73

5   Experiences and Spaces of Opportunity for Work with
    the Ngigua Language   86
    Teresa Damian Jara

6   The Use of Indigenous Languages in Community-Based
    Indigenous Education in Oaxaca, Mx   112
    Beatriz González and Cornelio Hernández Pérez

7   Toward a Methodology of Urban Indigenous Youth
    Language Learning   124
    Ernesto Colín

    Poem: Gidro' Lihdxan/Placenta   138
    Felipe Ruiz Jiménez

Part 3: Redefining Language Learning in Diverse Spaces and Modes

8   Nłt'éégo bénáłdiih: The Dissemination of Ndee Epistemology
    in Contemporary Times   143
    Louie Lorenzo and Philip Stevens

9   Reconnecting to Homelands through Digital Storywork   152
    Jessica Matsaw and Sammy Matsaw

10 Learning from Narratives: Life Stories of Indigenous Students
    in Chilean Graduate Science Programs as Voices of Advocacy
    for University Space Reclamation   165
    *Marta Silva Fernández, Jennifer Brito Pacheco and
    Paulina Griñó*

11 Reflections and Actions on Linguistic Resistance in Formal
    and Informal Spaces as a Proposal for Decolonization in
    Wallmapu/Wajmapu   176
    Carolina Kürüf Poblete, Silvia Calfuqueo and Kelly Baur

    Poem: Kuú teku/Ser de colores/Being of Colours   195
    Celerina Patricia Sánchez Santiago

Epilogue   197
*Julieta Briseño-Roa, Paulina Griñó, Vanessa Anthony-Stevens,
José Antonio Flores Farfán*

Index   203

Contributors

Angel Sobotta, Találtlilpt (Sunset), is Niimíipuu [the People] raised on the Nez Perce Reservation, she lives in Lapwai, Idaho, with her husband, Bob Sobotta Jr. Together, they have four children: Payton, Glory, Grace and Faith Sobotta (ages 24, 22, 21 and 18). In 2024, Angel became an Assistant Professor at Washington State University (WSU), where she teaches Niimíipuu Language and Story and Indigenous Research Methodologies and Methods. Since 1997, she has also served as a language teacher and coordinator for the Nez Perce Language Program (NPLP) and continues to support the program part-time and through her service at WSU. A lifelong learner of the language, she is proficient and deeply committed to its revitalization. With a passion for the arts, Angel integrates storytelling and performance into her teaching to engage students. Her interest in traditional stories has guided her research, focusing on reconnecting students to stories and their historical sites. From 2014 to 2024, she pursued this work in her Master's and Doctoral programs at the University of Idaho. Angel is an active member of the Nez Perce Appaloosa Horse Club, riding the historic Nez Perce Trail in honor of her ancestors. She is also part of the Luk'upsíimey – North Star Collective, a group dedicated to revitalizing the Niimíipuu language through creative writing.

Beatriz González I have lived my work and experience in the area of community-based education. Since 2009 I have collaborated in the project of Indigenous Community Middle Schools in the State of Oaxaca, México, as a community educator, and I am responsible for the area of teacher training. From 2019 to 2023 I had been the State Coordinator of the Indigenous Community Middle Schools. I have collaborated with collectives of teachers of different educational levels in the state of Oaxaca and in the country through workshops and courses in relation to the construction of learning projects and community-based education. I am the regional coordinator of the program, 'Writing as Readers in the State of Oaxaca', developed in Indigenous Community Middle Schools since 2019. From 2020 to 2022 I was part of the team of the Centro Universitario Comunal de Valles Centrales of the Universidad Autónoma Comunal de Oaxaca (UACO) at the Degree in Communality and in the Masters in Communal Education.

Carolina Kürrüf is a Mapuche woman. She is Professor of Physical Education at the University of Santiago de Chile and works at the Catholic University of Temuco as a Professor in Intercultural Pedagogy in the Mapuche context. She will soon be working in the Mapuche Language and Culture Department as well. Her research focuses on ancestral Mapuche games and sports.

Celerina Sánchez was born in Mesón de Guadalupe, San Juan Mixtepec, Santiago Juxtlahuaca, Oaxaca, México. Celerina Patricia Sánchez Santiago is a Ñuu Savi ('People of the clouds' 'Mixtec'), poetess, storyteller, and cultural activist. She holds a degree in linguistics from the National School of Anthropology and History in Mexico. Celerina has participated in several projects for the dissemination and revitalization of Tu'un Savi, the 'language of the rain'. She is a member of the female collective radio broadcasting effort for peace, NOTIMIA, where currently she is the coordinator of the training area. She is a teacher of the Mexico project 'Multicultural Nation' at Mexico's National University (PUIC-UNAM). Last, but not least, together with Victor Gally, a talented armonicist, graphic designer and painter, she developed the musical project Natsika, 'journey', which combines reading her poetry in the language of the rain and resonating her tonal language with Victor's blues and armonica, a unique and innovative musical production of which they have already published a CD and have made many presentations. More information is available at: https://www.mexicanisimo.com.mx/2020/08/natsika-un-viaje-de-poesia-mixteca-y-blues/.

Cornelio Hernández I graduated from the Escuela Normal Bilingüe e Intercultural de Oaxaca (ENBIO). I speak Zapotec, variant Didza' Xidza', native of the community of San Juan Yaee, municipality of the same name, in the district of Villa Alta, Oaxaca, México. I began teaching at the Indigenous Community Middle Schools in 2005; I have almost 20 years' experience in this educational modality. I have participated in educational events with the purpose of sharing my experiences in educational work of this modality with teachers of other secondary modalities. I have served as a community educator and community coordinator in two work centers in the Sierra Norte region of Oaxaca.

David E.K. Smith is from Eagle River, Alaska. Currently, an Assistant Professor in the Center for Indigenous Reaserch at the University of Idaho. An avid musician, composer, and educator, David has taught, written, and performed in Nepal, Uganda, Spain, New Zealand and Alaska. He holds a PhD in social and comparative analysis in education from the University of Pittsburgh, an MA in international education management from the Middlebury Institute of International Studies, and a BA in music composition from Bates College. David's research interests are broadly focused on how the arts can provide transformational educational tools that could be better integrated into both formal and informal schooling, especially among Indigenous populations. His most recent work is an extensive ethnography of two Iñupiaq dance and drumming groups exploring participation of other-than-human members and highlighting potential insights for building more culturally relevant learning experiences.

Erika Candelaria Hernández Aragón is a Zapoteco woman – comunera – from Sierra Sur in Oaxaca. She is an elementary education teacher and higher education educator. She has participated in the co-construction in foundational documents and programs for indigenous education in Oaxaca. Her academic work and research on educational and community projects are oriented to understanding the communal life of native communities and re-signifying local knowledges, identity and languages. Her research interests are community education, gender and syndicalism, teacher education, and educational policies. She was part of the founder team of the Universdidad Autónoma Comunal de Oaxaca, UACO, and co-founder of Department of comunal learning at the Candelaria Loxicha 'Yes Mxil' de la UACO. Currently, she participates in Proyecto Ciencia de Frontera in a 'CONACHyT 2023' – (a funded project through a gobermental agency Consejo Nacional de Humanidades, Ciencias y Tecnologías) with an initiative for the zapotec community in Canderia Loxicha, Oaxaca, MX.

Ernesto Colín is a visual artist, Aztec dancer, and the son of immigrant parents from Mexico. He is an associate professor in the Department of Teaching & Learning at Loyola Marymount University in Los Angeles, California. He holds Bachelor's degrees in Chicana/o studies and Spanish, and a Master's degree in secondary education. He received his doctorate in the anthropology of education from Stanford University. A former public high school teacher, he is a trustee of Anawakalmekak school in Los Angeles. His international research interests include indigenous education, culturally responsive pedagogy, and teacher education. He is the author of *Indigenous Education Through Dance and Ceremony* (Palgrave, 2014), a long-term ethnography of an Aztec Dance group in California.

Felipe Ruiz Jiménez is from Rancho Piedras Negras Quiatoni, Tlacolula Oaxaca, México. I am a speaker of Zapotec from the Central Valley of Oaxaca. I have a bachelor's degree in elementary education with a focus in Indigenous contexts. I studied in the year-long professional certificate program Project SEED in Indigenous education at the University of Arizona in 2012–2013. I am currently an elementary school principal. I have 24 years teaching service.

Haydée Morales Flores is from the state of Oaxaca. She has a PhD in anthropology from Universidad Nacional Autónoma de México (UNAM). Currently, she is part of Universidad Autónoma Comunal de Oaxaca (UACO) as a postdoctoral fellow and as a facilitator in posgraduate programs. Since 2015, she coordinates with Dra Teresa Valdivia Dounce the seminar on 'Anthropology of Power' at the Institute of Research in Anthropology, UNAM. Her main research lines are: territory, common good, and power; socio-environmentalist conflicts and extractivism; communal food systems; and visual anthropology, with a focus on photography. She has conducted research and consultancies to communities and social organizations in the state of Oaxaca.

Jennie Ramona Burns is an advocate for preserving the languages of the Great Basin area in Nevada. She works with three languages: Wasiw, Numu, and Newe. Jennie also worked as a Paiute language instructor for the Washoe County School District for high school students. She gained teaching experience in the classroom, which helped her become more confident to teach adults and pre-school aged children. Currently, her job allows her to work with the Colony's Head Start program. This program is for preschool-aged children and also the classroom teachers. In order for the language to be retained, it is important that all staff be involved with learning the language. Jennie also works with her father, Ralph Burns, first- language speaker of the Paiute language. Her father currently teaches the Paiute language at the University of Nevada–Reno. Jennie's father has mentored her on her journey to preserve the Paiute language.

Jennifer Brito Pacheco is a Chilean mother, teacher and a woman, Master in Education, researcher, and plant and decorative painting lover. Currently, she is a candidate in the doctoral program in Human Sciences, with a focus on discourse and culture. She has worked at different school levels, with projects in drama education, and in teacher professional development. Her research interests are in teacher professional development, inclusive education, and age and aging in southern Chile. She is currently recipient of a Doctoral Fellowship from the Research and Development National Agency (ANID – Agencia Nacional de Investigación y Desarrollo).

Jessica Matsaw (Shoshone–Bannock) is a mother of four children, a wife, gatherer, and matrilineal leader of her family. Jessica is currently a PhD student at the University of Idaho in the College of Education, Health and Human Sciences. Jessica holds a BS in sociology with a minor in psychology, a certificate in diversity and stratification, an MEd in curriculum and instruction, and certifications in secondary education. Jessica works as a research assistant and is the Sho-Ban site coordinator for the University of Idaho's Cultivating Relationships teacher development program focusing on Indigenous land pedagogy and STEM education. Jessica is an alumnus of the Indigenous Knowledge for Effective Education Program (IKEEP) at University of Idaho, which prepares and certifies culturally responsive Indigenous teachers to meet the unique needs of Native American Students in K-12 schools and is currently working with Indigenous high school students interested in becoming teachers. Jessica Matsaw is the co-founder of River Newe (rivernewe.org), a program for Indigenous and minoritized youth to find healing and wholeness in connection with homelands and rivers.

José Antonio Flores Farfán is full Professor of Linguistics and Anthropology at the Centro de Investigaciones y Estudios Superiores en Antropología Social (CIESAS), his home institution, and was recently appointed as Professor Emeritus of the National Council for Research, Humanities and Technology in Mexico (CONAHCYT). He represents Linguapax in Latin America. He has undertaken extensive research on Indigenous languages in Mexico, especially the pragmatics, sociolinguistics and revitalization of Nahuatl. He has also facilitated, produced, and written a series of educational materials aimed at the revitalization of minoritized languages, the accompanying processes of language revitalization and reclamation developed by speakers themselves. One of his passions is writing books for children, together with producing voiceovers, scripts and even music for the materials he envisions.

Julee Dehose is a teacher at Dishchii'bikoh Community School in Cibecue, Arizona. She grew up in Cibecue. Her home is located on the Fort Apache Reservation and she is from the White Mountain Apache Tribe. Julee's clan are Tło'gaa Dogain (Row of White Cane People) born by the Doole' (Butterfly Clan). Julee's parents are Judy Dehose and the late Virgil Dehose Sr. Upon graduating from Dishchii'bikoh High School Julee pursued higher education and went to school in South Korea at Yonsei University Korean Language Institute. She then set forth to New Mexico Highlands University, where she received her Bachelor of Arts and her Master's in sociology. Julee recently achieved her Master's in Elementary Education from Grand Canyon University. Julee's main mission in life is to be a positive role model for the children in her community and to instill culture and language back into the youth while healing historical traumas and giving them back their identity.

Julieta Briseño-Roa is Professor at the Centro de Investigaciones y Estudios Superiores en Antropología Social (CIESAS) in Mexico City. She has focused on the understanding of Indigenous educational realities through ethnographic approaches. She had been working with Indigenous teachers of Indigenous Community Middle Schools in Oaxaca since 2009. Her current research topics are land-based education, community-based pedagogies, and multilingualism.

Kelly Baur is a documentary filmmaker and community organizer who dreams of a future with no police and no borders. She is currently working on a PhD in linguistics/applied linguistics at Arizona State University. Her research focuses on Mapuche language revitalization, language policy, and discourse analysis.

Louis Lorenzo Jr (San Carlos Apache tribe) has 20 years' experience working in prevention program services with adults and youth in the San Carlos Apache community. He is deeply committed to using Apache cultural knowledge to inform strategic-planning efforts such as economic development, higher education, health care, and schooling on the San Carlos Apache Nation. He has participated in the establishment of the Bylas Strategic Tribal Empowerment Prevention Plan, the San Carlos Apache Medicine Society, and the Traditional Healers Advisory Committee. He is currently project director for the Native Connections in the Apache Youth Mentorship.

Marta Silva Fernández is mom to Leonardo, a science fiction fan, and a cat lover and with a Valdivian heart. She is an anthropologist from Universidad Austral de Chile and holds a PhD in education from the University of California. She is Professor for Undergraduate Courses in Social Science Research Methods at Universdiad Austral de Chile. Her research focuses on how indigenous students develop their interest in becoming scientists, with the aim of understanding the dialogue between ancestral and scientific knowledge for the purpose of building universities that are open to diverse knowledges.

Paulina Griñó is mom to Amaya, and is a Professor at the College of Education, Universidad Autónoma de Chile. As a teacher educator, she focuses on science teaching for the Elementary Education and Science Education programs. Her research has focused on documenting science teaching and learning in diverse cultural contexts, exploring our relationships with place and environment.

Philip J. Stevens (San Carlos Apache tribe) is Associate Professor of Anthropology and Director of American Indian studies in the College of Letters, Arts and Social Sciences, University of Idaho. Philip's research interests are in the field of Apache mathematics, 'educational raiding', and the cultural values imparted through the educational process. Philip is married to Vanessa Anthony-Stevens, with whom he has two daughters, Carmen and Hazel.

Richard K. Atuk was born in Wales, Alaska, to Walter and Virginia, who were Wales residents from birth. His grandparents were born in four different locations on the Seward Peninsula and Siberia prior to the 20th century. The family spoke only Inupiaq until they moved to Nome immediately after the end of World War II. Richard graduated from the original Nome High School, then received a degree in geological engineering from the University of Alaska Fairbanks and a Master of business administration from University of Alaska Anchorage. He worked as a petroleum geologist, served two years in the US Army, then worked 30 years for ANCSA (Alaska Native Claims Settlement Act) corporations and affiliates and the state of Alaska and Kenai Peninsula Borough, all in jobs relating to land and general management and administration. He served on the Advisory Committee to the Federal State Land Use Planning Commission. He participated in the Kingikmiut Singers and Dancers of Anchorage and is currently working on documentation of the Kingikmiut (Wales) Inupiaq language.

Sammy Matsaw Jr is a father, husband, grandfather, and extended family member with the Shoshone–Bannock tribes. He is a pipe-carrier and Sundancer with both his mother and father's tribes. Now serving his community on the Fort Hall Business Council, he is an elected member to the Tribal Council of the Shoshone–Bannock Tribes. He was formerly a research scientist where he attained 10+ years of science and management experience involved in Indigenous sovereignty and treaties with the Shoshone–Bannock tribes' Fish and Wildlife department. He also brings 10 years of military experience and leadership as a combat veteran. Lastly, he holds a PhD in Water Resources – Science & Management from the University of Idaho, a Master of Science in conservation genetics, and a Bachelor of Science degree in ecology from Idaho State University. Sammy Matsaw is the co-founder of River Newe (rivernewe.org), a program for Indigenous and minoritized youth to find healing and wholeness in connection with homelands and rivers.

Silvia Calfuqueo Lefio is a Mapuche woman, mother, elementary school teacher, and a weaver. Her work focuses on Mapuche cultural, economic, and linguistic development. She is a teacher at Kom pu lof ñi kimeltuwe, a Mapuche-run school in Mapuche territory, and supports Mapuche youth through a summer film program in her community.

Teresa Damian Jara I was born on January 24, 1980. I am a native speaker of the Ngigua language. I graduated as an elementary education teacher with a focus on Indigenous education in 2005, and earned my Master's degree in educational practice from Universidad Pedagógica Nacional (UPN) in 2020. I participated in a postgraduate program for Strengthening Primary Education for Indigenous Children in Mexico at University of Arizona, USA. In 2019, I participated in the Third Meeting of Living Socio-natural Laboratories Educational *Milpas* in San Cristobal, Chiapas, Mexico and she was selected a fellow scholar by the National Fund for Culture and the Arts (FONCA) for 'Verbal arts records'. During my trajectory as a teacher in Indigenous education I have tried to systematize ways to work with Ngigua language, designing curricular activities that place it as an immersive language. This strategy allowed me to be co-author the book *Pedagogía intercultural 2020 bilingüe desde la cultura ngigua*. In order to reflect upon my daily teaching practice while wanting to transform my own practice within the frame of 'Indigenous language', I attempted to elaborate a strategy that I named 'Dikun, thian, ntha'a ku tangi'. This experience was shared at the Symposium on American Indian Languages – SAIL 2021.

Vanessa E. Anthony-Stevens is an associate professor of social and cultural studies in the Department of Curriculum and Instruction, University of Idaho. Her research examines identity, language, and the production of opportunity through school discourse and educational policies. She specializes in Indigenous education in the Americas and is principal investigator of numerous initiatives centering Indigenous needs and desires in systems of education. Vanessa is married to Philip Stevens and is mother to two daughters.

Map

Indigenous education in critical times

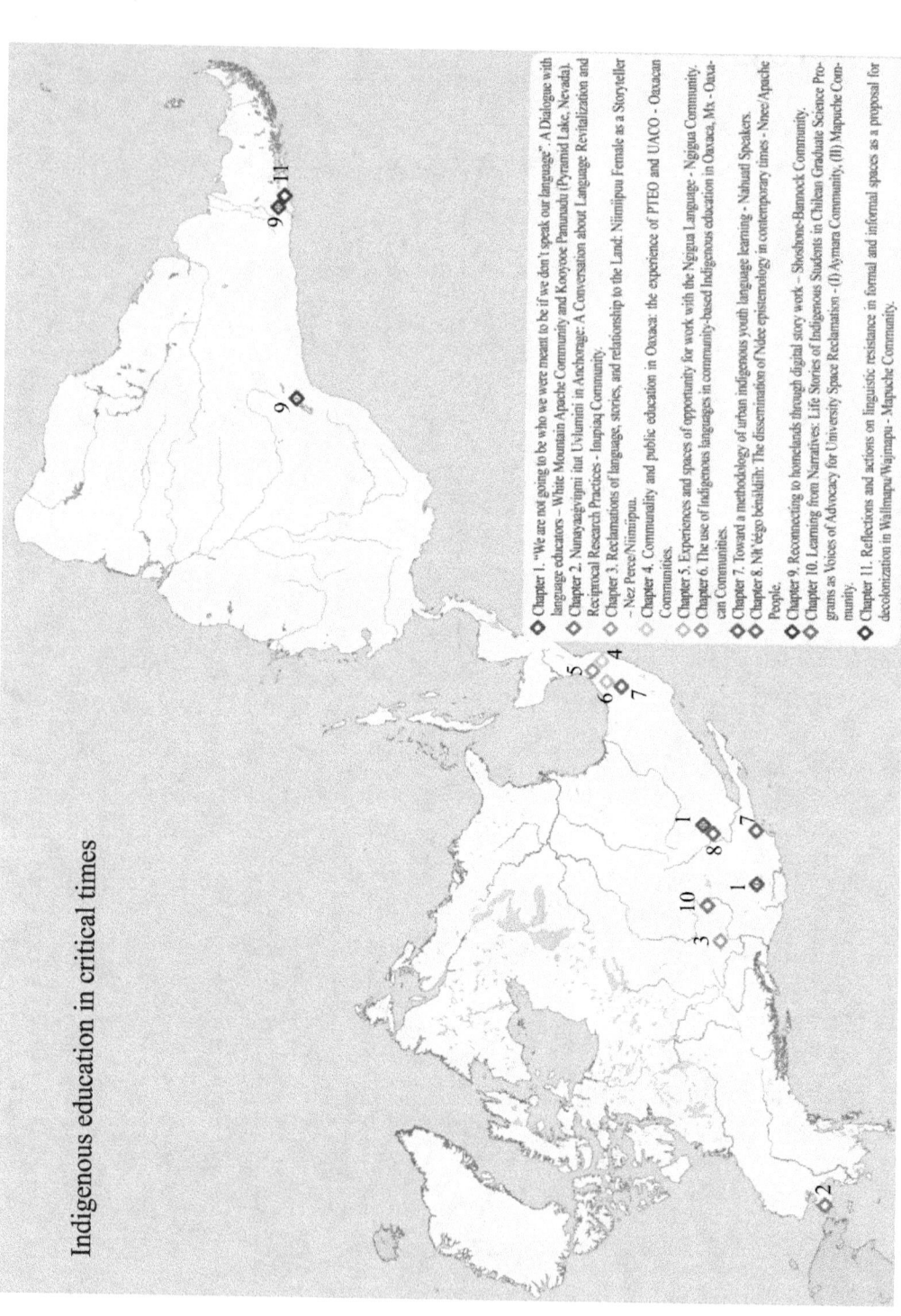

- Chapter 1. "We are not going to be who we were meant to be if we don't speak our language": A Dialogue with language educators – White Mountain Apache Community and Kooyooe Pannundu (Pyramid Lake, Nevada).
- Chapter 2. Numayaagviigmi itut Uwlumini in Anchorage: A Conversation about Language Revitalization and Reciprocal Research Practices - Iñupiaq Community.
- Chapter 3. Reclamations of language, stories, and relationship to the Land: Niimiipuu Female as a Storyteller – Nez Perce/Niimiipuu.
- Chapter 4. Communality and public education in Oaxaca: the experience of PTEO and UACO - Oaxacan Communities.
- Chapter 5. Experiences and spaces of opportunity for work with the Ngigua Language - Ngigua Community.
- Chapter 6. The use of indigenous languages in community-based Indigenous education in Oaxaca, Mx - Oaxacan Communities.
- Chapter 7. Toward a methodology of urban indigenous youth language learning - Nahuatl Speakers.
- Chapter 8. Nłt'éégo benáłdih: The dissemination of Ndee epistemology in contemporary times - Nnee/Apache People.
- Chapter 9. Reconnecting to homelands through digital story work – Shoshone-Bannock Community.
- Chapter 10. Learning from Narratives: Life Stories of Indigenous Students in Chilean Graduate Science Programs as Voices of Advocacy for University Space Reclamation - (I) Aymara Community, (II) Mapuche Community.
- Chapter 11. Reflections and actions on linguistic resistance in formal and informal spaces as a proposal for decolonization in Wallmapu/Wajmapu - Mapuche Community.

Foreword: Weaving Indigenous Words and Worlds and the Work of Everyday Hope

There are many Indigenous worlds that make up this whole and good planet, Teqsimuyu.¹ In the Andean world, there is a principle in Quechua called Yanantin, which is widely understood by Andean Indigenous people as at once philosophical and pragmatic. Yanantin refers to the carefully mediated duality between life and death, darkness and light, and other elements that may appear to be opposites in dominant mainstream thought but that are understood in the Quechua worldview as necessary and interdependent components of existence in the universe. I first learned about this principle as a teenager from my aunts and my cousin,² who apprenticed under them. Known herbalists and healers in our Wanka communities, they grew their own gardens and harvested wild native plants. As we walked through our community or the medicine markets, they would point out male and female parts of plants, differentiating their seeds, and instructing me on how each corresponded with the treatment of the people or animals who needed them. Despite being denied formal schooling, they held knowledge that was passed to them by other women in our family and healers in the region as they cultivated their own learning through rigorous study and experimentation with the natural world. Native women born of the sacrifice and hope of generations of Native women before them is the not-so-distant history that has also birthed me.

For our people across the Tawantinsuyu [the four quarters of Indigenous and Quechua lands], the five centuries that we have spent as subjects is brief in the span of human history – it is not even enough time for an Apu³ to raise themselves and walk across the land, from one place to another. Yet within this blink, across the Andes the colonial workings of European imperialism, including gender-based violence, set forth a modern chronology of oppressive structures and horrific events and patterns, creating a false Yanantin – the accelerated performance of destruction of Andean thought and a new kind of reality to accept. Andean Indigenous people would have to confront the ways in which their 'difference' would be invented and dealt with accordingly through policy – one was either an Indian or a Spaniard, a man or woman, a follower of the European god or the European devil, either bellicose or obedient. The conditions of those identities, crafted by generations under firstly colonization and then coloniality, are today modeled after a capitalist imaginary of so-called modernity (and communicated through English), which its architects fail to see as shortsighted and destructive at small and large scales across the Andes and everywhere. In the Andes, what has resulted among Quechua communities has been a disruption of the Yanantin *within* us as people and, correspondingly, our ability to recognize its workings across the natural world and to act *together* in ways that protect, fix, and (re)generate.

However, also over the last five centuries, there has been negotiation and adaptation, reflecting a kind of co-existence (not to be confused with conviviality) between the differentiators and the differentiated and their descendants who are not in and of themselves complementary opposites but who make up what Aymara scholar Silvia Rivera Cusicanqui calls a ch'ixi world (Rivera Cusicanqui, 2010). Ch'ixi in Aymara (cheqchiy in Quechua) translates to English as spotted or marbled, or distinct colors that can give the appearance of gray or one color from afar. Emerging from this ch'ixi world is the uneasy co-habitation of severely threatened 'local' languages alongside dominant 'global' ones. In Peru alone, the heart of the Tawantinsuyu, among a national population of almost 35 million people, including an Indigenous ancestry majority, approximately 4 million identify as Quechua speakers. There are many reasons for these estimates, which in some regions reflect a gradual decline and in others, a rapid one, but still widely occurring. Some reasons are held in common by the cases presented in this book: explicit and tacit language restrictionism in schools and educational policy, and systemic racism in the name of progress and development, for example. Also, like the stories of reclamation in this volume, there are movements by grassroots community leaders, intellectuals in universities, and Indigenous pop stars who are reclaiming the daily as well as public symbolic presence of Quechua and its different varieties by exhibiting its relevance and beauty across multiple functions. In my view, these efforts are about recovering our recognition of Yanantin, which is indeed a principle of/for/with the universe but also the method by which energies are balanced in the Andean world. For example, in our language, Quechua is nunashimi (Wanka variety) or runasimi (Collao variety), which roughly translate as person-mouth, implying human sound or speech.

Runasimi, like runakuna – people (plural) – is generally not used in reference to non-Quechua languages or people. Runasimi is *our* sound of *our* people, and this is neither discriminatory nor separatist. Instead, the distinction offers clear acknowledgement that *every living being has a language*, that *every language is a gift*, and that *every gift is bound to a set of responsibilities* to people and places, including more than human beings.

When early weapons of human and Earth destruction were wielded in Peru in the 1500s, the breath of living beings was taken and, over time, the people became separated from their sound. This trajectory has nothing to do with capability, and everything to do with politics: it is part of a pattern of Indigenous people being denied their gift and of responsibilities waiting to be reclaimed. In this volume, Richard Atuk (Chapter 2) likewise reflects:

> The biggest challenge to Inupiat teachers on a global level is to communicate to their own people the benefits of learning an additional language, their own language, when English is taught in school and their parents speak English. The English language excels as a means of communication in the modern world.... However, the English language is distant, sterile, and clinical when applied to Inupiat history, lifestyles, and ways of being and believing. When you consider the biological and genetic long-term connections of people to their past, using English only effectively severs Inupiat from their own history and their own sense of being.

In this precious space, authors like Richard and his co-author David E.K. Smith, who are working with these languages, have opened windows to their Indigenous worlds, generously sharing both painful severances and the strategies for healing that they have embraced or created. They have chosen to be in fellowship with each other and readers by telling the stories of what it means to actually live language learning and teaching daily, and to hold faithful to what Ngigua teacher Teresa Damian Jara (this volume, Chapter 5) refers to as the 'pact' to safeguard their languages as they acknowledge both the brutal odds stacked against them and their beloved communities and the 'resistance and vitality' of their languages and speakers. They bare their hearts to those of us who are on the other side of the pages that they have written. And what they have written *together* is a book about aliveness and spirit. It is a book about how people process what has been taken, and how they labor and dream for their and your children to make a better reality. As Matsaw and Matsaw (this volume, Chapter 9) eloquently write:

> Our children moved fluidly with us, mimicking our hunting trips or gathering medicine as they sat in observation within massive lecture halls, still gathering teachings but in a different way. We would bring

little brown faces to academic events that were not inviting for our children. We knew [that] the importance of traditional parenting in these moments of disrupting institutional norms were opportunities for folks in academia to take pause. For our children to feel secure regardless of being away from our tribal community and culture, we had to model to the best of our ability what it meant to be Shoshone–Bannock.

Theirs is a moving testimony, a kind of life poetry that is emblematic of the purpose in each contribution in this volume and all Indigenous writers, thinkers, orators, teachers, little ones, and our more than human relatives – those who know how speak *from within* and not above.[4]

As a family and community member who is a language learner, I too am discerning the spaces where I am not and will not be represented and where I can fully be myself – my grandparents' farm fields, the ceremonial houses, walks by our rivers, praying on the mountain, cooking with my relatives, are all places and times when we hear and speak, when we work to restore the balance. As an educational researcher, I also am deeply invested in all the different gifts that our people and children need to draw upon to remember who they are, including how we engage language with each other and across the life that emerges from our lands, that *is* our lands. Thus, the editors' vision for this collection – to be in good relationship with the very efforts of reclamation in and through the offer of this gift of words and worlds – is a stunning reminder that honors 'the people doing the work in places that matter', a powerful assertion as Indigenous communities in the Americas and globally battle their own erasure.

In spite of the chaos and confusion that coloniality wreaks upon Kay Pacha, This Earth, I believe that we, all Indigenous relations and our friends, have not yet lost ourselves. We are not done. Each of us holds what the editors call stories and teachings of 'everyday survival'. We also hold in our bodies and hands *everyday hope*, described by Māori scholar Joanna Kidman as:

> Everyday hope is not a grand or sweeping gesture. It is quieter and much more mundane. It speaks to the small, quotidian moments that happen in the passage of a day or a month or a year and which are the building blocks of our daily lives. That is often where real change begins. (Kidman, 2018: 7)

Kidman called for Indigenous research to transform education not only through rigorous scholarship but also through highly personalized and interpersonal gestures that emerge from the connections between researchers and their cultures – acts that are brilliantly illustrated by Dehose, Burns and Anthony-Stevens (this volume, Chapter 1), whose stories and conversations reflect 'decolonial possibility that lives with communities, land, and non-academic life'.

Decolonial possibility is beauty, and beautiful possibility is decoloniality. I conclude this foreword with one of the most beautiful beginnings to something that was shared with me a few years ago. This is an artist's statement for a painting titled 'Light from Love', by Tewa artist Eliza Naranjo-Morse (2023). Her work reminds us that we each have something important to do, paths to travel, and while the trails may be hidden or unclear, we move together. Thank you to the authors of this volume, the visionary editors, and all your communities, for letting us (who are your audience and relatives from different places) hear your breath, thank you for sharing your light.

Trails had disappeared their own lifetimes ago
and the pilgrimage continued.
At some point along the quiet way each realized time was left
behind and color within their prayers became focused on the
particular hue of previously unknown possibility.

Hearing breath beyond their own fed their limbs.

It was the light of love for others that had been guiding each of
them all along.

Elizabeth Alva Sumida Huaman
Minneapolis, Minnesota, United States
August 31, 2024

Notes

(1) Literally translated from Quechua to English as 'beginning circle' (Mannheim, 1986) and can be used to describe Planet Earth. Spoken and written Quechua can take various forms. Even across the same variety, speakers will have different ways of saying words that are mutually intelligible but that may at the same time hold a local or regional flavor to their pronunciation. It is the opinion of this author that spellings of these words ought to try to honor these differences, even if they may not always follow written precedent. The Quechua words used in this foreword are influenced by the Collao variety of Quechua, and any errors are the author's own.
(2) I name these teachers: Mama Yola (Yolanda Herrera Borja), my mother's sister-in-law through marriage to Acisclo Huaman Carhuamaca; Mama Mari (Marina Huaman Carhuamaca), my mother's sister; and Herminia Salazar Huaman, my first cousin, daughter of Flora Huaman Carhuamaca and raised by our grandmother.
(3) Apu is the term for a mountain being, a more than human deity with a history, family, and an ecosystem of life that the Apu stewards or watches. Here I am referring to the story of Huallallo Carhuancho, also known as Waytapallana, who is said to have walked over time to reach our lands.
(4) I acknowledge my mentor, friend, writing partner, and Ko'o Dr Tessie Naranjo (Tewa/Kha'p'o Owingeh) for this way of explaining writing that enters one's heart and that moves with the listener rather than top-down.

References

Kidman, J. (2018) Comparatively speaking: Notes on decolonizing research. *The International Education Journal: Comparative Perspectives* 17 (4), 1–10.

Mannheim, B. (1986) The language of reciprocity in southern Peruvian Quechua. *Anthropological Linguistics* 28 (3), 267–273.

Naranjo-Morse, E. (2023) Artist's statement. In E. Sumida Huaman and N.D. Martin (eds) *Indigenous Research Design: Transnational Perspectives in Practice* (p. xii). Canadian Scholars.

Rivera Cusicanqui, S. (2010) *Ch'ixinakax utxiwa: Una reflexión sobre prácticas y discursos descolonizadores*. Tinta Limón.

Introduction

Julieta Briseño-Roa, Paulina Griñó,
Vanessa Anthony-Stevens and
José Antonio Flores Farfán

During the height of the pandemic year, we met digitally, reflecting upon several issues: the impact of confinement on our lives, both positive and negative; on our academic work and our social-epistemic commitment and, outstandingly, the possibilities of collective construction of knowledge and reclamation practices between Indigenous peoples and academics. Inspired by critical decolonial scholar Leigh Patel (2015), we asked ourselves: 'Why this? Why us? Why now?' to bring a heightened sense of intentionality and to attend to relationality in the compiling of this book. In this respect *Indigenous Language Education in Critical Times: Voices of Community Reclamation in the Americas* arose from those collective reflections looking to address those questions, and from our desires to invest in academic conversations grounded in meaningful change for, by, and with Indigenous people and communities. Drawn from individual backgrounds and history of professional work in Indigenous education, and beyond, we dived in, blending languages, planning across global time zones, and transcending borders, to engage with our colleagues in forwarding the *practice* of space-making for a diversity of voices: namely, Indigenous teachers, community activists and committed academics. We desired to invest our academic skillset to highlight Indigenous language reclamation as critically vital community-driven social action. Our concerns for Indigenous education de-center mandates from state systems of education, i.e. schooling. Rather, we were drawn to consider the efforts of teachers (defined broadly), community activists, and scholars who are developing initiatives to invest in and support Indigenous language reclamation practices in, around, and beyond schooling; therefore, emphasizing diverse processes of language reclamation in complex and diverse lands and settings, led by people and collectives in a variety of roles.

The global pandemic acutely underscored the shortfall of official educational policies in effectively facing larger social, economic and digital inequities in the Americas for decades, if not centuries; inequities which continue to impact Indigenous populations the hardest –

for instance, the passing of many elders, limited health care services, and rural isolation experienced during the pandemic, not to speak of monolingual, one-language-one-nation schooling ideologies. Even so, the pandemic also allowed, in specific contexts, reflection upon, and reconnection with, Indigenous pedagogies and land (e.g. territorial) education, still very poorly documented in the academic literature.

But the global climate crisis is a fact that impacts us all. In many latitudes the consequences of neocolonial exploitation have placed responsibility on Indigenous peoples to subvert this situation, yet as Davi Kopenawa, Yanomami spokesperson and tribal justice advocate, states: the responsibility belongs to us all. In this context, it is fundamental to reflect on how the relationship between education and cultural and linguistic landscapes connect, and how physical, social, and linguistic territories have been re-shaped in recent years.

Who are we to promote this work? We have found, across our careers, that waiting for the colonial-formed academy to be/come a partner in projects of Indigenous sovereignty is a waste of our time. Instead, we – descendants of settlers to the Americas and Indigenous peoples from the Americas alike – commit to *participating* in the work of dismantling colonial-informed knowledge hierarchies, and to engaging in interdisciplinary, cross-contextual, and applied projects to support Indigenous sovereignty, well-being, and land rematriation. It is important to know who we are in this work.

Julieta has accompanied community education processes and Indigenous teachers for more than 11 years. She is starting her professional career as an anthropologist of education, considers it fundamental to contribute to land-based education as a form of cultural reclamation, defense of the territory, and actions against the climate catastrophe.

Poli, daughter of a Spanish-language art teacher and born in Santiago, Chile, land of Picunche people, is a science teacher educator. Her experience is centered around elementary teacher education and classroom connections to the territory and locality, contributing to the vindication of traditional community practice in teaching and schooling. Currently, she is part of educational initiatives that re-connect community knowledge into school curricula.

Vanessa was born of second- and third-wave European immigrants to the USA and raised in the region referred to as 'Chicagoland', homelands of the Peoria, Myaamia, Ho-Chunk, Potawatomi, and other Indigenous peoples. As a former schoolteacher and current teacher educator and educational anthropologist, Vanessa's more than 20-year career in Indigenous educaton and Tribal Nation-building efforts centers on practices and policies of educational sovereignty. She is a partner in an Apache family through marriage and mother to Apache daughters, making the professional also intimate in the space of Indigenous knowledge persistence and political action.

José is a sociolinguist and activist in support of linguistic rights. Born in the Yucatan, Mexico, José's ancestry includes his Maya grandfather. José was deprived from the Maya language at a very early stage, seeking reconciliation with this trauma through his work with several Indigenous communities over the past few decades, producing materials in diverse Indigenous languages that not only allow gaining visibility but occupying and innovating spaces for the vindication of minoritized languages.

Experiences navigating during two years of pandemic crises highlight the call for scholars, activists, and educators to re-consider deeply what is language reclamation today and to re-prioritize material and symbolic investment in decolonial futures. We join voices in this book to consider the possibilities offered by liminality and new seasons. Facing several contradictions and conflicting forces, such as the schooling paradox, sites where critical knowledge is suppressed, we look to center the wisdom that in-between spaces offer. By in-between spaces, we mean the creativity and agency of speakers in intersectional settings, such as celebrating Indigenous peoples coming back to their lands and languages, and Indigenous language speakers exploring new ways to gift their languages to a new generation. Voices in this volume offer an unapologetic break from received parasitic paradigms that perpetuate inequitable power structures, such as considering Indigenous peoples as perpetual informants whose knowledge is appropriated by colonial institutions. Together with several creative expressions and proposals carried out by the agentivity of Indigenous peoples themselves, this book features a wide collection of contemporary formats – poetic, musical, and narrative, among others – to cultivate conditions for language expression as thriving guidelines and philosophies for how to 'live well' in our planet.

By reclamation, we are inspired by Myaamia linguist Wesley Leonard's (2017) definition to catapult the efforts of Indigenous communities to claim, enact and expand their rights to speak and live in their languages holistically. Leonard describes reclamation as beginning with community histories linked with contemporary needs. Further, he underscores language work as never independent from the environment in which speakers live: hence, reclamation requires an ecological approach that expands the frame of engagement to include 'non-linguistic' forms of community knowledge transmission and meaning-making, in place and across generations. In other words, reclamation does not disentangle language as a separate 'object' from speakers but, rather, it treats language as the very core of our multilayered social lives. We are careful to state that we are not focused on reclamation as a new or novel practice. The voices in this volume shed light on the persistence of Indigenous peoples and worldviews through times of violence, oppression, and massive environmental change. As Leonard points out with other Indigenous language scholars in the global north, centering Indigenous education in its many modes and forms 'represents the forward-looking legacy of the survivors of assimilation programs' and 'offers broader lessons on the role of language in individual and communal well-being' for all peoples (McCarty *et al.*, 2018: 161). Centering the everyday experiences of Indigenous educators committed to Indigenous continuance, those who act and reflect, and act again, allows us to spend time learning from the diversity of ways people are doing extraordinary things and to braid together new and old curriculum maps for nourishing Indigenous languages. These practices do not occur in one form or one mode, but in relationships that link people, land, water, and other-than-humans as critical orientations that have been central to Indigenous self-determination and current and future well-being.

Indigenous Ecologies at the Center of Language Reclamation

We asked ourselves several related questions in order to understand the complex ecologies of power in language reclamation. For instance: Why do we need another book on this matter? What are some of the conditions we have (still) not thought about that are relevant for this work? First of all, we found ourselves interested to further dislodge colonial notions of language hierarchies, such as the concept of 'endangered' languages, which in and by itself already entails a fatalistic, passive view on the future of minoritized languages. Such concepts facilitate a disconnect from engaging in the social and economic conditions enabled and obfuscated by colonialism, a paradigm that sees knowledge as hierarchical, lands as exploitable, and minoritization as a natural consequence of universalizing truth. We believe more attention should be paid to the ways that scholars of multilingual education study language use and language instruction through an ecology-of-language approach, an approach which recognizes the dynamics of power between language and its speakers, and the importance of cultivating and sustaining the use of languages that are marginalized in other sectors of society (Haugen, 1972; Hornberger, 2009). The ecological approach asks us to see interactions between languages and their environment(s) as relational, and co-existing. The symbiosis between language and environment is social and includes relations of power and identity (Hornberger, 2009), for better or worse. We emphasize an ecological approach to language as foundational to theorizing social movements, by, with, and for local peoples. However, we also recognize that such ideas, while novel in the academy, are not new *per se*.

Indigenous thought has always been rooted in ecologies of relational and situated meaning-making. Tewa philosopher, Greg Cajete (2000: 46), states: 'Indigenous people are people of place, and the nature of place is embedded in their language'. Indigenous Knowledge of the natural world is based on a massive accumulations of empirical knowledges continuing over generations and through relations among humans and place (Cajete, 1994; Kawagley, 2006; Stevens, 2021). Indigenous philosophies underscore the necessity of a holistic, ecological approach to education as necessary for 'Life's sake' (Cajete, 1994: 227). Placing Indigenous language education within Indigenous *ecologies of knowing* provides a more holistic paradigm to understand knowing, being, and living in relation to place, human and more-than-human-beings. As such, an ecological approach that privileges place 'represent(s) significant epistemological and ontological departures from those that have emerged in Western frames' (Tuck & McKenzie, 2015: 51). Said this way, we can recognize that languages do not become constrained in isolation, and Indigenous Peoples, language, and Indigenous Knowledge Systems have not been passive over centuries of interaction with colonial institutions and policies.

With this book, we believe it remains important to trouble the inequitable power dynamics of who gets to decide how to document languages and what efforts are acknowledged as meaningful in the revitalization process. Turning away from the passive mainstream paradigm of language documentation and even revitalization, which continues to decontextualize language from social and cultural practice and force Indigenous languages into the blandness of grammar and rote memorization common in Euro–Western school formats, conceiving speakers as 'informants', is sorely needed. While we have strong examples of Indigenous-led grassroots efforts of language education, most academic language documentation and applied linguistic work continues to deny the agency of speakers to reclaim and re-create their languages and cultures (McIvor, 2020), bordering on a 'covert racism' (Kroskrity, 2021), in which even telling phrasings such as 'salvage' linguistics are formulated. As scholars of Indigenous language revitalization point out, partnerships and collaborations in language reclamation efforts must be developed based in understandings defined by the 'self-determined and self-governed' (McIvor, 2020: 91). Stances such as engaged (socio)linguistics, active documentation or even biolinguistics, are all contemporary paradigms that can work to close divides between language activism and committed academics, call into account the responsible agentivity necessary for constructive practices led by Indigenous people themselves to define processes and conditions that support the flourishing of their language and cultures (for more on this see Flores Farfán & Ramallo, 2010). We also overwhelmingly center our efforts in adult education (e.g. teachers) and institutional spaces (e.g. schooling), which, no matter how important they are (and they are indeed crucial inasmuch former colonial spaces are reoccupied), are never enough to reverse language shift and advance language reclamation practices.

When we consider what is still needed to further the field of Indigenous language reclamation work, centering reclamation practices that demonstrate the beauty of collectives, explicitly bringing together educators with formal, experiential, an outside-of-institutional education is critical. In this regard, inviting authors to engage in collaborative writing to reach multiple audiences, including mainstream populations, together with land, children and youth in multiple settings and formats, is a goal of this book. It is no accident that each chapter underscores attention to land-based education and place-based pedagogies (Penetito, 2009; Simpson, 2014; Styres, 2017), an important theme threaded throughout this book. Land-based education implies a connection with self-in-relationship with the land. As a philosophy and educational strategy, land-education allows linking new generations in different ways with ancestral homelands and with the knowledge that is transmitted by being in relationship with territory and with the animacy of the living and other-than-living beings that inhabit it. Placing relationality with the land (e.g. territorio) and with all the living beings that inhabit it at the center of the education of children and youth maintains and promotes holistic, contextual, place-based ways of knowing central to Indigenous and Native peoples since time immemorial. As seen in many of the chapters in this volume, practices of land-based education mean returning to ways of sharing and learning that have been silenced for decades, and in some cases centuries. As Louie Lorenzo and Philip Stevens (this volume, Chapter 8) write, homelands enable an individual to 'remember who you are, where you are coming from, and where you are going'. As Nnee (the people), Apache consider themselves to be children of the earth with all other living beings that exist within their homeland as co-equals. Indigenous paradigms remind us that land is a partner in knowledge co-production, not just a source of extraction and manipulation, as is common in Euro–Western views of land and place. Therefore, education *is always* in relationship with land: recontextualizing learning with Indigenous homelands is a way of reclaiming one's own existence. For Sumida Huaman, land as a central theme of Indigenous education restores and maintains the connections between the spaces, the language, and the ritual practices, which is why the school itself 'becomes a "sanctuary" space for Indigenous knowledge' (Sumida Huaman, 2020: 268).

In recent decades, efforts have been made to (re)build land-based education spaces, outside, inside and alongside schools, in Indigenous territories. Tinirau *et al.* (2020) show the importance of strengthening traditional ways of learning between children, the young, and the elders with river-based activities. Including elders in these examples of learning is indispensable for the reconnection between generations and the value of knowledge based on local experiences and wisdom. Practices such as walking through the different landscapes have demonstrated the value of recognizing the place where the new generations belong, the ancestral knowledge and the responsibility towards kinships. Additionally, the power of the arts – and especially music and multimedia formats, should not be undermined in the processes of language reclamation. Several experiences around the world have shown us the diversity of positive performances that have allowed Indigenous creators to flourish in different ways while producing different pieces of art, becoming role models for their communities, elevating Indigenous social prestige, not to speak of enabling Indigenous creators to construct a modus vivendi. In this respect, in the last few decades, we have seen the emergence (reaching general audiences) of different linguistic and cultural expressions in Indigenous languages that previously remained as local experiences. Together with a growing cinema production in Indigenous languages (Córdova, 2017), new generations have joined artistic movements such as rap, hip-hop, TikTok videos, to (re)claim the use of platforms and social networks as their own (Cru, 2018; Flores Farfán & Cru, 2020; Llanes Ortiz, 2020). Although many examples in this text focus on school experiences, we have included other expressions which celebrate the wealth of Indigenous languages and cultures and, of course, remind us that we cannot conceive language reclamation as an (one space) isolated effort but must do so as a whole ecosystem. Therefore, we include three poems to show the power of the arts in language reclamation. The world of poetry in Indigenous languages has produced a growing and robust corpus – for instance in Mexico – providing visibility and demonstrating the equal value of minoritized languages, not only among Indigenous communities but even among the public, enabling Indigenous authors to raise their voices. The poems are by Ñu Savi ('Mixtec') poetess Celerina Patricia Sánchez, who also carries out the musical project Natsiká, 'Travesía/Journey' and Diixazá ('Zapotec') poet Felipe Ruiz, who is also a teacher and language activist.

We hope that the themes that weave their way through this book will inspire readers to contemplate how Indigenous language reclamation is essential for planetary well-being and colonial healing. In turn, we invite readers to consider ways to develop new awarenesses of multilingualism as a societal benefit and to deepen our collective commitments to living multilingualism in whatever ambient one has influence. We would like to open up these contemplations by sharing them with the reader, not as closed answers but rather as open questions that the book hopefully will inspire various responses to and that continue a trajectory of sharing diversity in complex forms and representations: for instance, the connections and conflicts between institutional life (e.g. schools) and ways of everyday survival and (institutional or not) adaptation and accommodation, negotiating and constructing different (at times conflicting) identities, appealing to speakers' agency and creativity as a never ending important topic which criss-crosses all the book's contributions.

Other outstanding issues raised by this book encompass facing colonial trauma without reproducing victimizing schemes. Examples of facing colonial trauma take shape in persisting to learn and grow while appropriating colonial heritages and aesthetics (see, for example, Chapter 7 by Colín, on the Cantares Mexicanos); striving to heal colonial wounds in innovative and creative manners (see Chapter 9 by Matsaw and Matsaw), such as opening up space for talking about one's life histories (see Chapter 3 by Angel Sobotta); and appealing to autobiographical methods (see Chapter 5 by Teresa Damian Jara), in which people open themselves up to vulnerability while at the same time raising their voice against oppression, pursuing personal and collective emancipation. Therefore, the different texts in this book show the importance of focusing on the actions people perform in their language reclamation contexts, from a situated perspective.

Thus, the interest of the book and of us as editors, is to be in good relationship with efforts of reclamation and to gift the academic community with a fresh perspective from the field. Brought together with intention and long-term relationships, we asked ourselves how we can elevate the work of those conceiving languages as part of the counter-power that forms different (e.g. cognitive) territories of reclamation, and engages collective resistance to the climate crisis and genocidal governmental policies. Collectively, the pages of this text show how small and local efforts that may be invisible to those not directly involved build powerful networks of love and strength. Like the mycelia of the fungi kingdom, invisible but strong, the actions of local communities described in each chapter look to unite – throughout the continent – teachers and committed community members and engaged activists, who daily work to develop practices for the defense of their territories, environment and those who live in them, reclaiming the teachings in their languages.

Let us insist that although the focus of this book is mainly on instances that take place inside schools, we recognize the fundamental role for the reclamation and retention of languages taking place in and around schooling. As a basic premise of our reflections, intergenerational relationships and community practices outside schools are paramount, including the crucial role of grandfathers and grandmothers in passing on minoritized languages to the new generations, transmitting the sensitive cultural and linguistic practices linked to the agricultural, domestic, economic values, rooted in their cultural and linguistic diversity. In other words, we recognize that new generations are formed by learning together in practice with the elders, a 'hands in' approach, transforming each other together (Lave, 2019). In this respect, Indigenous communities have long histories of participatory learning structures that socialize young children into a community's 'curriculum' through 'being there', e.g. seeing, hearing, feeling, as adults carry out essential responsibilities and community roles (Romero-Little, 2011). Each chapter is a window into worlds where educators and activists are laboring to give children and new language learners the best possible seat or role for actively observing, listening-in on events, and participating in purposeful activities under the care of knowledge community members.

Language Reclamation in the Americas

Recovering sustainable and respectful relationships with mother earth should be the center of language reclamation work. We state this without romanticizing the complex and diverse reality in which Indigenous people live. Many Indigenous communities today are in severe crisis. Recognizing the outstanding place of Indigenous communities' past, present and future wisdom in facing colonial adversity and confronting all types of climate and planetary change, is a matter of social justice for oppressed peoples. We draw hope, despite all the genocidal and linguistic global threats to mother earth, in listening to and sharing the everyday practices of an otherwise, that is theories of being outside the colonial gaze and their innumerable solutions to our pressing challenges. As Wanka Quechua scholar Elizabeth Sumida Huaman and Nathan Martin (2020) advocate, humanity must be defined along local and non-Western terms to enable consideration of decolonial openings, and to engender greater understandings of equity and rights. Here, we too want to prioritize philosophies and practices outside the colonial gaze and offer local examples to contribute to 'the idea that we can re-envision the world through an alternative perspectives and ways of being by recognizing the epistemic limitations of our current conditions and embracing our own agency to articulate, remember, and create something different' (Sumida Huaman & Martin, 2020: 10).

In this respect, this book is also an invitation to go beyond pessimistic received paradigms in the academic world, subverting the orthodox making of research and its ideologies. For instance, turning to land pedagogies and community-based education, contesting predominant necro-linguistic biases reflected in labels such as 'rustic', 'semi-speaker', 'obsolete', or even 'endangered languages', uncritical notions of passive documentary linguistics, to which we oppose a biolinguistic approach, highlighting and accompanying the agency of speakers that allows the emergence of neo-speakers or the awakening of dormant languages, among other reclamation efforts, which of course are linked to leveling power relationships, asserting political, ideological and territorial vindications together, healing colonial wounds.

Context Review of Indigenous Language Reclamation Efforts in the Americas

Elevating the voice of Indigenous educators allows understanding of the ways in which teachers negotiate national and local ideological assumptions about curriculum mandates and pedagogical processes, recognizing policies as situated sociocultural practices involving 'modes of human interaction, negotiation, and production mediated by relations of power' (McCarty, 2004: 72, cited in Castagno & McCarty, 2018). Quechua linguist Serafín Coronel-Molina (2017: 1) writes: 'The Americas are a multilingual, pluricultural, and multiethnic territory where asymmetrical relationships of political, economic, sociocultural, and linguistic power have existed for centuries despite all the efforts that have been made to alleviate these situations'. Asymmetrical power relationships make sharing and documenting the rich practices, negotiations, and sociolinguistic transformations within social institutions that constrain Indigeneity remarkable. The sophisticated sense in the making of critical education policies among Indigenous teachers and collectives illuminates how teachers are active policymakers playing critical roles as frontline mediators through their own language epistemologies and identities, accommodating and responding to formal schooling (Menken & García, 2010). Even in cases where national policies allegedly support multilingual education, such as Mexico and Federal Indian Self-Education policy in the US, interrupting long-standing deficit assumptions about Indigenous languages and their place in the broader society is at stake (Cortina, 2014). The everyday and innovative figuring of educator and community activist actions are complex and central to our motivation to explore how decolonization occurs alongside and outside the colonial gaze. In times of crisis, such as the global pandemic, exacerbated economic inequality and global climate change, the paradoxical co-existence of vibrance and innovation alongside devastation and oppression, affirming Indigenous voices is a resource of radical hope for a new century.

The so-called Americas are as diverse as their people. Despite centuries of ongoing oppression, a series of vindications has nonetheless occurred in such a huge territory, re-naming and re-inventing Indigenous spaces in the face of colonial histories, movements which have in common different ways of decolonizing Indigenous peoples and Indigenous societies. From the Wallmapu to the Inuit territories, Indigenous peoples have been and are struggling not only to survive but also to revitalize, recover, regain, and reverse language shift, reclaiming and vindicating their ancestral practices, while at the same time inhabiting the modern world, in which languages play a definite role, linked to a holistic view of sociocultural life. Indigenous agency opposes the compartmentalization and mystification to which Western society has looked to subjugate their indigeneities, among other things, setting up museums' views of decontextualized 'cultural artifacts', or studying 'Indigenous languages' thought of as close-knit systems, as totally detached objects from their speakers – an extractivist gesture in itself – so typical of contemplative mainstream colonial extractivist anthropology or linguistics.

Opposing and conflicting such individualistic conceptions of the self, Indigenous peoples have become global references in terms of the hope that humanity requires for its continuity as a species, appealing and practicing ecological respect for mother earth and related inhabitants, going beyond anthropocentric views of the multiple contradictory and conflicting worlds we are living in. From opposing the Dakota Access Pipeline oil pipeline by several tribes in the north of the hemisphere, passing through the Maya Zapatista movement which has become an obligatory referent of Indigenous autonomy and sovereignty, to the endured resistance of the Mapuche people, to retain their territory in the southernmost part of the continent, in the Wallmapu, all these mobilizations have commonality as one of their utmost values, together with a set of other core axiologies and ontologies, such as reciprocity and collaborative communal work (Tequio, Minga), to which committed anthropologists or linguists are turning to as a much more sociocentric, collective approach to human life and its production and reproduction.

Abya Yala (The 'Americas') is the homeland of one of the most diverse (linguistic) landscapes of the world, a relational inter-twinning of people and place. The unique and diverse language experiences linked to its vast territory and cultural practices include almost all types of languages, ranging from tonal ones, as represented in this book by Diixazá or Nguiwa, to rich vocal systems that allow the production and reproduction of robust sociolinguistic identities with a wealth of unique sound repertoires and distinct ways of speaking and verbal art, endemic to their territories, linked to language ecologies struggling to maintain their ever changing and dynamic oral storytelling diversity, adjusting and accommodating to contemporary contexts, multiple worlds and struggles.

Abya Yala has historically experienced diverse ways of colonization, ranging from the (almost) total devastation of original languages and cultures and, of course, their people, especially in the north and most southern parts of the continent, where extreme genocide took place (almost) wiping out entire Indigenous populations, to other more subtle ways of colonial oppression, such as that which occurred in what today are the countries of Mexico and Peru, in which, to a certain extent, a more 'humanistic' approach to (religious) Indigenous assimilation was apparent, based on the study and use of original languages by Spanish missionaries, such as Nahuatl and Quechua. As is well known, these general languages were recast, and ironically even expanded, for purposes of evangelization and religious conversion. The creative ways in which, in their heterogeneity, Indigenous people faced and are still facing religious and other forms of colonial imposition and oppression speak of peoples' resistance and resilience: for instance, often incorporating their ancestral theologies into the new imposed one, producing a series of cultural and ideological amalgams, telling of the capacity of Indigenous people not only for survival but for ensuring their languages and cultures endure.

The People Doing the Work in Places that Matter

Contributors in this book encourage the readers to see, hear, feel, and live language reclamation efforts as multifaceted and relational, embodied in mundane, explicit, and innovative ways. We highlight living experiences drawn from Indigenous knowledge that move to reclaim, restore and protect local-based epistemologies (Sumida Huaman & Martin, 2020), anchored in the role of the arts, wellness, school, and community efforts alike in the voice of their own practitioners.

The authors encourage readers to question categories constructed from top–down approaches to identity and language use, such as 'Indigenous' and 'Indigenous education', or 'language' itself, as well as the colonial relationships that anthropology, especially linguistic anthropology and linguistics, has constructed within the spaces and people it 'studies' as objects. Across the chapters, the guiding thread is a transition to the familiarity of narratives as knowledge regarding community-based collaborations, an embrace of the local and lived experiences to subvert asymmetrical power relations between academia and educational practitioners and activists. Thus, the book itself is an invitation to interrupt hegemonic academic paradigms. By opening up other ways of narrating and constructing experiences of language reclamation and their contributions toward a better future, the authors take readers beyond academic ventriloquism and establish the terms of language work is one concept, and it is based on the direct voices of Indigenous reclaimers and practitioners. At the same time, authors invite academics to re-think their role and position in research production from a most needed (auto) critical and committed perspective.

Organization of the Book

The book chapters are organized in three main parts. However, as mentioned, the texts are connected in different ways, even though they are situated in different contexts and latitudes.

In '"We Are Not Going to Be Who We Were Meant to Be if We Don't Speak Our Language": A Dialogue with Language Educators', authors Julee Dehose (White Mountain Apache, USA) Jennie Burns (Paiute, USA) and Vanessa Anthony-Stevens (Euro-American/White,

USA) center the life journeys, work, and visions of Julee and Jennie, two Indigenous language teacher–activists, as discussed in conversation with Vanessa, a settler scholar–educator–collaborator. The chapter tells various stories, counter-stories, and details of practice important to highlighting the creativity and persistence involved in language work, as well as the deeply personal relationships guiding language work in specific communities and cultural landscapes. The questions that guide the stories are: 'Describe your journey to language reclamation. What factors have influenced your journey?' 'Where are the places and spaces that you teach and practice your language?' 'What experiences during the COVID-19 pandemic taught you about the needs for language education?' 'What would you like to see for your community in the future?' The chapter presents reflection among language advocates as a valuable practice of recognizing the centrality of self-in-relation to place, time, and family/community, and underscores knowledge co-production as fundamental to Julee and Jenny's practices of 'doing' language reclamation.

In 'Nunayaaġviŋmi itut Uvlumini in Anchorage: A Conversation about Language Revitalization and Reciprocal Research Practices', coauthors David E.K. Smith and Richard Atuk take us through a wonderful collaboration experience inspired by an Inupiaq elder and guardian of the language, Richard Atuk, and a young, committed anthropologist, David Smith, who is also a musician, highlighting the need to develop culturally sensitive, sustainable resources for language reclamation and revitalization. Starting with a dialogical format, they take us through the experience of their co-work, reminding us of the poignant necessity of overcoming asymmetrical power relationships perpetuating the commodification of speakers and their languages; instead, they show us how they created opportunities for common growth and for constructing tangible products dear to the communities' reclamation expectations. The production of a children's book to share Inupiaq values with young people provides an example of engaged scholarship guided by Indigenous own needs and desires, which inspires communities' hope to continue reversing language shift and develop local reclamation practices with global implications, opening up possibilities of inspiring new and growing collaborations.

Angel Sobotta Talaltlílpt's chapter, 'Reclamation of Language, Stories, Relationship to the Land: Niimíipuu Female as a Storyteller', analyzes Indigenous relationships with the language, stories and land. She discusses her research on Indigenous law within the Niimíipuu stories, language, and land as a process to reject settler-colonialism and patriarchal hegemony, to awaken the role of the Indigenous women as storytellers. Using gendered talking circles to create space for the Niimíipuu Female Educators to share knowledge, Angel explores female perspectives on traditional Niimíipuu stories, and shares a process that contributes collectively to new negotiations of meaning, often meaning lost by colonial censorship in translations. Angel describes an effort to re-establish the Niimíipuu knowledge within the stories as an action to 're-indigenize', taking back Niimíipuu truth and reuniting the truth and power in the stories of Indigenous people with an Indigenous worldview. To tell a titwáatit (story) from a Niimíipuu perspective re-establishes Niimíipuu knowledge within the titwáatit and provides a means to advance individual and collective empowerment, supporting females to reclaim their role as storytellers and as stewards of important Niimíipuu values.

In Erika Candelaria Hernández Aragón and Haydée Morales Flores's chapter, 'Communal Education, Existence of Shared Autonomy', the authors describe the political context of Indigenous leadership in which both a program for Indigenous elementary education and a communal university are developed. The authors center the concept of *comunalidad* (communality) and define it as an ancestral way of living for Indigenous communities in the contemporary state of Oaxaca (Mexico) and they theorize transformational academic efforts through this lens. They describe the teacher movement in 2006 that catalyzed the development of PTEO (Plan para la Transformación de la Educación en Oaxaca), as an alternative to the state-run, public, hegemonic education, in particular for Indigenous elementary school students. The strengthening of such a movement, with its contradictions, difficulties, and challenges, gives origin to the Autonomous Communal University of Oaxaca, UACO. This institution, founded a few years ago, claims to be built within the values of Oaxacan communities, integrating relevant members of the pueblos themselves. Both experiences, PTEO and UACO, present their challenges: one of them is how they navigate the state system for education while also negotiating with community and community members to develop and create an alternative system that resonates with their people. Thus, this chapter emphasizes the resistance experienced and perseverance necessary in the pursuit of autonomy and self-determination in the educational path.

In 'Experiences and Spaces of Opportunity for Work with the Ngigua Language', Teresa Damian Jara, a Ngigua speaker with decades of experience in the Indigenous primary school system in Mexico, takes us through her long-time experience struggling to survive and navigate a system that is more declarative than practical in terms of favoring the use of the Indigenous language. Recognizing that the Mexican Indigenous primary school system ghettoizes Indigenous teachers, Teresa analyzes the ways in which Indigenous language education is more often a linguistic bridge to reach the hegemonic one – Spanish – and functions to impose a national curriculum. Pinpointing a series of hidden contradictions that dwell in her everyday practice, Tere takes readers through her journey to creatively occupy an instructional space to vindicate her own epistemologies, reaching the point in which a

Ngigua community of practice emerges. She shows us how appropriating features of received language documentation allows for the development of a Ngigua-led documentation process with language reclamation in mind, going beyond uncritical paradigms commonplace in institutional and research practices. This chapter highlights the agency of Ngigua speakers to reclaim their Ngigua language and culture in an institutional space, recovering and constructing robust links to community-based education and its communal structures, outstandingly the land and landscape.

Beatriz González and Cornelio Hernández Pérez, Indigenous teachers with more than 18 years of experience, offer 'The Use of Indigenous Languages in Community-Based Indigenous Education in Oaxaca, Mx', as an example of the flexible use of Indigenous languages in a model of Indigenous community education unique in the state of Oaxaca. The Indigenous Community Middle Schools of Oaxaca in Mexico, encompassing 12 schools that have existed autonomously since 2004, provide public education for Indigenous children and youth. Through a narrative about their own experience, these authors develop two ideas. The first is the organizational efforts of Indigenous educators in these schools to maintain an educational model relevant to community life and knowledge. These efforts are visualized in the processes of collective professional training, in the sharing of experiences, and in the search for economic resources for community continuance. Beatriz and Cornelio highlight how they develop and apply Indigenous languages as a mode and medium of instruction. Using the example of a school located in an Indigenous community Xidza' Didza', a continuous and flexible way of doing schooling in daily life is presented, without being limited to a specific timetable. This text contributes to visualizing the linguistic and cultural reclamation rooted in community-driven school life and the daily efforts of teachers advocating for Indigenous futures.

In Ernesto's Colín's chapter, 'Toward a Methodology of Urban Indigenous Youth Language Learning', a unique educational experience of a high school in Los Angeles is described with rich detail. Stemming from the long-standing tradition of Chicano vindications, which historically have turned to Indigenous, especially Nahuatl, language and culture to reassert their own identity, we learn how this project incorporates Indigenous art in the form of one of the oldest existing Nahuatl texts, stemming from the 16th century, the Cantares Mexicanos, which has for a long time been misleadingly only considered 'poetry'. On the contrary, looking to assert a contemporary holistic perspective on this text, studying the Cantares means bringing together a myriad of (educational) voices, ranging from a Nahuatl speaker to an art teacher, in a creative ecosystem, allowing re-creating Indigenous epistemologies, especially sounds, as part of a dynamic Indigenous mindset, conceived as a powerful educational resource, rather than as a conventional, received 'research problem'.

Louie Lorenzo and Philip Stevens share the work of bringing youth into relationship with Ndee (Apache) ways of knowing, doing, and being in 'Nłt'éégo bénáłdiih: The Dissemination of Ndee Epistemology in Contemporary Times'. Louie and Philip, both San Carlos Apache tribal citizens (USA), bring us into the Apache world, where Apache values, philosophies, and teachings are the life map for well-being and for confronting n'daa, the negative things associated with life. In the context of a contemporary community initiative to educate young Apache men to avoid drug and alcohol addictions, Lorenzo and Stevens emphasize that avoidance of n'daa should not be the focus of one's life. They explore Apache ontological and epistemological perspectives as core pillars necessary to inform how non-Apache initiatives (e.g. federal health funding) should be appropriated to apply Apache-led education for Apache youth. Describing the Apache Youth Mentoring (AYM) program, led by Louie, the authors state: 'N'daa, the negative things of life, proliferate when we forget what we were taught and lose sight of the goals of gozhooné' (p. 144). They offer the work of mentoring youth through traditional Nnee methodologies, transmitted through Apache language and cultural practice, as a source of well-being that stretches from the past into the future.

In 'Reconnecting to Homelands through Digital Storywork', by Jessica Matsaw and Sammy Matsaw, who are Newene (Shoshone–Bannock people), we learn about a reclamation experience in close relation with their ancestral homelands, the Middle Fork of the Salmon River, as a way to reconnect to Indigenous and land-based pedagogy, in River Newe, Fort Hall Indian Reservation, Idaho, USA. In a family effort, the River Newe project is discussed as a community-oriented initiative, based on a non-profit organization working with young people to de-center the Eurocentric devaluation and discrimination to which Newene language and culture has been subjected through colonial policies, forced land removal, and deficit logics in schooling. The River Newe project looks to close divides between recovering ancestral homeland pedagogies and the digital world of STEAM (Science, Technology, Engineering, Art and Mathematics), strengthening land-based education, together with developing practical intergenerational educational communities looking to revitalize their language and culture. Most importantly, the experiential learning that is foundational to River Newe does not disentangle language and culture revitalization from everyday sociocultural life, otherwise linked to river-based pedagogies, such as the knowledge related to salmon wisdom and otherwise forms of Indigenous knowledge and methodology.

In 'Learning from Narratives: Life Stories of Indigenous Students in Chilean Graduate Science Programs as Voices of Advocacy for University

Space Reclamation', Marta Silva Fernández, Jennifer Brito Pacheco and Paulina Griñó explore the life journeys of graduate indigenous students in science programs in Chilean universities. The chapter starts by providing a theoretical framework that describes hegemonic relationships between scientific knowledge and other epistemologies. In this, the authors suggest missing opportunities to weave indigenous knowledge into scientific knowledge, so that we can understand the world from multiple perspectives. Student narratives are written in a way that the reader can see the journey of these students, from their childhood memories to their lives in their graduate programs, making visible the stories of discrimination and cultural dispossession. To finish, the authors reconnect with theory to highlight the character of the experiences through adaptation and culture reclamation. Through their stories, students build on, and reveal, their own indigenous identities while at the same time participating in science territory, grounded in hegemonic grounds.

The closing chapter, 'Reflections and Actions on Linguistic Resistance in Formal and Informal Spaces as a Proposal for Decolonization in Wallmapu/Wajmapu', by Carolina Kürüf Poblete, Silvia Calfuqueo and Kelly Baur offers us three experiences of language revitalization within the context of Chile, and particularly in relation to Mapuche territory: Wallmapu. These three experiences are framed within the Chilean landscape of Indigenous languages, Indigenous education, and the long history of colonization, land dispossession, and the compensatory policies to address such conflicts. The first experience corresponds to an analysis of how Mapuche people are portrayed through the Chilean press as 'terrorists', providing a critical perspective on how it perpetuates social discrimination against Mapuche people. The second experience focuses on the revitalization of Mapuche language, Mapuzungun, in a school taken by community members, where a curriculum was built to address the strengthening of Mapuche cultural identity. Finally, the last piece argues that ancestral Mapuche games embed philosophy, knowledge and cultural practices that today, given the neocolonial context, can result in strategies for language revitalization, where youth become actively involved in play. The three experiences emphasize aspects of the Mapuche life and its involvement in the development of spaces of resistance. Such spaces encompass practices deeply rooted in Mapuche epistemologies.

References

Cajete, G. (1994) *Look to the Mountain: An Ecology of Indigenous Education*. Kivaki Press.

Castagno, A.E. and McCarty, T.L. (eds) (2018) *The Anthropology of Education Policy. Ethnographic Inquiries into Policy as Sociocultural Process*. Routledge.

Córdova, A. (2017) *Following the Path of the Serpent: Indigenous Film Festivals in Abya Yala*. Ms. Available at: https://www.academia.edu/43840958/Following_the_Path_of_the_Serpent_Indigenous_Film_Festivals_in_Abya_Yala.

Coronel Molina, S.M. (2017) Introduction: Indigenous language regimes in the Americas. *International Journal of the Sociology of Language* 2017 (246), 1–6.

Cortina, R. (ed.) (2014) *The Education of Indigenous Citizens in Latin America*. Multilingual Matters.

Cru, J. (2018) Micro-level language planning and Youtube comments. Destigmatising indigenous languages through rap music. *Current Issues in Language Planning* 19 (1), 1–19. Available at: https://www.researchgate.net/publication/325629437_Micro-level_language_planning_and_YouTube_comments_destigmatising_indigenous_languages_through_rap_music.

Flores Farfán J.A. and Ramallo, F. (2010) Exploring links between documentation, sociolinguistics and language revitalization. An Introduction. In J.A. Flores Farfán and F. Ramallo (eds) *New Perspectives on Endangered Languages* (pp. 1–12). John Benjamins. Available at: https://www.academia.edu/372334/New_Perspectives_on_Endangered_Languages.

Flores Farfán J.A. and Cru. J. (2020) Reviewing experiences in language (re)vitalisation: Recent undertakings in the media and the arts. *Journal of Multilingual and Multicultural Development* 42 (3), 941–954. Available at: https://www.academia.edu/107994183/Reviewing_experiences_in_language_revitalization_recent_undertakings_in_the_media_and_the_arts.

Haugen, E. (1972) *The Ecology of Language*. Stanford University Press.

Hornberger, N.H. (2009) La educación multilingüe, política y práctica: Diez Certezas. *Revista Guatemalteca de Educación* 1 (1), 95–138.

Kawagley, A.O. (2006) *A Yupiaq Worldview: A Pathway to Ecology and Spirit*. Waveland Press.

Kroskrity, P. (2021) Covert linguistic racism and the (re-)production of white supremacy. *Linguistic Anthropology* 31 (2), 180–193.

Lave, Jean (2019) *Learning and Everyday life: Access, Participation and Changing Practices*. Cambridge University Press.

Leonard, W.Y. (2017) Producing language reclamation by decolonising 'language'. *Language Documentation and Description* 14. Available at: https://www.lddjournal.org/article/id/1179/.

Llanes Ortiz, G. (2020) Art, music and cultural activities. in J. Olko and J. Sallabank (eds) *Revitalizing Indigenous Languages. A Practical Guide* (pp. 273–283). Cambridge University Press. Available at: https://web.archive.org/web/20220522050255id_/https://www.cambridge.org/core/services/aop-cambridge-core/content/view/F2B5AE97CFEBCF994D63F310F5559236/9781108485753c16_273-296.pdf/art-music-and-cultural-activities.pdf.

McCarty, T. (2003) Dangerous difference: A critical-historical analysis of language education policies in the United States. In A.E. Castagno and T.L. McCarty, 2018 (eds) *The Anthropology of Education Policy. Ethnographic Inquiries into Policy as Sociocultural Process* (pp. 71–93). Routledge.

McCarty, T.L., Nicholas, S.E., Chew, K.A., Diaz, N.G., Leonard, W.Y. and White, L. (2018) Hear our languages, hear our voices: Storywork as theory and praxis in indigenous-language reclamation. *Daedalus* 147 (2), 160–172.

McIvor, O. (2020) Indigenous language revitalization and applied linguistics: Parallel histories, shared futures? *Annual Review of Applied Linguistics* 40, 78–96.

Menken K. and García, O. (2010) *Negotiating Language Policies in Schools. Educators as Policy Makers*. Routledge.

Patel, L. (2015) *Decolonizing Educational Research: From Ownership to Answerability*. Routledge.

Penetito, W. (2009) Place-based education: Catering for curriculum, culture and community. *New Zealand Annual Review of Education* 18, 5–29.

Romero-Little, M.E. (2011) Learning the community's curriculum: The linguistic, social, and cultural resources of American Indian and Alaska Native children (pp. 89–99). In

M.C. Sarche, P. Spicer, P. Farrell and H.E. Fitzgerald (eds) *American Indian and Alaska Native Children's Mental Health: Development and Context*. Praeger.

Simpson, L. (2014) Land as pedagogy: Nishnaabeg intelligence and rebellious transformation. *Decolonization: Indigeneity, Education & Society* 3 (3), 1–25.

Stevens, P.J. (2021) A woodcutter's story: Perceptions and uses of mathematics on the San Carlos Apache reservation. *Anthropology & Education Quarterly* 52 (4), 430–450. https://doi.org/10.1111/aeq.12399.

Styres, S. (2017) *Pathways for Remembering and Recognizing Indigenous Thought in Education: Philosophies of iethni'nohsténha ohwentsia'kékha (Land)*. University of Toronto Press.

Sumida Huaman, E. (2020) Small indigenous schools: Indigenous resurgence and education in the Americas. *Anthropology & Education Quarterly* 51 (3), 262–281.

Sumida Huaman, E. and Martin, N.D. (eds) (2020) *Indigenous Knowledge Systems and Research Methodologies: Local Solutions and Global Opportunities*. Canadian Scholars.

Tinirau, R., Pauro, C., Pauro, C., Maraku, P. and Mihaka, R. (2020) Kua kā kē ngā ahi: The fires are already alight and alive – Rekindling relationships, practices, and knowledge of kai amongst Tamariki and Rangatahi of Ngāti Ruaka, Whanganui river. *Mahika Kai Journal* 1 (1), 15–36.

Tuck, E. and McKenzie, M. (2015) *Place in Research: Theory, Methodology, and Methods*. Routledge.

Useful Links

Garabide is an Euskera ('Basque') NGO based in the Basque country pursuing linguistic cooperativism around the world. https://www.garabide.eus/espanol/.

The UNESCO website related to the International Decade of Indigenous Languages, 2022–2032 is available at. https://idil2022-2032.org/.

IKEEP stands for Indigenous Knowledge for Effective Education. Based at the University of Idaho it develops a culturally responsive program for Indigenous teachers and Native American students. https://www.uidaho.edu/ed/resources/student/ikeep.

Linguapax is an NGO working in favor of linguistic diversity pursuing peace linguistics around the world, with a consultative status to UNESCO. https://www.linguapax.org/es/.

Part 1
Narratives of Reclamation: Lifework and Learning in Dialogue

1 'We Are Not Going to Be Who We Were Meant to Be if We Don't Speak Our Language': A Dialogue with Language Educators

Julee Dehose, Jennie Burns and Vanessa Anthony-Stevens

Introduction

Experiences of Indigenous resistance and reclamation are deeply individual journeys and occur in relationships between the place we live and those we share place and time with (human and more-than-human). These experiences are simultaneous and often multilayered. Indigenous resistance and language reclamation work takes shape as ideological, political, and material commitments to navigating tensions between community values and needs and the hegemony of contemporary, colonial-influenced institutional practices. This chapter centers the life journeys, work, and visions of two Indigenous language teacher–activists (Julee and Jennie), discussed in conversation with a settler scholar–educator–collaborator (Vanessa). As educators invested in Indigenous well-being, we chose to tell stories of what matters to us, our relatives, and our communities from Indigenous perspectives and informed by Indigenous worldviews. In conversation, we tell stories, counter-stories, and practice the craft of remembering what makes us feel: joy, pain, sorrow, relief, acceptance, and so much more. This chapter is constructed initially from a single conversation, but reflects ideas that flowed into, and extend beyond, a single telling of our experiences. In using our dialogue as a basis for developing meaning, we draw from the work in Indigenous methodologies, particularly the practice of 'yarning' described by Kovach (2010) where storytelling, re-storying and re-membering, center conversation as dialogic and relational meaning making. Sharing knowledge is never without obligation, responsibility, and reciprocity, and demands attention to place, time, and context. We use relational conversation as a practice of recognizing self-in-relation to place, time, and community, essentially centering the relationship of knowledge co-production as foundation to understand Julee and Jennie's practices of 'doing' language reclamation.

Setting the Groundwork for Storytelling

The three of us – Julee, Jennie and Vanessa – met in the summer of 2022, when Julee and Jennie took a summer course titled 'Centering Indigenous Language and Culture Education in Times of Rapid Change', taught by Vanessa through the American Indian Language Development Institute (AILDI) at the University of Arizona. Vanessa, a professor, had been involved with AILDI for more than 15 years as both a student and course instructor. During the summer of 2022, coming off two years of COVID disruption, we had an intimate class of five students, all of whom were passionate language teachers. We spent five days a week for four weeks during June involved in daily 3-hour discussions. Our classes were intended to be hybrid, with some students place-based in Tucson, Arizona, and others connecting from our various home locations; but the class fully moved to all zoom after the second day of class due to an abundance of caution as a few cases of COVID were reported by Tucson-based AILDI participants.

The course content was built around study and discussion of applied efforts to expand Indigenous language use in contemporary contexts, focused on Indigenous-led language reclamation work occurring around the globe. Through hearing from and reading about other Indigenous language activists (most of whom would not refer to themselves as activists), we put our heads together to think from our various locations, physical and ontological, to describe and enact relationships to foment a love of language. Through artwork, song, storytelling, performance, and digital images, we taught each other important aspects of each other's cultural practices, protocols, and relationships. Following the conclusion of our intense weeks together, Vanessa asked Julee and Jennie if they would be interested in sharing their experiences of teaching language as embedded community members and seasoned teachers in the form of a publication. Indigenous language work involves a humility often not found in the English lexicon, and that runs counter to the Euro–Western identity of a 'teacher,' e.g. expert, all-knowing, authority. Vanessa asking Julee and Jennie to think about what it meant to them to be Indigenous language activists, led us to question what activism is and means, and to talk about, and re-examine, activism not as people protesting in the street but as everyday acts that center Indigenous thoughts and local relationships with Indigenous languages. In English, the word activism means one who brings about social change; we agreed that working on behalf of Indigenous languages, whether Apache or Numu, is a conscious practice of engaging in social change. To initiate this chapter, we met for one hour via zoom in July 2022. Vanessa posed a few questions to Julee and Jennie, and together we listened to each other's stories of cultivating conditions for Indigenous languages to be gifted, seeded, and tended. We decided to record our conversation so we could use the conversation to guide collaborative writing. The questions posed were:

- 'Describe your journey to language reclamation. What factors have influenced your journey?'
- 'Where are the places and spaces that you teach and practice your language?'
- 'What experiences during the COVID-19 pandemic taught you about the needs for language education?'
- 'What would you like to see for your community in the future?'

What follows reflects the transcribed and edited transcript of our conversation, and a series of subsequent zoom meetings, phone calls, and text messages between July 2022 and July 2023. Vanessa identified three themes in Jennie and Julee's reflections and stories, essentially a constellation of the values important to language reclamation:

(1) understanding the relationships between language and identity;
(2) the gift of languages for place-making; and
(3) the role of visioning to cultivate the conditions where Indigenous languages can thrive.

First, we begin by introducing how we have come to this conversation by presenting ourselves more thoroughly.

Where We Come From

Julee is a citizen of the White Mountain Apache Tribe in traditional Apache homelands and what today is referred to as central Arizona, USA. Julee is the daughter of Judy Dehose and the late Virgil Dehose Sr; maternal grandparents were the late Kenzie and Ida Early, paternal grandparents were the late Francis and Sarah Dehose. Julee comes from the Row of White Cane People (Tło'kąą dogain) and born by the Butterfly clan (doolé). Julee was raised in a traditional Apache household, having her puberty ceremony, otherwise known as the Apache Sunrise Dance, at the age of 14. This ceremony is done for young Apache women to prepare and strengthen them for the hardships of life, and, through the songs and prayers, Julee attributes her accomplishments in life to this ceremony that she feels strengthened her mentally, physically and spiritually. Julee has worked with her tribe in various ways through land restoration, leading projects in the Ndee Bini Bidaa Ilzaah (pictures of Apache Land) summer project for the youth of Cibecue. In this program high school students learned how to be proper stewards of their land traditionally. Julee also worked with her tribe's water resource department, surveying wetland areas of the Fort Apache Reservation. Today, Julee teaches K-5 Apache language in her hometown and in the school she attended and graduated from in Cibecue, Arizona. She hopes that through her personal accomplishments she can spark hope and motivation in the youth of her community that one day they will follow in her footsteps, that if someone from a small reservation can do what they want in life, they can too.

Jennie is Numu (Paiute) and Newe (Western Shoshone) from the Great Basin area that is now Nevada. She is an enrolled member of the Pyramid Lake Paiute Tribe (Kooyooe Tukadu – Ancient fish eater). Her father is Ralph Burns, also an enrolled member of the Pyramid Lake Paiute Tribe. Jennie's Hootse'egapu (paternal grandmother) is the late Bernita Winnemucca, Numu (Paiute) from the Kooyooe Tukadu band. Her Kunoo'ogapu (paternal grandfather) is the late William Burns, Numu (Paiute) from the Kedu Tuka'a band (Groundhog eaters from Fort Bidwell, California). Jennie's mother, Anita Sanchez, is Western Shoshone and is an enrolled member of the Reno–Sparks Indian Colony. Jennie's Moo'agapu (maternal grandmother) is the late Katherine Pete-Sanchez, Newe (Western Shoshone) from Reese River, Nevada. Jennie's Togo'ogapu (maternal grandfather) is the late Tony Sanchez Sr, Newe (Western Shoshone) and Mexican from the Smokey Valley area in Nevada.

Jennie was raised in Reno, Nevada by her maternal grandparents at the Reno–Sparks Indian Colony. Her grandmother raised her in the traditional ways of the Newe (Shoshone) women – to be a strong resilient woman. These teachings taught Jennie to prepare for life in this modern world. Jennie's maternal grandmother was a fluent Shoshone speaker, who tried to teach her children the language and to teach through storytelling. When her children did not want to learn the language, she gave up and told them that the language will die with her. It was not the children's fault: to live in the city of Reno, it was imperative for them to speak the English language. Jennie's maternal grandparents wanted to make sure she knew her paternal grandmother, who lived on the Pyramid Lake reservation in Nixon, Nevada, a rural town about 65 miles out of Reno. Jennie was very young when she would make these visits; it was during this time that Jennie knew her paternal side mostly spoke Numu (Paiute) and not English.

Jennie is the mother of four children, Kendallgapu, Ashley, Jordan, and Wesleygapu. Jennie was employed at the Reno–Sparks Tribal Health Clinic, Saint Mary's Hospital, Pyramid Lake Jr/Sr High School and the Pyramid Lake Paiute Tribe.

In 2008, tragedy hit Jennie and her family. Her son Kendall died by suicide at the age of 21. For several years after his death Jennie tried to find meaning in her life. She went back to school and finished her associate's degree in finance. During this time, she started to drive her father to the language classes he taught at the Reno–Sparks Indian Colony. She watched him work tirelessly to keep the Paiute language alive. Her father started to teach a community language class in Wadsworth, Nevada on the Pyramid Lake Reservation. Her son Wesley was learning the language at school and wanted to keep learning during the summer. Jennie, still not knowing what she wanted to do in life, was encouraged by Wesley to go to summer class with him. At that time, Jennie started her journey to learn the Paiute language – something she thought her son Kendall would admire and encourage.

The Washoe County School District was looking for an on-call Paiute language instructor. With encouragement from her father, who told Jennie that she knew enough of the Paiute language to teach the language to beginning students, she applied for the job and thus began her new care as a Paiute-language teacher. The school district offers Paiute as a World Language credit in three high schools. Jennie has taught at all three schools but has mostly been stationed at Reed High School in Sparks, Nevada since 2016. All students are encouraged to enroll and learn the Paiute language and culture.

Jennie currently works for the Reno–Sparks Indian Colony in the education department. She works with language and culture as a language specialist. She works with three languages: Numu (Paiute), Newe (Shoshone) and Washiw (Washoe). Jennie also works with her dad in his community classes and helps him create lessons for his classes at the University of Nevada–Reno.

On March 31, 2023, Jennie's youngest son Wesley died at the age of 23. He was learning the Paiute language and culture along with his mom. We lost a future teacher. Jennie considers herself a 'forever student' and does not consider herself a fluent speaker. She and her father will continue the journey together as teachers. Reclamation of the Numu language has been Jennie's focus for the last 12 years. In order for the Numu language to survive, we need to continue to encourage our youth to learn and to be proud of who they are.

Vanessa is the daughter of European ancestors who emigrated to the eastern USA during the settler colonial migration trail of the 1840s–1900s. Vanessa was raised in ancestral homelands of diverse Indigenous peoples – Miami, Potawatomi, Menomenni, Ho-Chunk, and others – in a context of colonial amnesia. That is to say, Vanessa was raised in what is commonly called Chicagoland and she had little education in the Indigenous history and knowledge of the place where her feet first touched the ground. In her early twenties, she met and married her husband, Dr Philip Stevens, who is a citizen of the San Carlos Apache

Nation. As a mother raising daughters to be proud of their Indigenous and European heritages, Vanessa has learned to participate in Apache socialization practices, including traditional Apache coming-of-age ceremonies and hunting in Apache homelands. As a scholar–educator in higher education, Vanessa works with Indigenous teachers and teachers serving Indigenous youth to conceptualize multilingualism as a human superpower and to invest in Indigenous-led education also in classrooms.

The three of us have a shared connection to the Southwest and, specifically, Apache homelands. Jennie's daughter is married to one of Vanessa's in-laws and resides in the eastern territory of San Carlos. Julee has overlapping relations with Vanessa's in-laws, both in White Mountain and the San Carlos Apache regions, including having been the teacher of a relatives' children. These extended familial and overlapping relationships are often assumed among tribal peoples in the US, where standard protocols of naming one's relatives is a way to orally 'map' connections and responsibilities. Such connections are also a source of humor as it's common for people to say, 'Everyone in Indian country is related! (so be careful who you take up with or talk about!)'. Our shared connections as women, as mothers/aunties to Native children, make us accountable to practices of honoring family connections in how we approached our conversations.

Language as a Gift: Sustaining Relationships

Stories of relationships flowed when we talked about language: language as a living relationship; language as a conduit between relatives, across generations; and language as place. Jenny and Julee never describe themselves as language experts, yet their commitments to sharing what they know with others illuminated the ethic of gifting one's language as a central practice of sustaining relationships with people and place.

Familial bonds in healing and purpose

In 2008, Jennie was driving her dad to teach his Numu language class. During this period, Jennie had lost one of her sons and was in a state of deep grief. She did not want to leave the house and she felt lost. Her father would say, 'Come on, come with me to class'. Across long car rides and conversations, Jennie began to notice what he was doing for their language. She observed her father deeply focused on his teaching. One day, after one of his classes, she asked, 'Who helps you with all of this?' and he replied, 'No one. I do this on my own'. Her father didn't get paid in the community to do any of this kind of work. He just took it upon himself, because he always said, '... if our language dies so are we... we're not going to be who we were meant to be as the Paiute people. We're just going to be brown-skinned White people'.

During the long car rides and conversations with her father, Jennie was noticing what he was doing for the language. Her father's language work had been his passion in his mature years, yet he was doing it on his own. From there, she too began to feel her father's purpose and she developed a conscious need to do something for their language. She reflects on that time with happiness, as it was the start of what she calls becoming her father's 'little assistant' at a time when she felt uncertain ('I didn't even know much about the Paiute language then') and in grief.

In a way, Jennie's father was bringing her to a better path. He knew that staying home and remaining sad was not going to help her live well. Working with her language was a source of strength after suffering the loss of her son. Jennie reflected on that time in this way:

> I felt like I had this purpose in my life after my son had died, I was like gosh. I was always home upset and crying, and my dad kept inviting me to come with him. He really got me involved with the language, instead of being home and being sad all the time.

Language work, for Jennie, became about relationships with family and a system of supportive healing. Jennie began working as a teaching assistant for her dad's classes, driving him to and from the university, all the while learning with him and spending time with him. She was his Vanna White (reference to a popular American TV show called *Wheel of Fortune*), doing whatever role her father needed to support his teaching. This was a fluid apprenticeship – neither of them was paid, they just did this work on their own. From the side of the classroom, Jennie observed how her father reached people – college students, non-Native and Native learners. Observing her father bring the language to his students helped her to see how he built relationships with his language and brought a spark to his audience. When the Wycliff alphabet[1] was introduced for written Paiute – a system based on suffixes, so if you know the core word, you also need to learn the suffix to make the word change – Jennie and her father would have a little competition with each other to see who could teach their students to master the 'most' suffixes in Paiute. As her father's adult college students were dominant in English, they found this system compatible with English structures. Jenny and her father would share teaching strategies and reflect on what worked well for helping the students retain their learning from the day's lessons. Jennie, who saw herself as a novice, began to take more of a role in co-teaching with her father. She recalls when he first gave her compliments on her teaching. Their connection with each other felt good.

Pride in who we are

Julee, who currently works as a K-5 Apache language teacher at a public school in her home community, shared this statement when describing why she teaches: 'I want to be a role model to my community'. Julee now teaches at the same school she attended as a child. Pride in her home, her family, and her people motivates her to work with young people today.

Julee remembers, when she was a young girl, not wanting to speak Apache in school. It wasn't that she couldn't speak Apache. As a lighter skinned child, many people assumed she was white or treated her as if she had white parents. Living in a small community combined with race-based associations of identity as a phenotype made it awkward to speak Apache outside her home. Julee did understand and did speak Apache, but did not see herself as a fluent speaker, like her mother, uncles or grandparents were. She *chose* not to speak Apache in school and saw that students who did speak Apache experienced different treatment from teachers. She observed the many ways her fellow classmates were not encouraged to excel in school, or not offered opportunities beyond remedial classroom instruction. Being knowledgeable about Apache language and life was not rewarded in school.

As a young adult, right after graduating from high school, Julee took an opportunity to participate in a student exchange partnership with a university in South Korea. She lived abroad in Korea for about a year and became a student of the Korean language. As a speaker of Apache and English, learning Korean presented new opportunities to develop language acquisition consciousness. She returned to the US to study sociology and political science at the University of New Mexico, where she completed her BA.

Motivated to be a role model, Julee maintained attention on her home and returned to Cibecue in 2013 to work for her tribe's water resources department. 'Then reality hit me hard', Julee remembers, 'when I saw that we are losing our language at an alarming rate, and I also took a look at myself and realized that I was not fluent enough as I should be'. Julee felt compelled to make a choice:

> I stepped out of my comfort zone and decided I wanted to be a part of our language revitalization program at my work. Though I was not fluent enough I ignored this and decided that if I was going to become better at my language, what better way than to teach the language and in turn also teach students what I do know. My main goal was to show that if someone such as myself, not confident in my language, can actually learn and teach our Apache language, that they [students] can do the same too, they can see that it is possible for anyone to learn our language, no matter what level of Apache they are at, basically to show people that we can speak Apache, show people that they can learn.

Apache people are and can be many things. Apache language holds brilliance. Yet, Julee knew these were not the dominant messages the youth in her community received about their identity in institutional contexts. There are lots of people who believe that her high school is not equipped to support students to live full adulthoods after they graduate. Recognizing the inherent damage-centered colonialist logics that cast Apache-ness as uneducable, choosing to commit to language reclamation is an act of agency to reject deficit and strengthen Apache relationships between people, place and knowing, Julee committed herself to sustaining and expanding her ability to name and image the world through the Apache language.

At their entry points to language work, Julee frequently described herself as 'not even fluent at all', and Jennie described herself as 'I didn't even know much about the Paiute language then'. Their language consciousness underscores language use and practice as dynamic and alive and available to be activated in each period of one's life. Their parents' generation experienced Apache and Paiute languages in ways different from Julee and Jennie, and differently from their current students. Seeing language as a living relationship forming, sustaining, and deepening bonds among community, relatives, across generations, facilitated an entry point for language activism – an ethic of gifting one's language to nurture well-being as an ecosystem.

Navigating Local and Institutional Tensions with Patience and Endurance

Discussion among us about where language is used, with whom, and the ways in which language flows or has to navigate through dams, underscored institutional spaces as holding a significant role in contemporary language instruction. Yet, the impacts of colonial ideologies and their technologies for privileging Euro–Western knowledge hierarchies and pedagogies devoid of context, cannot be denied as deleterious in their effects upon Indigenous relationships. Schools and institutions have systematically minimized Indigenous knowledge, perpetuating disruptions to Indigenous knowledge transfer. For Jennie and Julee, sharing Indigenous languages in institutional spaces required a generosity of patience and endurance to navigate institutional frames not based on Indigenous values.

'Pretend you are a 3-year-old'

Prior to COVID, Jennie and her colleagues at the language and culture department spent time teaching the Paiute language to young children on a weekly basis. They would go to the Head Start[2] and daycare in Reno–Sparks Indian Colony. Before COVID we would work two times a week by bringing elders to the little children. Jennie would make short language lessons around the content theme within the Head Start curriculum. I would take the themes – numbers, colors, clothing, animals within the region – and make little lessons that the elders could use to share the language with the youngsters. Recounting pedagogies of performance and language-in-interaction makes Jennie smile. At the Head Start, teaching language through song was always powerful: 'Little kids don't have shame, they are happy to sing. My advice for adult language learners is to "Pretend you're a 3-year-old," because the children don't question whether they are speaking well or not, they are eager to perform'.

Languages are carriers of knowledge systems, ontological and axiological. Paiute language is inherently an expression of Paiute values, yet, as many young people are English dominant, teaching Paiute values also comes in the form of stories told in both English and Paiute. The incongruity between Euro–Christian values, which frame standardized institutional curricula, and Paiute values present an incommensurability that is obvious and elusive. Jennie offered the example of making a language lesson from the Cumusi (rabbit guts) story for elders to teach the small children. The Cumusi story is about a girl rabbit who was *really* lazy. The girl rabbit slept while the grandmother took the siblings out to gather food. The girl rabbit was so lazy that when she saw ants working hard, she made fun of them for working. But the girl rabbit, being as lazy as she was, fell back asleep again. The ants took her guts while she was asleep. She was left skinny – 'rabbit guts, we all eat rabbit guts, fat girl'. Rabbit has a burnt foot. Young women have to be industrious and they '*can't be lazy*' they must learn the value of getting up early and making a fire for the household (Paiute story). Lessons about power during menstruation, too powerful it can weaken. These gendered stories are complicated to teach to young people today, and, especially as contemporary discussions of gender fluidity in popular culture are more normalized and left to the individual, greater context to teach about the place of distinct gendered roles and their relationship to community well-being is frequently needed.

Jennie's reflections underscore the salience of context, and its *mattering* for language, the specificity of process, and relationships within language education. Jennie's work is located in and around a 'colony', a tribal community in a city made up of multiple tribes with different languages. The colony/reservation is the home to tribal services, such as the language and culture courses. Classes offered by her tribal government are primarily geared toward adult learners in classroom settings. Three languages are taught: Wasu, Shoshone and Paiute. The fast pace of a high-density region, the multiculturality of the city, and the manipulation of land for urban commerce form additional layers around and through Jennie's work. Navigating the tensions is central to the work. It is the work with the children, the 3-year-olds, that keeps Jennie grounded:

> ...what we do is go out into the community and have classes like with the little guys at the Head Start or daycare. Sometimes we'll see [the children] and we know we're doing good when they see us, they automatically give us a greeting in the language. So, to me, that's part of reclaiming the language. Where it may not seem like we're doing a lot, but in a way, I feel like we *are* doing a lot.

Giving your language

'It can be really hard to try to give your language to them', Julee said of teaching Apache language in an elementary school. 'You have to repeat and repeat; some kids don't care, some are naughty, and some really, really want to learn. You have to try to motivate them' said Julee, referring to schooling and the many demands related to funding, standardized assessments, and Eurocentric assumptions about 'proper' participation. The impact of standard language pedagogy frequently undermines 'giving your language to learners' and can thwart language learning. But reclamation continues –Julee and her Apache language colleagues struggle on to put Apache language in its rightful place during the school day.

A school practice Julee has developed with her colleagues is the teaching of handling verbs. For the Apache language, handling verbs are essential for everyday talk and interactions. English has a simple verb form to express commands, basically the verb stem. However, for handling verbs and commands, Apache uses an inflected verb form, which has to be inflected for second person singular, dual, or plural. Verbs in Apache also employ stems that classify objects according to size, shape, number, texture, etc. (Bray, 1998). As a teacher, Julee and her colleagues ask themselves, 'What can we teach that we can use every day?' 'Shanti', which means 'Hand me that (a long skinny thing)', or 'shantsoos,' which means 'Hand me that (the flat flimsy object)' are all handling verbs that kids can practice every day in and outside their classrooms. Julee finds approaching language teaching through situational language to be the most realistic or practical way to support kids to *actually* talk with each other and their relatives, rather than just being passive listeners to the language. Julee relates to this pedagogy from her own experience as a learner: 'When you're not fluent you are not confident', so teaching practical things, situational language, she encourages children to have small dialogues with each other to get them comfortable to speak aloud to each other and then supports them toward making more complex sentences.

Outside the classroom, Julee has been involved the Ndee Bini Bidaa Ilzaah (pictures of Apache Land) summer project for the youth of Cibecue, a land and language project based around white anthropologist Keith Basso's language documentation, in his book *Wisdom Sits in Places* (1996), of places and place names in Julee's homelands. The program started with the Rodeo–Chediski fires that devastated nearly 300,000 acers of Apache territory in 2002 and incorporates hands-on field experiences where community members and youth visit places around the reservation, discuss their names in the Apache language, study the Apache knowledge and Western scientific knowledge about the vegetation and ecosystems (Long & Dehose, 2015). Studying the place names in

Apache language teaches people about the place and which living things and matter are found there, the life and the environment. For example, the place near Julee's house, tiscat, is the place of cottonwood. In Julee's experience, children learn the place names rapidly during these summer experiences on the land. She feels that is likely because the children are physically in contact with the place and 'language always comes into play when we are in our land'. Julee finds learning Apache language in context helps students understand the places they live in and allows them to gain a sense of the ways the climate and environment around them are changing as they connect to the deep relationship of language to land. For example, the Apache name for what today is Phoenix, Arizona, is *Tiis bił ogoteel*, which in English means cottonwood trees as far as the eyes can see. Today, Phoenix has few cottonwoods and little water.

Creating the conditions for gifting language has been a personal choice for Julee's family. Upon the arrival of her nephew, her household collaborated as a family to decide that Apache would be her newborn nephew's first language. Noticing that she and her younger siblings were speaking less and less Apache, at the behest of her mother the family agreed that everyone in the household would speak only Apache to the newborn. Julee remembers:

> My mom decided we should instill rules that everyone in the household has to speak Apache to my nephew. We wanted to maintain it as our first language. Once my nephew started school, we decided at school he can speak English. But if he knows someone is Apache, he has to speak Apache to that person.

Her nephew is now six years old and is dominant in Apache but quickly becoming competent in English. Over the years, Julee has seen her youngest siblings learning, speaking, and having less difficulty communicating in Apache; 'it has helped all of us to re-learn... we wanted our youth to keep our language alive. When we all speak only Apache, Apache flows better in our household'.

Learning from Crisis *and* Dreaming Beyond

Our dialog occurred in the summer of 2022, two years after the COVID-19 pandemic. Like many settler–colonial societies, Native Nations persist alongside histories of racist policies in wealth distribution and in access to land and institutional services. Our communities, similar to other Indigenous and minoritized communities around the globe, felt the undeniable effects of racist conditions where Indigenous peoples had disadvantageous access to health care, adequate diet and safe housing (Stevens *et al.*, 2021). These material deprivations grounded in crisis epistemologies wield the potential 'to silence and deprioritize language work, reducing it to a non-critical activity' (McIvor *et al.*, 2020: 409).

From a Western-centric nation-state perspective, Indigenous language work often fights for space on the large societal agenda. This is particularly true in schools and is reflected in damage-centered resource allocations to Tribal Nations and communities. However, flipping the perspective to center Indigenous voices, those working to share language within their households and communities, we can tell a different story. As described by McIvor et al. (2020) in their study of Indigenous language practices during COVID-19 in Canada and the USA, 'just like water, our languages always find a way' (2020: 409). In this way of thinking, our discussions of language work in critical times do not lose sight of the hopes, dreams, and aspirations of Indigenous people. Even as COVID was a fearful time for all of us, we all reflected on the power of having each other and living together during the uncertainty of COVID. The virus severely impacted people in both Julee and Jennie's home reservations, as it did in San Carlos, the homelands of Vanessa's in-laws. Strength was prayer and family sticking together even as many ceremonial practices for prayer were disrupted. We each reflected on coming out of COVID with this feeling, as stated by Julee: 'I don't want to take life for granted'. As we came out of COVID, Jennie observed: 'the kids raring to learn when they returned to school. It mattered to be with each other again'. The value of social interactions and relationships between ourselves and with our environments was re-centered, centering a-new awareness about the role of language in communal well-being, inside our homes, throughout our communities, and within our institutions. Nothing about this awareness translates directly to language revitalization practices; however, it has contributed to what Maori scholar Margie Kahukura Hohepa (2015) describes as regeneration – growth, regrowth, development and redevelopment – acknowledging that nothing regrows in exactly the same way as it had previously. Hence language, too, must continue to be generated and, in doing so, it takes on constant new life.

Dreaming: Returning Language to its Rightful Place

At the core of our conversations, Julee and Jennie repeatedly shared ways in which values are encoded/encrypted in the language. In reflection, we asked ourselves, How can we expand the conditions to recover and nurture the values in the language? And how might we regenerate value systems through language, especially when many of these ontologies and cosmologies have been blocked by historic and ongoing inequalities that have led to Indigenous language marginalization to begin with? Dreaming of language reclamation sometimes involves dreaming between both worlds. For example, having access to Apache language facilitates a different way of thinking and living than the English-speaking world. Apache language holds Apache solutions to Apache problems.

We will end by describing two examples of dreaming about connections and regenerating space for language to flow. For Julee, future-oriented visions include dedicating energy to the babies. Julee dreams of a community childcare center, much like the language nest models practiced in New Zealand, Mexico and the US:

> We can provide a babysitting service all in Apache language, all in Apache, like a community daycare. Elders could work there, make an income, and be able to teach the babies. Our children and babies need the support and many people in the Cibicue community need employment.

This community childcare setting could feed regeneration of Apache language in the elementary school setting as well. Julee envisions designating a wing of the current school building as an Apache-language-only building, where only Apache is spoken. 'The kids need to hear Apache every day. Right now, our children don't speak very well, but they can be strengthened'.

For Jennie, bringing language to learners through experiences on the land is the future of language work that she wants to envision. Over the years, Jennie has had some opportunity to garner school-based resources to take students on field trips to Pyramid Lake to teach them in her language and to expose them to traditional fish-harvesting practices. She builds her vision from experience with young people in the urban Indian colony where she works:

> Some kids have never been outside the city, or to Pyramid Lake. Seeing young men be excited to be on the land is so beautiful. There is *so* much we can teach people in our environment.

This vision is similar to what Indigenous scholars describe as land education – a form of Indigenous learning that comes through the land, that occurs in an Indigenous context and uses Indigenous processes for knowledge transfer (Wildcat et al., 2014). Jennie envisions teaching and learning on the land as something that must be driven by her community, but which also has a place for helping non-tribal people to understand and appreciate the Paiute lifeway. Land-based language education, re-emplacing language in relationship with land and contexts of Indigenous life and knowledge transfer, is an alternative to settler modes of thinking and teaching. As Wildcat and colleagues write (2014: iii): 'Land-based education, in resurging and sustaining Indigenous life and knowledge, acts in direct contestation to settler colonialism and its drive to eliminate Indigenous life and Indigenous claims to land'. This vision is possible.

In closing, we return to the topic of dialogues, yarning, and documenting the experiences of language teachers like Julee and Jennie. What is important about recording our conversations? Language work, as described by First Nations scholars, 'reconnects Indigenous peoples to place and the social relations' (Wildcat et al., 2014). Prioritizing spaces in institutions, in our households, and in relationship with the land and other-than-human life, engages a 'double movement of anticolonialism and rematriation—restoring the futures that Indigenous land and life were meant to follow' (La paperson, 2017: xxvi). Reflecting, re-membering, and making meaning from the experiences and struggles of Julee and Jennie, is to invest energy in futures where Indigenous people flourish. Jennie and Julee's acts engage diverse educational interventions and relational work, where we see through them that creating the conditions to 'greet people', 'use language everyday' and 'feel proud' are forms of structural agency against the injustice of colonialism. Similarly, returning to the wisdom of Jennie's father: 'being who we were meant to be' by reclaiming Indigenous language use is to abide by a decolonial value system, one that is lived through self-in-relationship with land and people. The everyday acts of language reclamation shared across the personal stories of this chapter represent decolonial possibility that lives with communities, land and non-academic life. We thank you, reader, for listening.

Notes

(1) The Wycliffe writing system refers to the orthography created by one of the 20th century's largest North American faith missions: the dual-organizational combination of the Wycliffe Bible Translators (WBT) and the Summer Institute of Linguistics (SIL). This writing system was spread widely among North American missionaries working to translate the bible into Indigenous languages.
(2) Head Start refers to a US federal program for early childhood development and education.

References

Basso, K.H. (1996) *Wisdom Sits in Places: Landscape and Language Among the Western Apache*. University of New Mexico Press.
Bray, D. (ed.) (1998) *Western Apache–English Dictionary. A Community-Generated Bilingual Dictionary*. Bilingual Review Press.
Kovach, M. (2010) Conversation method in Indigenous research. *First Peoples Child & Family Review* 5 (1), 40–48.
Hohepa, M. (2015) Te reo Māori – He reo kura? Māori language – A school language. In C.A. Volker and F.E. Anderson (eds) Education in languages of lesser power: Asia-Pacific perspectives (pp. 244–260). John Benjamins.
La paperson. (2017) *A Third University Is Possible*. University of Minnesota Press.
Long, J. and Dehose, J. (July 9, 2015) Learning that Wisdom Sits in Places: Apache Students Reconnecting to Land and Identity in Arizona, US. In Terralingua. https://terralingua.org/2015/07/09/apache-students-reconnect-to-land-identity-arizona/ (accessed September, 2024).
McIvor, O., Chew, K.A. and Stacey, K.N.I. (2020) Indigenous language learning: Impacts, challenges and opportunities in COVID-19 times. *AlterNative: An International Journal of Indigenous Peoples* 16 (4), 409–412.
Stevens, P.J., Lorenzo Jr, L. and Ahumada, M. (2021) Tribal sovereignty is bestowed upon us by the Creator. *Journal of American Indian Education* 60 (3), 123–132. https://doi.org/10.1353/jaie.2021.a851808.
Wildcat, M., Irlbacher-Fox, S. and Coulthard, G. (2014) Learning from the land: Indigenous land-based pedagogy and decolonization. *Decolonization: Indigeneity, Education & Society* 3 (3), i–xv.

2 Nunayaaġviŋmi itut Uvlumini in Anchorage: A Conversation about Language Revitalization and Reciprocal Research Practices

David E.K. Smith and Richard Atuk

> Aipaani inuiit inupiraaqtut ilughatiŋ. Qaniqłiġuut agliġinaimilat. qaniqłiuut quliaqtuq kina qituuvituutlu nahmun qaiviutlu. Aglaġuktuut qaŋiqłiġuut kinŋimiutin qanuataa uuviilatlu tiyuaatlu ilisimaaġuqtut qituuvatlu kina aŋayuġaatpatlu itpat. Kattimmauraatġuktuut qanuataa piłhuziatniq naġġuŋuaqłilqtuq.

> *Long ago, all Inupiat spoke Inupiaq. Our language was not written. Our language tells us who we are and where we came from. We want to write our language Kinikmiut dialect to give our children and grandchildren a deeper understanding and pride in our ancestry. Real community involvement and shared control of resources can help to accomplish meaningful outputs to community needs.*

Language revitalization requires resources; acquiring resources is aided by visibility; yet the visibility provided by academia is so often insular. This research on language revitalization hoards the necessary resources rather than using them to help communities. This chapter is a dialogue between Inupiaq Elder Richard Atuk and David E.K. Smith, discussing the revitalization of the Kingikmiut dialect and reciprocal research practices. Our conversation is situated in the people, land, and environment of Alaska, which is home to at least 40 distinct Native languages, depending on whom you ask.[1] We focus on the Inupiaq language family, which is spoken throughout much of the northern regions of Alaska, and specifically upon the Kingikmiut dialect, which is centered in the village of Wales (Kingigin) at the tip of the Seward Peninsula in northwest Alaska.

We met as part of David's dissertation research on the educational outcomes of Alaska Native dance. Richard is a member of the Kingikmiut Dancers and Singers of Anchorage, a dance group based in Anchorage, Alaska, that carries on traditional dance practices originating from Wales. To help pursue his dissertation research, David received funding from a National Science Foundation grant. The use of external research funding – and external research as a whole – in Alaska Native communities has historically been extractive and exploitative (Parker Webster & John, 2010). Communities often have little say in how the funds are used, and the knowledge produced through this research is turned outward and removed from the community. To counteract this problematic trend, David wrote the grant proposal to allocate the majority of the funding to an unspecified project. This money could be used on whatever project the Kingikmiut Dancers and Singers of Anchorage collectively found most useful. Through a series of lunches, we settled on two goals. Our first goal is to help document the songs and dances of their dance group as well as the stories and composers behind these songs, to ensure that this knowledge is easily accessible and can continue to be passed down intergenerationally. The second goal is to create a children's book about these songs with the hope of engaging more Alaska Native youth with their culture.

In this chapter we first introduce ourselves, then discuss Richard's experience and efforts on revitalizing and documenting the Kingikmiut dialect. Our use of the term dialect is purposeful. Dialect is the term most commonly used by both Alaska Native and non-Native people to describe the variations of Inupiaq spoken in different regions of Alaska. While we recognize that it has a pejorative connotation among other Indigenous groups, for Inupiaq communities the term dialect is not used to diminish different language groups but is instead a signifier of pride and identity for each individual dialect. This pride and ownership of dialect directly counteracts Western colonial attempts to standardize and homogenize the Inupiaq language. We conclude with a discussion of the children's book and reciprocal research. Well-rounded, contextual, and culturally congruent research involving Indigenous communities requires ensuring that these communities are active collaborators who also benefit from the research practices and outcomes (Kirkness & Barnhardt, 1991). This reciprocal research forefronts shared decision-making and reaffirms Indigenous collaborators as owners of their narratives and intellectual property (Crouch et al., 2023).

We hope that by placing conversations such as this one into an academic context we can highlight the importance of the continuance of the Kingikmiut dialect, that we can argue for the necessary resources required for this continuance, and illuminate the meaningful work currently being done by the Kingikmiut community. At the same time, we hope this chapter to model reciprocal research practices between researchers and communities and encourage creative, accessible outputs that can be shared with the community.

***

Richard: Both my parents were from Wales, Alaska. Their parents and grandparents and ancestry were from the Seward Peninsula area, including Shishmaref, Rocky Point, the Diomede Islands, Siberia, and King Island. I spoke my Kingikmiut language only until first grade at 7 years old. My older siblings and their peers were subjected to physical abuse for speaking their language. My younger siblings and their peers spoke English. I was raised in the traditional Inupiat hunting ways and blessed to be part of the last of our 8-man umiaq hunting crews using the traditional skin boat.

I received a high school diploma, then a degree in geological engineering and a Master's in business administration and served two years in the US Army, including a tour in Vietnam. After working in various jobs, I was involved in recovery of our dance and song tradition. Now I am working on promoting our language.

David: My name is David Elikak Kancewick Smith. I was born and raised in Eagle River, Alaska, on the traditional lands of the Dena'ina Athabascan people. My parents migrated to Alaska from other parts of the United States to work as Native rights lawyers with Alaska Native communities. My middle name, Elikak, is a Yup'ik name passed down by a close family friend after the death of her brother. It means 'one who stands by your side'. I am not Alaska Native but I grew up in Alaska and I call it home.

As a non-Indigenous scholar–educator I work to live up to my namesake Elikak, to support and stand by the side of Indigenous scholars, educators, and communities. Recording ideas in collaboration for others to read, such as this chapter, is part of my effort to support and stand by through bringing attention to the Kingikmiut dialect.

Richard: Our Kingikmiut dialect, along with the dialects of the communities of Diomede, Shishmaref, Teller, Brevig Mission, and King Island, are some of the oldest continuing languages in America. People moved from west to east in the north and rarely, if ever, from east to west. Language groups were Inupiaq in the north, Yupik to the south, and Aleut and others further south. Time of people moving is easily traceable back in recent time to 5,000 years and up to and beyond 15,000 years. Whereas many people and languages tend to become centralized, the Inupiat and their language have continually advanced and occupied a continuous lineal space of 2,500 plus miles.

David: But this has become complicated by Western influence and the increased ease of communication and travel – major factors in dialect loss (Amanao et al., 2014). While these different groups have historically communicated and interacted, these interactions have been limited by the sheer size of the larger Inupiaq-speaking region and difficulties in travel. More recently, with radio, television, phones and the internet to communicate between villages, combined with planes, snowmachines, and other travel advances, everyone feels closer together. Despite all the dialects you mention, most non-Native people generalize Inupiaq into a single language, something that I certainly believed for most of my childhood. This is consistent with Western efforts to help preserve the Inupiaq language which primarily focus on the Inupiaq spoken in the North Slope region and centered in Utqiaġvik.

Richard: The efforts of the Western English-speaking people to standardize Inupiaq like they can standardize English does a disservice to Inupiaq people.[2] This type of treatment that all Inupiat should be the same as each other and have identical languages becomes distilled to the idea that Inupiat are descended from savages who were heathen and somehow less. Today's schools teach mostly the 250-year American history (leaving out slavery and Indian genocide years and so much more). Today's Inupiat students are expected to accept that they somehow materialized in the north and the role of their parents and grandparents was to give them birth. Non-Inupiaq English teachers could only teach what they knew and were constrained to abide by the United States educational system to receive their paycheck.

In a community with a language of oral tradition, the local history is within the language speakers. The Europeans artists and writers highlight traditions for good reason. If you do not know who you are, or where you came from, you will struggle to advance and 'keep up' in life. Furthermore, as they do in America, educators have mostly not taught the Indigenous history that they do know.

In the short time we spent learning our dialect, we also learned some of our history. To understand our history, we need to understand our language. To understand our language dialect, we need to understand our local history. Teachers of Inupiaq are needed. The primary role of our language documentation is to provide the tools necessary to preserve knowledge and records of local regional history and tie the young people strongly to their parents and grandparents and to recognize the strength, endurance, and intelligence that it took to achieve this survival in a good way into good people.

David: As you have started to work against these oppressive colonial forces, what have been your current efforts to teach the Kingikmiut dialect?

Richard: We started with teaching what we knew, then expanded to what our members could teach, then expanded to include what recorded writing and speech was available. At this point, we realized minimal resources were available to teach our dialect and that most of the material that was available to teach the Inupiaq language was expressed in dialects other than our own. This was evident when we started reaching out to elders experienced in our dialect. At this point we shifted our main effort into correcting that shortcoming by transcribing audio recordings of several stories told by individuals from Wales and Little Diomede.

David: Now, so many Native children in Alaska primarily speak English and have grown up in Western educational structures. How do you work to teach Inupiaq within this context?

Richard: As far as we know, Inupiaq adults and leaders did not cede their language. Children were punished for speaking their language. Your question, and the existing teaching efforts and teaching material and programs, highlight the major frustrations we are experiencing now. All of this is done using Western world language, ways and means and American education practices. Children were punished for speaking their language. Repeating this sentence is purposeful. In the first instance, adults and leaders probably had little to say on this. When I studied the history of my parents and their peers and the history of my grandfather and his peers, I realized they were much more aware of national and global affairs than scholars, writers, historians and politicians would dare suggest to each other. I believe our leaders and elders were aware of the events in southeastern Alaska when United States of America Navy ships artillery bombed villages for trying to stand against being dictated to. I also believe our leaders were aware of the circumstances in which and the reasons why American ships decimated to near extinction the Bowhead whales. If they were not fully aware of American and European kidnapping and enslavement of African Nation people, I feel any indigenous people would sense the horrible aura of those crimes.

Regarding the second instance, there are more impacts. One is that readers tend to move on. 'Oh, their hands were slapped; let's move on'. Try to imagine being a happy confident six year old, then being suddenly attacked by an adult for speaking the only language you ever knew. Mostly, they hit the back of your hands with a 12- or 18-inch oak ruler or a long pointer. Or they forced a Fels naphtha bar of soap into your mouth. Some people say they had to stand with their nose on the blackboard until they had permission otherwise. Lives were forever changed. Some became angry and rebellious, others became timid and apathetic. Witnesses of this abuse became untrusting and afraid. Parents were helpless to protest for fear of naval warships. Communities became unsafe and uncertain. Parents and their children's bonds were weakened for allowing such abuse.

Also understand that other community practices like dances were frowned upon or banned by other groups like church leaders. (Today, we have communities where dances and customs were crushed compared to others where dances and customs were supported.) It resulted in pain lasting a lifetime, and in some cases, a firm determination to stop speaking their native language and to protect their children from the pain and possibility of shame by insisting they learn only English.

We realized we needed to start over as far back as we could but still use the English language to communicate to people the value of learning their parents' or grandparents' language.

We appreciate efforts of people attempting to document and teach Inupiaq using the English alphabet. Since many people are familiar with it, we started with the English alphabet framework. Our concept is if Inupiat teach their own language using their own teaching material, what would that look like? We use as much of the English alphabet as is close enough to our language to use, then make new characters for ourselves as fits our tongue. This is our first biggest challenge. How do we sell this concept to people already accustomed to being dictated to by Western people's ways and means?

Our language is structured so differently from the English language that efforts to teach it in American standard ways are almost fruitless. It seems counterproductive but due to the widespread knowledge of English among contemporary youth and young adults, it may require that much of teaching Inupiaq to English-speaking people must be done in English first to explain the differences. Adults learning Inupiaq are perceptive and willing to adapt. Unless they know the differences, they tend constantly to force their English structure into the Inupiaq language. Said another way, they try to force Inupiaq to be English. We learned to advise people to ask, 'How do you say?' rather than 'What is the word for?' If you learn our language, you will learn we do not have existing words as such but, rather, we make 'words' as we speak. This is the biggest challenge.

David: These fundamental differences in structure and form must make creating a dictionary or direct set of translations between English and the Kingikmiut dialect very difficult.

Richard: There is no commonly recognized 'dictionary of our language dialect'. At best, the 'North Slope' dictionary corresponds to 60% of our dialect if you take the time to find them. Imagine, trying to understand a paper or document where 40% of the words are alien to you. The 40–60 figure is based on our own sampling research of the most common words/bases we listed. After the most common, the disparity increases.

David: Without a codified written language resource – an expected tool for much of Western teaching and learning – how, then, do you teach Inupiaq?

Richard: Before we can teach something, we must know it. Before we can learn our language from our elders and experienced speakers, they must be willing to teach us. They will be more willing if we use their language but, even more so, if we use their dialect. The English teacher does not face the same situation. English is ubiquitous. If our elders have confidence that their dialect will be used, their time in teaching becomes so much more meaningful. If they are compensated for their time, their lives become so much more meaningful. They would be working on something they know, something they love, something they want perpetuated for their people. They are the elder and experienced Kingikmiut speakers that we rely upon for confirming our documents of Kingikmiutin. Each village needs its own experts, but we can share, we already know how to share. We do not certify them: they certify us. We hope to work with Bering Straits School District and others as they will recognize the value of teaching children their indigenous language.

David: Drawing on Elders and experienced speakers as the teachers and knowledge bearers provides one part of the learning community, but teachers need interested and invested students. How do you motivate the younger generation of Inupiat to learn the language?

Richard: The biggest challenge to Inupiat teachers on a global level is to communicate to their own people the benefits of learning an additional language, their own language, when English is taught in school and their parents speak English. The English language excels as a means of communication in the modern world. It has no equal language when it comes to modern science, business, legal, historical, artistic and religious concepts. However, the English language is distant, sterile and clinical when applied to Inupiat history, lifestyles, and ways of being and believing. When you consider the biological and genetic long-term connections of people to their past, using English only effectively severs the Inupiaq people from their own history and their own sense of being.

David: This past March, you hosted a workshop on Inupiaq language reclamation with the goal of bringing together Inupiat to discuss these concerns. With more than 100 people participating over three days, what came out of this workshop?

Richard: Our recent workshop to gather Inupiat to reflect on their own language and history was revealing. There is a continuing latent urge in our people to connect with their own people, their own past and history and to know who their own parents, grandparents and ancestors really were and are. We found that just the effort to learn our own language and history is extremely healing and therefore very important.

While our original effort was to teach what we knew, we found we were lacking in resources and knowledge, and we could not teach beyond a small circle. We found that while some forms of Inupiaq would exist in the future, our local dialect would be subject to loss within the next generation. Despite any best advice or process, we found ourselves in the position of gathering and documenting our language while making a best effort to teach it as we learned.

David: What resources would help address these challenges?

Richard: We need accurate documentation of our dialect in written form. Experienced dialect speakers can team up with facilitators who are computer literate and have been trained in Inupiaq structure to document the dialects involved. We are encouraging village residents from the Northwest Seward Peninsula to take an interest in and see the benefits of revitalizing the language of their parents, grandparents and ancestors. When that is awakened, we have a product to offer that parents and grandparents can use to share culture in their own dialect. We believe it will give hope that someone is working on their dialect and that others can join in to learn and help. The documents are the key product. Whether each village has its own table, or several agree to a 'master table' is up to the village or villages. We hope to have cooperative community efforts, so the details of what this will look like have yet to be determined.

David: We had this type of conversation the first time we met when I asked you about how my research project could be geared to potentially provide support for your language teaching efforts. One of my biggest concerns as I started this research was figuring out how to not be extractive in my research practice and provide some sort of benefit to the community I was working with. I talked extensively with different people – both academic mentors and community mentors – before I started the project to try to build out a reciprocal element. As my research centered on dance, music, and education, I assumed that my contribution would fall somewhere in one of those areas, although I was urged to remain open and simply to ask what I could do to help and respond accordingly. Embracing this uncertainty as I applied for grants and fellowships to fund the project was immensely difficult, but I ultimately wrote into these proposals that I needed funding for a reciprocal project and that it was not possible for me to know what that project would be until I was able to work with the community. Luckily, the National Science Foundation Arctic Social Sciences Program was open to this ambiguity.

As scholar–educators with access to many resources, coming to language revitalization work with funding that has no specific strings attached to them allows for cooperative, collaborative and meaningful reciprocal research outcomes. The way these resources are used is dictated by the community to address a need and is not prescribed by an external force. Having decision-making power held by the community instead of the entering researcher is especially important in Indigenous contexts as the Indigenous populations control resources and retain agency, working against pervasive and entrenched asymmetrical colonial power structures in academic research.

Nunayaaġviŋmi itut Uvlumini: A Day at Camp

We, along with other community members, brainstormed ways to use the grant funding and ultimately decided that the bulk of the money would be put toward producing educational materials in the Kingikmiut dialect. With the goal of creating a book to help parents foster an early interest in Inupiaq language and culture, we felt it was important for the book to prominently feature representations of modern Inupiaq life. Karen Eben Garcia, the Inupiaq artist who illustrated the book, did a wonderful job of conveying this slice of life through artwork that includes traditional summer parkas, drums and dance movements alongside riding in a modern red pick-up truck.

We titled the book *Nunayaaġviŋmi itut Uvlumini*, in English *A Day at Camp* (see Figure 2.1). It tells the story of a summer day at camp with their family. Children learn about water safety and participate in cultural activities, including gathering greens, preparing food, getting firewood, and traditional Inupiat dancing. The book features information about four dance songs shared by the Kingikmiut Dancers and Singers of Anchorage. Two of the songs ('Aluiiġaniaq' and 'Tipsizuklui') are more than one hundred years old, 'Kizhuq' was created around 1999, and the 'Float Coat Dance' was created in 2017 to help promote the use of life-jackets when boating in Alaska.[3,4] To help contextualize the book, we included the following as a preface:

> We chose to print the text of this story in both English and Inupiaq so that the story can be read in either language. The Inupiaq dialect used is that of the Northwest Seward Peninsula, specifically the dialect of the people of Wales (Kingigin), Alaska. For many centuries Inupiaq has existed as an oral language only. Young children learned by listening to stories told by their elders in Inupiaq. These stories were repeated often and memorized to be passed along from generation to generation. The traditional dances served as another way to record and celebrate events, activities, and observations about daily life. Each dance tells a story through the song and the motions.
>
> In the 1800s and early 1900s, Inupiat children were forced to go to school and learn English. They were often severely punished for speaking Inupiaq at school. The dances were also stopped in many places, including the village of Wales. During this time the Inupiaq culture and

Figure 2.1 Cover of *Nunayaaġviŋmi itut Uvlumini [A Day at Camp]*

language were threatened with extinction. Since 1990, the Kingikmiut people (and descendants from the village of Wales) have reclaimed their dances and they are now regularly practiced where Kingikmiut people gather at events large and small throughout Alaska, but particularly in Anchorage, Fairbanks, Nome, and Wales. Today the Kingikmiut and people from the other coastal villages on the Seward Peninsula are working to revive and preserve their own dialects by putting their language in writing and teaching it in their schools as other Inupiat people have done.

This book can be a resource for teachers and parents who want to promote awareness and understanding of the language and culture of the Inupiat people of the Seward Peninsula. We believe that this book and others like it can help our young children to gain a sense of pride and a clearer understanding of their own heritage. The stories and illustrations in this book can serve as a springboard for discussions about the readers' and listeners' own cultural experiences.

The community interest in the book, even in its current digital draft, has been remarkable. Richard's wife, Jane Atuk, recently took the book to an elementary school classroom and read it to a class. The teacher and the students were enamored with the story and the artwork and are now all clamoring to get a copy once it is printed. We have had similar reactions from everyone who has seen the book and are hoping to get it into classrooms and homes across Alaska. Much of the excitement is centered around the feeling that the illustrations highlight Inupiaq life and emotions combined with knowing the story is about their culture and told in their dialect. This is hopefully just the start. As this book spreads, we will be able to continue to produce more educational resources in the Kingikmiut dialect.

The resources available to academics – often driven by the perceived greater expertise associated with the number of letters after your name by Western purse-holders – are susceptible to being used in an exploitative self-aggrandizing cycle where the outputs and outcomes of the research are returned to the academic community (Leonard & Mercier, 2016). This process feeds into an endless resource loop that perpetuates the exclusivity of the academy. Resources are given to those who produce for academic audiences who then use those same resources to continue to produce and be increasingly eligible for more resources. The resulting feedback loop is only amplified within the alleged rarified air, remaining extractive while isolating the potential use and meaning of the research.

Projects such as our children's book work to break this cycle through creating and legitimizing outputs external to the academy using academic resources. The extractive feedback cycle, however, is so entrenched that many of our community members remain concerned about extractive research practices. Some have expressed fear that, by publishing a book, their cultural and intellectual property will be stolen, misrepresented, and used to profit others, as has too often happened in the past (Parker Webster & John, 2010). The key differentiators for our project are its specificity and who holds control. Projects working to disrupt the existing resource cycle must be community generated and context specific rather than a researcher replicating previous work simply because it was successful in other settings. Bringing these resources into a community, giving control over the resources to those most knowledgeable about local needs, and collectively accomplishing something meaningful on the ground that has no aim other than to accomplish what the community needs, breaks the extractive feedback loop. As communities secure the external resources it becomes progressively easier for them to continue to access more resources: they are allowed into the resource cycle. Over time, the snowballing admission and inclusion of communities has the potential to fundamentally transform the resource cycle. Once in the door, communities are now able to climb within the power structure of those receiving and giving resources. A shifting power structure could work to remove Western bias from the criteria of who receives resources and who benefits from the outputs and outcomes of research. We recognize the importance of research within the academy – but the outcomes and outputs of reciprocal research must expand beyond academic contexts to be recognized in both external and local settings.

Notes

(1) The Alaska Native Language Center at the University of Fairbanks created a language map that is widely used and that is available at https://www.uaf.edu/anlc/languages-move/languages.php. While this is a useful resource and provides helpful context, the demarcations on the map and the language groupings were created by a select group in academia and are disputed by some Alaska Native communities.
(2) Standardize may not be the best term. English-speaking people across the nation and across the globe understand each other with little difficulty. Inupiaq speakers from Wales have a commonality of understanding in the high 90% plus range within a 60-mile radius. At Kotzebue, about 70 miles away, it is less than 50%. At another direction 200 miles east, it is 70% and at Unalakleet it is 80% + with some segment of that population. Point Hope less than 60%. Barrow less than 60%. Canada, from 3% to 70%. Greenland, less than 7%. The primary reason is Inupiaq has been here somewhere up to 15,000 years across 2,500 miles lineal and English is concentrated among many people up to 700 years.
(3) Life-jackets are vital in Alaska due to the extreme temperature of the Arctic waters. Submersion can be fatal as you can go into hypothermic shock within minutes, rendering you unable to swim. Alaska Native people rely on the frigid lakes, rivers, and ocean for transportation and substance. Despite this reliance and its associated danger, life-jacket use in Alaska Native communities is low.
(4) A video of the 'Float Coat Dance' can be found at https://www.youtube.com/watch?v=uF_wQKeFf-U.

References

Crouch, M.C., Kim, S.M., Asquith-Heinz, Z., Decker, E., Andrew, N.T., Lewis, J.P. and Rosich, R.M. (2023) Indigenous Elder-centered methodology: Research that decolonizes and indigenizes. *AlterNative: An International Journal of Indigenous Peoples* 19 (2), 447–456.

Kirkness, V.J. and Barnhardt, R. (1991) First Nations and higher education: The four R's—Respect, relevance, reciprocity, responsibility. *Journal of American Indian Education* 30 (3), 1–15.

Leonard, B.R. and Mercier, O.R. (2016) Indigenous struggles within the colonial project: Reclaiming Indigenous knowledges in the western academy. *Knowledge Cultures* 4 (3), 99–116.

Parker Webster, J. and John, T.A. (2010) Preserving a space for cross-cultural collaborations: An account of insider/outsider issues. *Ethnography and Education* 5 (2), 175–191.

3 Reclamation of Language, Stories, Relationship to the Land: Niimíipuu Female as a Storyteller

Angel Sobotta Talaltlílpt

This chapter utilizes my research on Indigenous law as it is embedded within the Niimíipuu stories, language, and connection to the land. The Niimíipuu, also known as the Nez Perce, are a Native American people whose reservation is situated in North Central Idaho, bordering the state of Washington in the United States of America (see Figure 3.1). Niimíipuu, meaning 'the People', will be used consistently throughout this chapter.

Language is the heartbeat of one's culture. Indigenous people experience this through their relationship with the language, stories, and the land. Settler colonialism has interrupted these relationships, and

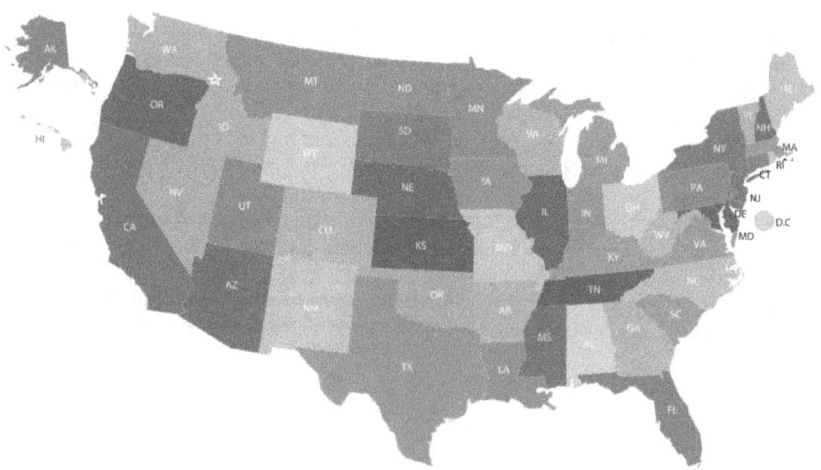

Figure 3.1 The star depicts where the Nez Perce Reservation is located in Idaho

the violence of colonization, alongside patriarchal hegemony, silenced Indigenous women, diminishing the role of the Indigenous female as a storyteller. Indigenous women were also made invisible in areas such as research and are overlooked as capable of contributing to knowledge.

I am a Niimíipuu woman, born on our aboriginal territory and raised on our Niimíipuu reservation in Lapwai, Idaho. In my 27 years of language reclamation, I am also a storyteller and I use Niimíipuu traditional stories and language in my reclamation work. Several other Niimíipuu Female Educators also use traditional stories in their work. Therefore, my doctoral research at the University of Idaho focused on using a gendered talking circle to create an equitable space for the Niimíipuu Female Educators to share knowledge, explore female perspectives on traditional Niimíipuu stories, and collectively contribute to new negotiations of meaning. Niimíipuu women play a prominent role as disciplinary figures and educators. Gendered exploration of Niimíipuu knowledge matters, as Sami scholar Rauna Kuokkanen (2012) cited in (Huaman & Naranjo, 2019: 226) has noted: 'un-gendered research on Indigenous self-determination conceals patriarchal structures and relations of power'. The Female Educators' Talking Circles provide a means to advance individual and collective rights to contribute to knowledge where violations of women's human rights prevented them from being contributors to knowledge in the past. When women contribute to knowledge and empower themselves with knowledge, they reclaim their role as storytellers and, in this way, they decolonize.

Land and Language of the Titwáatit

A lot of our titwáatit are tied to the land. There are reportedly over 300 documented Niimíipuum titwáatit (People's stories) (Taylor, 2010). American historian, Alvin Josephy Jr., describes where our Niimiipuu ancestors lived and where they traveled.

> The usual and accustomed places of the Niimíipuu [see Figure 3.2] are in the Plateau cultural area of the Northwest from the Rockies to the Cascade Mountains, Fraser River in British Columbia to the Great Basin in southern Oregon, and Idaho. The Niimíipuu aboriginal homeland covered approximately 70,200 square kilometers (27,000 square miles), covering areas in Idaho, Washington, Oregon, Montana, and parts of Wyoming. The Plateau tribes include the Nez Perce, Wallawallas, Palouses, Umatillas, Yakamas, and Salish-speaking peoples as the Coeur d'Alenes, Spokanes, and Flatheads. (Josephy, 2007: 2)

These Plateau tribes share many cultural practices and spoke closely related dialects of Sahaptian tongues of the Penutian language family, as well as Cayuses and Molalas, whose somewhat different languages also stemmed from the Penutian stock (see Figures 3.3 and 3.4) (Josephy, 2007: 2).

52 Part 1: Narratives of Reclamation: Lifework and Learning in Dialogue

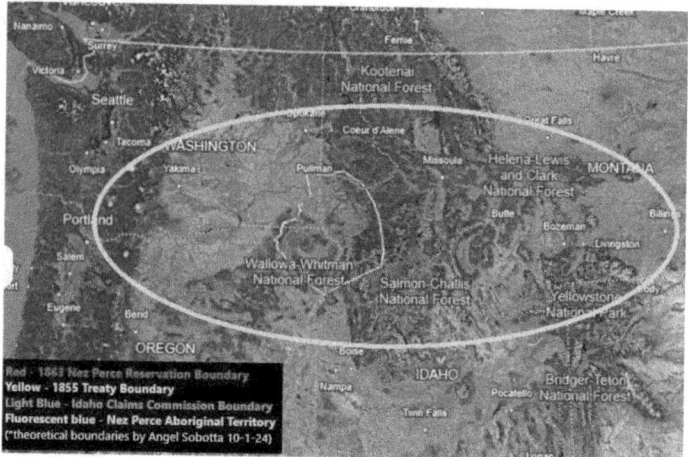

Figure 3.2 Nez Perce Tribe area of use and influence: 1863 Reservation Boundary

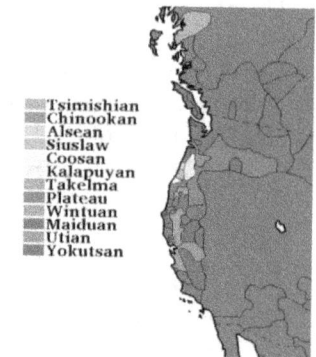

Figure 3.3 Penutian languages map

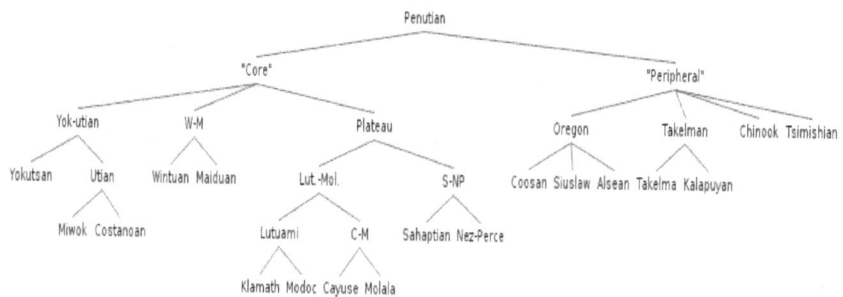

Figure 3.4 Penutian language family

The description of the Niimíipuu aboriginal territory and their language family shows where connections were made with other tribes. Connections were made throughout Native land in the United States and Indigenous People's land in Canada and Mexico. The Niimíipuu sent 'runners' to different parts of the country to learn new things. Some Niimíipuu runners journeyed east a few years before Lewis and Clark and the Corps of Discovery arrived in Niimíipuu country in 1805 (Pinkham et al., 2013).

Decolonizing Our Stories

To decolonize means to indigenize by reclaiming the knowledge within the language and stories. In North America, Indigenous stories were altered to fit a Western worldview, even when recorded in Indigenous languages. Traditional stories were lost partly due to the colonizers forcing American Indian boarding schools upon the Indigenous population. The Nez Perce who attended boarding schools were separated from the Nez Perce family structure, in several different boarding schools. The Indian boarding schools or Indian industrial schools that Nez Perce children attended were Chemawa Boarding School in Oregon (formerly Forest Grove Indian Boarding School) in 1879–1945, Carlisle Indian Industrial School in Carlisle, Pennsylvania, in the 1870s, Chilocco Indian Industrial School near Newkirk, Oklahoma, in the 1880s, Spalding Indian Boarding School at Spalding, Idaho, in the 1890s, and the Catholic Mission School at Slickpoo Mission near Culdesac, Idaho, in the 1880s–1940 (Slickpoo & Walker, 1973; Taylor, 2010). These dates align with the American Indian boarding school era elsewhere in the United States: approximately the 1850s–1980s. Indigenous story teachings were prohibited at these Indian boarding schools and industrial schools (Lomawaima & McCarty, 2006).

As First Nations scholar Jo-ann Archibald (2008: 24) states: 'Indigenous stories have lost much educational and social value due to colonization', in which Christian religious groups – such as that led by Presbyterian Christian missionary Reverend Henry Harmon Spalding, who arrived in Nez Perce country in 1836 – played a central role. The Niimíipuu already had a way of worshiping, though some were also open to learning the white man's way, and many were baptized (Slickpoo & Walker, 1973). The missionaries' quest to teach Christian values worked continuously to replace Niimíipuu teachings and values, not only in worship but also in the Niimíipuu relationship to the land, in assimilative farming practices, demonizing them for wearing their traditional clothing, essentially making them look and think like the white man (Slickpoo, 1973). However, the Niimíipuu always sought ways to empower themselves (Pinkham et al., 2013).

A technique to erase the values of the Niimíipuu in stories and oral traditions was through 'bowdlerization'. The term, coined in the 1800s by physician Thomas Bowdler, was used to describe creating 'purified literature' or omitting words considered vulgar from the Christian worldview. Missionaries like Henry Harmon Spalding practiced bowdlerization, and many Niimíipuu with newly acquired or forced-upon Western worldviews also practiced bowdlerization. The telling of traditional stories, specifically stories that had elements of sexual context, was subject to bowdlerization. Josiah Pinkham, Cultural Resources Ethnographer for the Nez Perce Tribe, explains this process in the following way:

> There's that story about 'iceyéeye's símqe [Coyote's penis], where he sees those girls across the water, and he starts to, you know, pound his símqe, make it longer, and he takes advantage of them, and he gets busted. So, he reels it back in and throws it over his shoulder, and off he goes. And he understands that he can't live his life carrying that thing around. So, he coils it up, and he severs it. If a young man is the kind of person that takes advantage of young women, they are going to remember it, and you're going to be stuck with your reputation. There is a landmark of this. Some call it 'Coyote's rope,' they bowdlerized it. But oral traditions still incorporate the word símqe because it reflects human nature. I teach my boys this, and they did not grow up ruined. They are not pedophiles. They're functioning members of society. They learn from the landmark. (Josiah Pinkham, personal communication, September 12, 2022)

To re-establish the Niimíipuu knowledge within the stories is to 're-indigenize', taking back our truth of the titwáatit (stories) where bowdlerization concealed our true telling of the titwáatit. To re-indigenize reunites the truth and power in the stories of Indigenous people with an Indigenous worldview. To tell a titwáatit from a Niimíipuu perspective re-establishes Niimíipuu knowledge within the titwáatit. In driving by the place that Josiah referred to as the 'Coyote's Rope', a physical place located west of Clarkston, Washington (USA) on US Highway 12 near Chief Timothy Park, west of Clarkston, Washington, a Niimíipuu elder, stated: 'My grandma told me that was Coyote's guts where the Army Corps of Engineers cut through some of it to make a road'. This titwáatit had elements of sexual context that were bowdlerized, replacing símqe (penis) with máymay (guts, intestines, entrails) or including the símqe as an internal organ. However, Nimipuuwíitki (in the People's way of thinking) Teecukwenéewit (way of teaching) did not bowdlerize and was told truthfully and to the point. In July 2016, on a long road trip to Montana, I told these Niimíipuu sex education types of titwáatit to my kids when they were younger. At the time, one of my daughters thought I was telling her a 'dirty story'; in astonishment, she expressed: 'Mom, how can you be telling us these stories? They're so inappropriate?' I discussed this with Josiah Pinkham, and he stated: 'They are appropriate. That's how we learned about sex. We didn't view sex as dirty, so when you tell your daughter these stories, tell her that sex wasn't viewed as dirty' (Josiah Pinkham, personal communication, 2016).

Our stories, as they are shared through language, tell of specific cultural values. For the Niimíipuu, learning about important lessons, such as sexuality and sex, was part of knowing the world, where life comes from, and being responsible and respectful members of a family and our wider society. Decolonizing the values shared in a story from the female perspective is the main goal behind my line of inquiry: What new knowledge did the Niimíipuu Female Educators' Talking Circles gain when listening to the stories? Here, I will describe what was shared and learned as Niimíipuu women gathered to listen to, and learn from, our original stories.

Methodologies

The Female Educators' Talking Circles consisted of nine enrolled Niimíipuu tribal members. All participants reside on or near the Nez Perce Reservation in North Central Idaho and within the traditional Niimíipuu territory (see Figure 3.2).

The gathering of this group was the focus of my doctoral research from 2020 to 2021. Due to the COVID-19 pandemic, the Female Educators' Talking Circles had three meetings through the Zoom application and attended one field trip together. I implemented an Indigenous methodology in the research. According to Indigenous scholar Shawn Wilson, this entails an Indigenous epistemology, a way of thinking, and a relational accountability to 'all my relations' (Wilson, 2004: 105). The Indigenous methodology I used was storywork, known elsewhere as personal narrative, or talking circles (Archibald, 2008; Kovach, 2009), or focus groups. It is about relationships, the importance of a relationship, and getting into a relationship. At times, our talking circle became a space of intimate spiritual connection as we used storywork to share our personal narratives of what we learned and took to heart from the titwáatit.

As the Titwatiyaw'áat (storyteller), a more culturally appropriate title rather than researcher, I approached this storywork by using the three R's: Respect, Reciprocity, and Relationality (Wilson, 2008) to guide me through the storywork. Talking circles are an intimate Indigenous methodology where respect is reciprocal (Haig-Brown & Archibald, 1996), and Zoom meetings are not the ideal way to capture the stories' spirit. COVID-19 precautions required distance and mask-wearing, impacting our talking circles' nature. However, to honor this space, I lit a bundle of our Indigenous medicines of sage and sweetgrass in the initial talking circle to smudge the co-Titwatiyaw'áat. In this way, we welcomed our first teachers, the Titwatityáaya (story people), who are the Animal People. As we heard their stories, reflected in their teachings, and poured out our hearts in our sharing, the Animal People's spirits through the stories were felt, but, more so, the group experienced that research is a ceremony, 'a ceremony for improving your relationship with an idea. It takes place every day and has taken place throughout our history...' (Wilson, 2008: 162). It served as spiritual medicine to strengthen us as we experienced this through the COVID-19 pandemic. It was a sacred space.

Forming a relationship with the Female Educators, and they with each other, became just as important as forming a relationship with the story, land and language. Within the Female Educators' Talking Circle, which I call píiten'wet ciílpcilp [discuss/talk with each other circle], a circle of trust and friendship developed. It allowed the women to open up and share their hearts, which became a deeply personal experience. This píiten'wet ciílpcilp gave us a safe place to talk. Indigenous knowledge from the Niimíipuu women's current reflections on old stories connected us with the past, and the fluidity of the old story to our modern-day experiences added to a new collection of Niimíipuu knowledge.

Female Educators' Talking Circle

The stories covered were with known story sites and told in Nimipuutímt by Niimíipuu storytellers Elizabeth Penney Wilson and Samuel Watters, documented and recorded in the 1960s. I provided the ladies with different ways of experiencing the stories. The steps I used are described below.

(1) Listened to the story recordings following the interlinear text and then read the English translations.
(2) Used Google Earth and other pictures to show the story's location. Asked first if they knew where the titwáatit site was and showed them the morphology of the story place name.
(3) Shared the Niimíipuu knowledge and the common themes I learned in titwáatit. Switched from sharing first to inviting the co-Titwatiyaw'áat to share what they learned from the titwáatit as a way for them to obtain and contribute to Niimíipuu knowledge without my influence. This process resulted in rich discussions.
(4) Discussed the songs and chants in the titwáatit.
(5) Challenged each participant to develop their relationship to the story place by calling it by the name in Nimipuutímt.
(6) Took a field trip to the Hatwai area in the Clearwater River Casino vicinity to view five titwáatit sites and a quick review of each titwáatit.

While my approach builds on contemporary work in Indigenous research methodologies of North America, the Niimíipuu also used this traditional method of inquiry, a píiten'wet ciílpcilp (talking circle). Niimíipuu leaders would sit in a circle and smoke with the peace pipe in a ceremony to discuss important matters. As the Titwatiyaw'áat, or researcher, I had a dual role of Titwaatiyaw'áat and a participant

Figure 3.5 Cemíitx (huckleberries), representing knowledge

of the píiten'wet cíilpcilp. The Niimíipuu Female Educators were the co-Titwatiyaw'áat co-researchers. During our discussions, it was like a journey of driving in the mountains in search of the color purple in the green bushes that would reveal the delicious cemíitx (huckleberries). When you find them, they are valuable, a delight, 'ahímkasayqsa (it tastes beautiful), like Niimíipuu soul food, the wisdom that connects you to your ancestors who took the same journey in search of cemíitx. Metaphorically, we were fed baskets of cemíitx, like round royal purple wisdom, wiitmiipn'itéen'ix (each pouring out their heart] filling up each one's basket, Niimíipuu liméq'is cúukwenin' (with deep Niimíipuu knowledge) (see Figure 3.5).

In an Indigenous research paradigm, it is respectful and part of our Indigenous axiology (ethics) to name the co-Titwatiyaw'áat. Trust relationships were formed, and timíipn'isine (poured out their hearts) filled with the cemíitx of wisdom. Furthermore, like the titwatityáaya (story beings) in our titwáatit, they always prepare for the Netíitelwit (human beings) to come. Likewise, the Female Educators wiitmiipn'itéen'ix (each pouring out their heart), told their stories to 'feed' the Niimíipuu with the liméq'is cúukwenin' (deep knowledge) of cemíitx. The Niimíipuu need to know who their teachers are, 'So if you are leaving out their name, how can people know that you have the authority to present this information?' (Wilson, 2008: 168). Therefore, I use the names of the co-Titwatiyaw'áat.

To empower the co-Titwatiyaw'áat with titwáatit knowledge, it was important first to provide them with titwáatit that had a known location. The three main stories discussed included K'assaynóomy'ac (Elbow Child/baby), Hayóoxchacwal kaa Paqáx̱paqax (Cottontail Boy and Small Rattlesnake), and Tukeyúutpe (Laying Down Place). For this chapter, I will discuss the Niimíipuu knowledge from the K'assaynóomy'ac story as shared by the Female Educators (co-Titwatiyaw'áat).

Female Educators' Storywork Contributing to Knowledge

The Female Educators' Talking Circles became a space for receiving, sharing, and contributing to knowledge. The decolonizing process un-silenced the Female Educators as they addressed the values shared in a story from the female perspective and addressed the research question: What new knowledge did the Niimíipuu Female Educators' Talking Circles gain when listening to the stories?

K'assaynóomy'ac

The morphology breakdown of K'assaynóomy'ac, the titwáatit summary, and some of the titwáatit discussion are as follows.

Morphology

k'assáyno	+	miyá'c
Elbow	+	Child

K'assaynóomy'ac summary

'iceyéeye [Coyote] had a baby boy that popped out of his Elbow: thus, the name Elbow Baby is used more frequently than Elbow Child. 'iceyéeye and his best friend Tilípe' (Fox) both had five daughters each. They spent the winter together 'elwíteespe (at the winter quarters). 'iceyéeye left his firstborn son with the girls when he went hunting. They tickled and tickled K'assaynóomy'ac too much. It was more than he could handle, and his sisters ended up tickling him to death. 'iceyéeye was so sad that his son died, so he got revenge on the daughters. As they slept in their pit house, the 'elwíteespe, he killed them and the daughters of Tilípe' by drowning them with his urine. But the laymíwt (youngest) daughter escaped. She told 'iceyéeye' that she is going to where the sun sets and will return in the Fall. The laymíwt came back as wind and fire, was loud as a storm, and chanted,

cimik'íisqiwne 'awi'líwaa'inpqawtaca.
(Hateful old man, I am going to scoop up in fire.)

ham'olíicqiwna 'awi'líwaasiqataqawtaca ham'óolic kem
(Cute old man, I am going over him, cute you.)

The laymíwt daughter got revenge by jumping over the nice man, Tilípe', and burning the hateful man 'iceyéeye. As time passed, Tilípe' got lonely and found the jawbone of 'iceyéeye, stepped over it three times, and 'iceyéeye returned to life. Stepping over someone's remains was believed to bring that person back to life (Aoki & Walker, 1989; Phinney, 1934).

The Female Educators' Talking Circles discussed the stories, and each shared how they connected to the stories, creating meaning for them. Mirroring what Wilson (2008: 24) described, the titwáatit allows the co-Titwatiyaw'áat 'to draw their conclusions and to gain life lessons from a more personal perspective'.

New knowledge gained through the story of K'assaynóomy'ac

The Female Educators' discussions revealed many themes by the co-Titwatiyaw'áat. The themes in this titwáatit include:

Figure 3.6 K'assaynóomy'ac (Elbow Baby)

Table 3.1 Themes revealed from the titwáatit of K'assaynóomy'ac

Most Frequent Themes:

Protection and Caring: The sisters help raise their siblings, taking care and protecting each other.

Ceremony and Ritual: Ceremony and Ritual help with the mourning period.

Boundaries, Responsibility: Respecting one's boundaries and being responsible for others are values that can have dire consequences if not followed.

Revenge, Forgiveness, and Healing: Revenge is bad medicine, but good medicine occurs through forgiving, which leads to healing.

Hostile Aggression/Violence/Unhealthy Coping: Revenge involves hostile aggression and violence and is an unhealthy way to cope.

Justice/Karma: Handling situations with revenge results in bad karma for the vengeful, with justice being served through karma.

Cross-cultural Epistemology for Deeper Understanding and Connection: Cultural teachings from other Indigenous people help connect knowledge and understanding.

Least Frequent Theme:

Discipline, Grief, and Mourning: Group discipline is a traditional teaching, and Grief and Mourning are sub-themes of Ceremony and Ritual.

When viewed through Nimipuuwíitki (in the People's way of thinking), reality, or ontology, these themes are the tamáalwit (law). The co-Titwatiyaw'áat see the stories as tamáalwit or axiology – ethics and morals and relate meaning from the titwáatit to the tamáalwit codes of conduct appropriate for our Niimíipuu.

The titwáatit are called 'Law' because they have teachings like guideposts to adhere to. There is a deep connection between learning stories and reclaiming Niimíipuu knowledge through the language. The morphology breakdown of Nimipuutímt is like a titwáatit unfolding as it reveals pieces of Indigenous or Niimíipuu knowledge and guidance within the words. Author John Borrows explains the relationship between worldview and language thus: 'learning Indigenous law can heighten the ability and the motivation to learn the Indigenous language of which the law is a part' (Borrows, 2016: 810). The co-Titwatiyaw'áat experienced a heightened awareness of the story name and appreciated learning the Niimíipuu knowledge, connecting them to the story more powerfully.

New Lessons Found in the Stories

Protection, caring and boundaries

Similar to having a heightened awareness of the story name, the co-Titwatiyaw'áat, through their storywork, made meaningful connections to the story relating to the themes of *protection, caring and boundaries*:

> Honestly, I always thought there was a lesson in the fact that the girls tickled the baby to death. But I could never figure out what the lesson

with that action was. They were just having too much fun. It was just too much for the little one, you know, maybe the little ones don't need that much stimulation. (Vivian)

Vivian touched on the tamáalwit codes of conduct with the themes of *protection, caring, and boundaries*. The cemíitx of knowledge ripened in her as she recognized the tamáalwit happening in the titwáatit.

For many in the Female Educators' Talking Circle (including myself), the findings identified *forgiveness* (identified by 5) as a main tamáalwit (theme). The co-Titwatiyaw'áat saw in Tilípe' who forgave his best friend 'iceyéeye. In the story, 'iceyéeye killed his and Tilípe'nim (Fox's) daughters in revenge. However, the laymíwt daughter escaped and warned that she would return in the Fall. Yet Tilípe' experienced grief not only for his daughters but also for his best friend 'iceyéeye. I was the only one who discussed grief. However, grief ties into mourning and ties into the theme of *ceremony and ritual*, which will be addressed further. 'iceyéeye experienced karma when the laymíwt daughter came back as a storm of wind and fire and scooped up 'iceyéeye with fire, and justice was served by the laymíwt as she killed 'iceyéeye in revenge. Tilípe' brought his 'best friend' 'iceyéeye back to life by stepping over him three times (*ceremony and ritual*, identified by 5). Now that's forgiveness. Tilípe' models that in life's most difficult situations, healing begins once one forgives and can continue with life more peacefully. Forgiveness is healing.

Ceremony and ritual

Tilípe' in his way, went through *ceremony and ritual*. Two co-Titwatiyaw'áat share traditional teachings of dealing with *grief and mourning* through *ceremony and ritual*.

> I can relate this back to waláhsat (Niimíipuu worship) as well when you go through the teachings and go through the ceremony. And you get to that point when you have the Crying Ceremony, and then they tell you after no crying at all after a year. You can't cry because you're holding them back. (Alicia)

> Yeah, that's usually done (Crying Ceremony) because you're holding in your tears while your loved one is still around, and then after the loved one is in the ground and then you can let it out, but you cry, not to get over it, but more to let it all out. And then the next year is the most important, to be able to get over it, so there's, you know, there's a whole year of mourning that is the usual timeline. I guess we're not the normal but the usual timeline, though. We practice. I guess it's hard to try to get over something so quickly. (Angela)

Alicia and Angela, in their sharing, added to the cemíitx (huckleberries) of Knowledge by addressing the themes of *ceremony and ritual* and *healing and mourning*. Like the purple cemíitx is tied to the land, so are the tamáalwit, not only in titwáatit but in experiencing ceremony, ritual, healing, and mourning as 'iceyéeye did in the K'assaynóomy'ac story. Indigenous scholar, Leanne Betasamosake Simpson (2017) explains:

> In Land-Based pedagogy theories, when we are experiencing these stories, we are experiencing these theories. 'Theory' within this context is generated from the ground up and its power stems from its living resonance within individuals and collectives. (Simpson, 2017: 7)

What Simpson describes as land-based pedagogy is important to implement in Indigenous research because of our relationship to the land, language, and stories. As Alicia and Angela underscore, our stories are guides, containing many lessons relating to each situated action. As Niimíipuu growing up with these stories and experiencing these stories, we are experiencing the theories of being, Nimipuuwíitki (the People's way of thinking), Nimipuunéewit (the People's way of knowing), and Niimíipuum tamáalwit (the People's law (theory)). Theory is not just for academics described in the European world like ontology and epistemology. We live it (Simpson, 2014).

When driving by this titwáatit site prominently lying on the top of the hill across the river from the Nez Perce Tribe-owned Clearwater River Casino is where K'assaynóomy'ac lies, like in a baby board, and appearing elderly, like a chief, thus also called the Sleeping Chief (see Figure 3.6). In our Nimipuuwíitki, once a person passes away, even if they are young, they are now referred to as our téeq'is (elder). Once passing over, they experience the afterlife that the living has no experience of, so they gain wisdom. 'Iceyéeye mourned the passing of his child K'assaynóomy'ac. Crying, he stated that his child would be rich and a great chief. So, at a certain angle, the land looks like a chief in a warbonnet sleeping on his back. The profile of the face is prominent.

Forgiveness and healing

The tamáalwit of *forgiveness and healing* provides a valuable teachings for the Niimíipuu to learn from. The co-Titwatiyaw'áat added royal purple cemíitx to the huckleberry basket of wisdom. The women's connections to the stories reveal that forgiveness is a cultural value that leads to healing. There is such beauty in these cultural values of *forgiveness and healing*.

> I like the cultural value of forgiveness, too. Just as it really resonates and, you know, my own personal journey on this earth and how important that really does play for your mental health, your spiritual well-being, I mean, everything. And sometimes, you know, forgiving someone or yourself, whatever it might be, is the most courageous thing you could ever do. You know, because it will hold you back. (Stacia)

> Especially where forgiveness with family. Yeah, even more so. Because you keep holding that in, and yeah, eventually, you have to forgive that person, and then you're off. It's worse for you than what it was before. Yeah. Because you couldn't say what you really wanted to say all because you're being too stubborn. (Alicia)

The cultural value of *forgiveness* leads to *healing*, and knowing the story and the story site serves as a reminder that, in forgiving, we heal. Therefore, the land is constantly teaching.

Revitalization of Niimíipuu Knowledge among Niimíipuu Women

Another Niimíipuu cultural value, tamáalwit or axiology, and a valuable teaching from this titwáatit is 'Responsibility'. Of particular interest is the gendered responsibility of the female as an auntie, like in our stories, cíice' qócqoc (Auntie meadowlark), who is responsible for telling the news, gives advice. When the laymíwt watches her older sisters get into trouble, she learns from their mistakes and becomes the most responsible of them. Coming from a family of five sisters and four brothers, I can attest to raising our young ones together and the caretaking of us by our aunties and grandmas. Stacia explains the role of Niimíipuu women with gendered lessons of responsibility and protection:

> Even the role with, you know, 'iceyéeye's ha'áyat mamay'ác [Coyote's female children] and the role of Niimíipuu women about how, you know, we raise up our young ones together, and that is the responsibility of sisters to be able to keep an eye on, you know, the family members, community members, and things like that. Now, it is all a community effort because it probably would take five people to help a young child, boy or girl. (Stacia)

The Wet'ew'éet (Whip person) 'Whipper' is a Whipman or Whipwoman who has the authority to discipline someone's child with a whip. The Wet'ew'éet is a cultural value of shared communal responsibility. A Wet'ew'éet would use their whip or tell the child or teen getting whipped to get a good switch from a tree. If one kid did something wrong and other kids were present during the bad behavior, they could all be sent to the Wet'ew'éet for not looking out for each other. They are supposed to take care of each other. Responsibility is another cultural value. If they got whipped for someone else's wrongdoing, that taught them responsibility. Shared communal responsibility is out of care and love for that person getting whipped, plus care and love for the parent needing help. It also relieved the parent from using their hand to discipline their child. And if a child was sent to the Wet'ew'éet, they knew it was serious.

I have wanted to send my children to a Wet'ew'éet, and this isn't out of cruelness but seeking help. However, the roles of the Wet'ew'éet have changed. They aren't called upon to discipline with whippings anymore. Assimilation forced upon the Niimíipuu led to a change in discipline, especially with the whip. In today's Western society, parenting is more lenient, so whippings or spankings are frowned upon. Parenting focuses on letting the child express their feelings and opinions openly with others. Years ago, a Niimíipuu child was told to be quiet, not speak, and to listen. It was acceptable for someone to receive a lecture from another adult. And now, even trying to discipline another person's child with words is no longer accepted. A few years ago, the Circle of Elders discussed how Nez Perce tribal members requested that the old way of the Wet'ew'éet be brought back and the disciplinary whippings implemented. However, not all Wet'ew'éet were comfortable doing that.

Na'qáac (my maternal grandmother) Wesese (wic'éese) (born and reborn), also known as Rena Katherine Ramsey, was a Wet'ew'eet for the Chief Joseph and Warriors powwow until her passing in 1999. Then, Ne'íic (my mother), Rosa Mae Spencer Yearout, inherited her mother's wet'éen'es (thing for whipping) or walliskó's (horsewhip). And then she became the Wet'ew'eet for the same powwow. Today's role of Wet'ew'eet has changed, but it still has a disciplinary role. A Wet'ew'eet holds the walliskó at a powwow to show authority. They help to keep order on the dance floor. They raise their walliskó's, indicating that people should stand, and if little kids are running around on the dance floor, the simple walking over to the children with a walliskó's sends a strong message to behave, and the kids listen.

On December 27, 2021, each co-Titwatiyaw'áat of the talking circle met at Héetwey Plaza west of the Clearwater River Casino parking lot. This field trip was designed to help the co-Titwatiyaw'áat and further develop our relationship with the wéetes (land) of the titwáatit sites we discussed in our talking circles through Zoom. At the parking lot, I reviewed the titwáatit and discussion points, located the titwáatit rock formations, practiced saying the titwáatit name Nimipuutímtki (in the People's language), and repeated some key phrases Nimipuutímtki from the titwáatit name.

During the traditional storytelling, the cold winter December day allowed the co-Titwatiyaw'áat to create a relationship with the land at the titwáatit sites. It snowed, and the rock formations were beginning to be blanketed with snow, providing a different perspective of the titwáatit sites compared to the other seasons. The snow brought a small amount of mystical magic into the air, swirling around the titwáatit sites. This beautiful winter day was captured with a group picture with the story sites as our background (Figure 3.7). I had visited the titwáatit sites previously in the spring, summer, fall, and winter, and completed my visit to the titwáatit sites in all four seasons. Relationships

Figure 3.7 K'assaynóomy'ac story site by Clearwater River Casino. Winter Field Trip 12/27/21

are strengthened with frequent visits throughout each season. Re-establishing the relationship gives the potential for the learner, like the co-Titwatiyaw'áat, to grow as Titwatiyaw'áat (storytellers) and grow into 'complex mindfulness' over one's lifetime (Iseke, 2013). The person's growing knowledge of the story weaves together pieces of knowledge throughout one's lifetime, like when a weaver adds strand by strand to create a whole basket, piece by piece, forming a collection of knowledge.

In a relationship, names are remembered. Some of the co-Titwatiyaw'áat remembered the Nimipuutímt name of the titwáatit site. When asked what the name of the titwáatit site was during the field trip, Wiitmíipn'ime (each person poured out their heart – remembering place) was remembered by a couple of the co-Titwatiyaw'áat as well as remembering K'assaynóomy'ac (Elbow Baby). They remembered Hay'óoxchacwal (Cottontailboy) but weren't sure how to say Paqaxpáqax (Small Rattlesnake), and all remembered Wexwéqt (Frog); however, there were four total wexwéqt stories that we discussed. Our Niimíipuu land has natural resources to offer us and to sustain us. A resource at these story sites is wisdom. Western Apache elder Dudley Patterson shared: 'It's in these places... wisdom sits in places' (Basso, 1996). Knowing the power of these places, I encouraged them to visit these sites each season, or at least to acknowledge them when they drive by, to reflect on the teachings and the Animal People in the titwáatit. In this deliberate attention to the titwáatit site, one will grow in knowledge and learn something new about the titwáatit or themselves. At the same time, it is an act to decolonize, preferably to state this act as Indigenizing our educational system.

As the co-Titwatiyaw'áat collectively contributed to titwáatit knowledge, reclaiming language, story, and relationship to the land, they practiced a main tenet of land-based pedagogy by decolonizing.

Indigenous stories allow us to practice a reclamation of Indigenous voice. The relationship with the land is reciprocal. The land sits and waits to offer its wisdom. When one thinks of Indigenous knowledge, one is most likely referring to the knowledge passed down to us from our Indigenous ancestors. Our ancestors learned from their ancestors but, somewhere along the line, one learns through trial and error, experiential learning, etc., and new ways of knowing are learned. In an Indigenous epistemology, the way of doing 'new' Indigenous knowledge within the Niimíipuu Female Educators' Talking Circles are woven together.

I use a cornhusk bag woven by Na'qáac (my maternal grandma) and myself as a metaphor for creating new knowledge and giving back through storywork. I display it when I speak about the stories told by my great-grandfather Sam Lott and my grandmother, his daughter Rena Katherine Ramsey. Their stories of knowledge colorfully weave together and create new meanings; like the beautiful and unique cornhusk bag, it now has a useful purpose. I will share the 'new' Niimíipuu knowledge that the Female Educators wove together in their talking circles, which are of great value. The richness of what they shared has given me new powerful perspectives on the titwáatit that will strengthen my relationship with the titwáatit, and, in sharing this new knowledge, I hope it will also strengthen the relationship with the titwáatit of others. Then perhaps many will drive by Wiitmíipn'ime and remember our teachers, the Titwatityáaya (Story People) or the Animal People 'each poured out their hearts'. The Titwatiyáaya sacrificed themselves for us, the Netíitelwit (human beings). My hope for the future is that we, too, as the Netíitelwit today, will learn the Niimíipuu tamáalwit (law) teachings and be moved to timíipn'it (pour out heart) remember, prepare, and sacrifice for the Niimíipuu. In the titwatitnáawit (traditional folktale), 'iceyéeye always hitoláyca (he is going upriver) on a journey. In our journeys, we can look to the wéetes (land), listen to the titwáatit and the Nimipuutímt within them, and fill our cemíitx (huckleberry) baskets with royal purple cemíitx of Niimíipuu knowledge.

In closing, investigating the Niimíipuu knowledge within the stories, language, and land strengthens our relationship and expands our knowledge and appreciation of these stories. Documenting discussions with the Female Educators, I can attest that we gained insight into values from the stories where we, as Female Educators, decolonized by collectively contributing to knowledge. The wisdom in these power places faithfully teaches, reminding us to be forgiving and loving like

Tilípe' and not revengeful and bitter like 'iceyéeye. Throughout our Niimíipuu lands, wisdom is abundant and generously gives us medicine.

References

Aoki, H. and Walker, D. (1989) *Nez Perce Oral Narratives*. University of California Publications in Linguistics 104.

Archibald, J.-A. (2008) *Indigenous Storywork: Educating the Heart, Mind, Body, and Spirit*. UBC Press.

Basso, K.H. (1996) *Wisdom Sits in Places: Landscape and Language Among the Western Apache*. University of New Mexico Press.

Borrows, J. (2016) Heroes, tricksters, monsters, and caretakers: Indigenous law and legal education. *McGill Law Journal* 61 (4), 795–846.

Haig-Brown, C. and Archibald, J.-A. (1996) Transforming First Nations research with respect and power. *International Journal of Qualitative Studies in Education* 9 (3), 245–267.

Huaman, E.S. and Naranjo, T. (2019) Indigenous women and research: Conversations on indigeneity, rights, and education. *International Journal of Human Rights Education* 3 (1), 1.

Iseke, J. (2013) Indigenous storytelling as research. *International Review of Qualitative Research* 6 (4), 559–577.

Josephy, A.M. (2007) *Nez Perce Country*. U of Nebraska Press.

Kovach, M. (2009) Story as Indigenous methodology. In M. Kovach *Indigenous Methodologies: Characteristics, Conversations, and Contexts* (1st edn) (pp. 94–108). University of Toronto Press.

Lomawaima, K.T. and McCarty, T.L. (2006) *'To Remain an Indian': Lessons in Democracy from a Century of Native American Education*. Teachers College Press.

Phinney, A. (1934) *Nez Perce Texts*. Columbia University Press. Volume XXV of Columbia University Contributions to Anthropology/. Available at https://books.google.com/books?id=T8B1AAAAMAAJ.

Pinkham, A., Evans, S.R. and Hoxie, F.E. (2013) *Lewis and Clark among the Nez Perce: Strangers in the Land of the Nimíipuu*. Dakota Institute Press of the Lewis & Clark Fort Mandan Foundation.

Simpson, L.B. (2014) Land as pedagogy: Nishnaabeg intelligence and rebellious transformation. *Decolonization: Indigeneity, Education & Society* 3 (3), 1–25.

Slickpoo, A.P. and Walker, D.E. (1973) *Noon Nee-Me-Poo (We, the Nez Perces): Culture and History of the Nez Perces*. Nez Perce Tribe of Idaho.

Taylor, A.M. (2010) Tradition to acculturation: A case study on the impacts created by Chemawa Indian Boarding School upon the Nez Perce family structure from 1879 to 1945. Master's Thesis, Department of Education, Loyola University Chicago.

Wilson, S. (2004) Research as ceremony: Articulating an Indigenous research paradigm. PhD Thesis, Monash University.

Wilson, S. (2008) *Research is Ceremony. Indigenous Research Methods*. Fernwood.

Poem: Nchií NaáKuú/¿Quién soy?/Who am I?

Author: Celerina Patricia Sánchez Santiago
Language: Tu'un ñuu savi (Mixtec)
From: San Juan Mixtepec, Distrito de Santiago Juxtlahuaca, Oaxaca, México
English translation: Lori DiPrete Brown

ñaa kuú

kuú
    mitu'únga ndivii ini
    ñaa kuni sa'á naá nuú kati
    yutu yàtàà
    nuú ndakita'án
    kue chiívì
    takua naa tui nuú tsikuaá
    raa kúú tuu ndùù
    nuú vatsi inka kue nikanchíi tsi yoo

kuú
    yaàka tsaná'a
    tachi ñaa nikondoo
    ñaa ndatuu ñaa ntsinduni ino
    yuchìì ñaa kue ndaá

kuú
    yuchi kua'á yivì
    nií tu'un tsana'á ñaa kuee nii ndakani naá
    yu'ú ñu'un tsana'á
    tu'un ñaa

kuú
    saanà ini naá
    ñû'ún yatàà

ñaá tsita statsaí
savi ya'í tíndo'óso
chichaà uín rii koo nii tu'ún

kuú
   ñû'ún yoso kuíà
   sììví kuí ndusu kue iyaa
   kue ñaá ndavàà nova'a nani Savi

I am *ñaa kuú*

I am breath, dust, fire, and Savi (rain).

I am *ñaa kuú*
   the last breath
   of hope in the shade
   of the ancient tree
   where the fireflies
   come together
   to infuse the night with life
   and light the dawn
   of a new era

I am *ñaa kuú*
   the dust of the past
   the aged wind
   that surrounds memory
   contradicting fragments

ñaa kuú
   the pluriverse
   the atom of untold history
   the voice of the earth
   the forgotten word

ñaa kuú
   the ancient fire
   the song that dances
   savi (rain) that pours down in buckets
   into the void with no answer

ñaa kuú
   the fire of a thousand years
   my name echoes the incantation of the gods
   that created me and named me *savi*

Spanish translation by the author

soy

soy
   el último hálito
   de la esperanza bajo la sombra
   del árbol antiguo
   donde las luciérnagas
   se dan cita
   para dar ánimo a la noche
   y alumbrar el amanecer
   de una nueva era

soy
   el polvo del pasado
   el viento añejo
   que envuelve la memoria
      fragmentos de contradicción

soy
   el pluriverso
   el átomo de la historia no contada
   la voz de la tierra
   palabra olvidada

soy
   el fuego antiguo
   el canto que danza
   Savi que baja a cántaros
      en el vacío sin respuesta

soy
   el fuego milenario
   mi nombre eco de los dioses
   conjuro que me creó con nombre de *Savi*

Part 2
Pedagogies and Practices of Indigenous Language Reclamation in and around Schools

4 Communal Education, Existence of Shared Autonomy[1]

Erika Candelaria Hernández Aragón
and Haydée Morales Flores
Translated by: Miguel Cervantes Aguilar

'Sembrar buena semilla' ha sido el sentido de lo que hacemos, desde el corazón, en un entramado y tensiones entre lo colonial y propio, este es el contexto donde buscamos construir en comunalidad otros aprendizajes. Comprender la vida, la memoria y el origen, fue un necesario el reencuentro con los maestros y maestras ancestras, y ha sido como aprender en clave comunal, de ahí que brota naturalmente la claridad política de vida, donde lo propio establece vínculos con otros maestros/as de vida, con los y las que coincidimos construir un proyecto de educación comunal o ser parte de él, el camino fue la reflexión de la expropiación de la memoria, de la historia, de la lengua y de lo propio. Y es aquí donde la celebración y el gozo como expresión natural de la vida y de re-xistencia ha sido nuestra compañía en este caminar. El pensamiento comunal como estrategia nos permite compartir una experiencia de vida que no intentamos romantizar sino plantear seriamente sus posibilidades y contradicciones al mismo tiempo que las vivimos. El llamado acaece del ombligo enterrado en la casa del pueblo `Yes Mxil' (pueblo de las mariposas) donde lo comunal te convoca naturalmente el regreso a la comunidad para no olvidar quién eres y que tu siembra sea buena semilla, es así como se es parte del proyecto que busca en la educación comunal y otras alternativas de vida con relaciones sociales más justas y el bien común.

At the end of the 20th century, communal education in Oaxaca, Mexico, emerged from the interweaving of diverse social movements and in the political struggle of the native peoples to take the space historically denied by the state. It is a living experience in constant tension between the defense of their autonomy and the institutional framework, which not only crosses the conceptual aspirations and needs but also the concrete of the territory that surrounds it. Communal education, as its own project, proposes the conformation of the 'communal being' for the care of life. Likewise, communal education proposes to co-construct knowledge based on experience, knowledge and community knowledge.

'Communality' emerged in the 1980s as a concept or word in the Spanish language to name the way of life and philosophy of the native peoples in Oaxaca. In the words of Martínez Luna, communality:

> is an experiential concept that allows the integral, total, natural and common understanding of making life.... It is the organic form that reflects the diversity contained in nature, in an integral interdependence of the elements that make it up. (Martinez Luna, 2015: 133)

In different spaces, the approaches of communality have become a horizon to challenge the violence of capitalism and the state towards knowledge and thoughts, including mother languages or Indigenous languages. In general, communality places co-existence in the collective, in the common, a vision concretized in practices such as the tequio or collective work for the common good and the festival as an element of celebration and enjoyment of what we produce or do. Likewise, government is conceived as a service and the Assembly is the maximum authority for making decisions regarding community life. Also, the territory is central: it not only allows subsistence but it is the space of memory and the sacred, where human, non-human and sacred beings co-exist. There is an academic consensus at first moment in considering these four elements of community life – the tequio, the fiesta, self-government, and the territory – as pillars of communality; although recent shared experiences have left us in academic reflection, an approach to a fifth element, *the language*, which we will share later. In a contrary logic, capitalism, as an economic system, centers life in the individual and, in its incessant accumulation, exploits territories, bodies, and everything that allows the generation of capital and, consequently, its reproduction, regardless of the *common good*.

In the construction of alternative education projects, communality is taken up again. Our educational experiences, which are not alien to challenges and contradictions, are diverse; what is essential is their progress, because they make it possible in practice to consider another type of education. In this chapter we share the experience of two pedagogical projects framed within public education and carried out in the state of Oaxaca. The first one is the Plan for the Transformation of Public Education in Oaxaca (PTEO), which corresponds to a program for elementary education developed over 13 years, from its implementation in 217 schools in its first year to the current implementation in more than 80,000 schools. The second project corresponds to the higher education initiative of the Autonomous Communal University of Oaxaca (UACO) in its firsts three years of operation.

Public Education and the Social Struggle in Oaxaca

Oaxaca, as one of the states located in the south of Mexico, is characterized by its mountain reliefs, vast forests, its water and its natural habitat, with a broad cosmogonic sense of the intangible, the relationship with the land and natural beings for *good living*, where language is a living and identifying element. There are 16 indigenous languages with their dialectal variants of ancestral origin, which characterizes each of the communities that speak a specific *communal variety*. Politically, 80% of communities are based in Indigenous practices of self-government, thus the territory is tangible and intangible, it is multiple and at the same time abstract, where its people organize their lives around the community, its Indigenous intellectuality and its social reality. This is the territory where a communal education is inscribed, one specific to its context.

The history of Oaxaca has been marked by the unfolding of different social movements that, in the 21st century, include the historical struggles of the peasantry, trade unions, students, teachers, electoral conflicts, agrarian worker and against regional bosses; and to these can be added the struggle of women and feminists, and socio-environmental conflicts, among other issues. In this respect, Zibechi points out that 'one of the most outstanding facts of the new scenario, from a viewpoint centered on the movements, is the difficulty of finding thematic axes capable of bringing together a wide range of local and regional struggles' (Zibechi, 2006: 223). Indeed, a wide range of social demands converge in the regions – some of them are historical, while at the same time new ones are incorporated; and, on their way, they appeal to mobilization experiences, and at the same time they face different challenges. A heterogeneity of struggles and conflicts that find spaces of convergence, dialogue, recognize common objectives, and articulate their agendas to strengthen their social demands.

One of the social movements with the greatest presence in the state of Oaxaca is the teachers' union, Section XXII of the National Coordinating Committee of State Workers (CNTE). CNTE was born out of a process of union democratization, which began between 1979 and 1980, in order to break away from the National Union of State Workers (SNTE), which was characterized by its verticality, political corporatism and its closeness to the government in power (Arriaga, 1979). CNTE considers itself as a mass organization that fights for union democratization and, although it officially belongs to the SNTE, it dissociates itself from it. The majority of the Oaxacan teachers' base is made up of men and women teachers from peasant families and salaried workers who found in education an alternative that allowed social mobility and a space for dialogue. Due to its political–social formation, the Democratic Movement of Education Workers of Oaxaca (MDTEO) is defined as democratic and it is affiliated to different union projects or ideological expressions. In this sense, teachers are involved in community life and, on many occasions, they fulfill their own obligations in the exercise of communal citizenship.

At the national level, in the last two 6-year terms (2006–2018), led by the National Action Party (PAN) and the Institutional Revolutionary Party (PRI), a systematic offensive was deployed against Oaxacan teachers, in which two moments were key: the first was the conflict generated in 2006, and the second was the struggle of CNTE against the educational reform being promoted by the government of Enrique Peña Nieto (2013). Regarding the 2006 conflict, Ortega (2009) states that, although it began during the state government of Ulises Ruiz with the failed eviction of the teachers' encampment in the Oaxacan capital, Zócalo, it is the consequence of a long crisis that was accentuated by the weakening of the PRI's hegemony and the construction of a very active civil society. The 2006 conflict, with its innovations and contractions, allowed the construction of a popular movement and, as a result of this experience, the Popular Assembly of the Peoples of Oaxaca (APPO) emerged. This was a heterogeneous movement involving the participation of diverse sectors, including unions, social organizations, municipal authorities, and the civilian population. Although participation was accentuated in the state capital and its periphery, there were demonstrations of support in all the regions and there was even occupation of municipal palaces and declarations of popular town councils. Today, the 2006 popular movement is still fresh in people's memory and it teaches us lessons of organization and political mobilization – an experience that cannot be left aside in the contemporary reading of social movements in Oaxaca.

In 2010, the teachers' union began another stage of struggle against the educational reform being promoted by the federal government, which teachers' union claim legitimizes the privatization of public education, that the reform is 'labor and not educational' and that it is punitive against teachers. On June 19, 2016, the movement reached a complex moment due to the incursion of the Federal Preventive Police (PFP) in the city of Oaxaca, and the teachers' union and the citizens decided to halt their march to avoid confrontation. However, in Asunción Nochixtlan, a municipality in the Mixtec region, the PFP responded with violence. The result was a massacre in which 8 civilians were killed – inhabitants of different communities who had come to show solidarity with the teachers – to which can be added about 100 wounded, 150 direct victims and 300–400 indirect victims (Hernández, 2019). The Nochixtlan massacre was considered a failed tactic of extreme violence perpetrated by the government to disarticulate the teachers' struggle; far from disarticulating it, it provided evidence of the unity between the education workers' movement and the Oaxacan communities.

In this sense, the teachers' movement and the pedagogical movement cannot be understood without consideration of the social and educational foundation that sustains them, and its historical memory in the face of national educational policies. The struggles mentioned above raise a slogan of educational resistance in Oaxaca, which in turn allows political encirclement of the national educational system, and, at the same time, generates autonomous construction gives rise to alternative proposals from the political, educational, administrative and legal framework. The alternative form of education being proposed by teachers in this sense is strengthened in its operability as a bastion of struggle and resistance based on the critical and communitarian approach that sustains the pedagogical practices in the communities. We refer to a movement that incorporates epistemological, theoretical, philosophical, and political positions that provides a philosophical framework in education public policy. This construction of an alternative education, as we have said, is not isolated from the social struggle: a proposal for communal or community education at different educational levels is proposed, based on the search for its recognition and institutionalization by the state. This communal education can be noticed as a first moment in the PTEO and, later, it has an impact on the construction of the Autonomous Communal University of Oaxaca (UACO).

Communal Education: Plan for the Transformation of Oaxaca's Education (PTEO)

As we have addressed, one of the education projects that has set an alternative reference in Oaxaca and the country is PTEO, which is part of the collective construction, and which aims to:

> Transform public education in the state of Oaxaca through the critical preparation of those involved, the understanding and modification of their environment by recovering knowledge, pedagogical and community knowledge, through the collective construction of programs and projects to achieve a comprehensive education of children, youth and adults. (CEDES22, 2013: 17)

In this sense, the plan proposes five action areas: teacher education and professional education for education workers; an Evaluation system; a State Program to Improve the School and Living Conditions of Children, Youth and Adults of Oaxaca; a program for school infrastructure and equipment; and a program for professional development for education workers. Although the systems and programs are sustained in an integral manner and in themselves, for the purpose of this chapter we will focus only on the area of professional preparation for education workers, in order to enunciate how the communal approach orients the foundations of this plan. It addresses the preparation needs of education workers that:

> will be based on culture, and other elements of it; multiculturalism, plurality, interculturalism, community and communality; in addition to epistemology, pedagogy, sociology, anthropology, philosophy and ethics, as formative elements to enable the link between the world of school life and the community. (CEDES22, 2021: 62)

This program, more than a decade after its implementation, contemplates four central axes:

(1) Theoretical–methodological elements of the Collective-Project.
(2) Student learning is considered an unfinished process.
(3) Teaching practice contemplates three fundamental forms of knowledge (pedagogical knowledge, multidisciplinary knowledge, and knowledge from community and socially shared life).
(4) Curricular construction based on the community and school context.

These four approaches support the recognition of teachers as part of their community and the incorporation of community knowledge and wisdom into their teaching practice. This system is established as one of the pillars of PTEO by orienting and developing its own training:, communal, and territorialized to the geographical, multicultural, and pluricultural realities of the Oaxacan context. In view of this, PTEO, as a political and educational alternative, builds collectively, in dialogue, so that learning is unfinished and cyclical. The plan proposes to analyze the reality from the communality, strengthen community life and co-construct the common good. According to Jiménez (2021) it is another learning process, it is a communal learning process that arises from exchange, collective work, dialogue, seeing, doing, giving and receiving, it seeks the common good more than the individual and, in close relation to the territory and the political forms of community organization. PTEO does not only consider school learning: it also addresses the formation of community subjects and the impact on social transformation. It is necessary to emphasize that Oaxacan teachers have built long-range educational research experiences. One example is the creation of the Center for Educational Studies and Development of Section XXII (CEDES), which recovers and systematizes the work done by teachers, and has a broad formative character based on the network of collectives. This experience has resulted in publications, inter-institutional collaborations, and a proposal for training and educational policy advocacy projects.

One part that seems necessary to emphasize is the need for critical reflection on the processes of PTEO. Although more than 80,000 education workers are implementing this plan, this has not guaranteed its comprehensive development. One of the most felt needs of the collectives is the lack of funding for its development, from the conditions for preparation and self-preparation to the resources for the implementation of educational projects. This is attributed to the lack of legal recognition in state education law, which implies a greater effort for teachers to carry out this alternative project. On the other hand, in relation to pedagogical practice in the communities, it faces many challenges, one of which is the community and parents' linkage, since communal education could not exist without the active participation of the community, which necessarily goes through the consensus of the parents' assemblies for its implementation.

Measuring the impact of PTEO is complex. We could advance that its viability was expressed in the times of COVID-19, since the work developed from the project–collective was key for the continuity of learning, at least in a great majority of teachers, due to the professional capacity to carry out a critical analysis of the social context and to build a curriculum that would meet the most pressing needs of society and that would have the community assembly as a central point; but, at the same time, it evidences the necessary and urgent concern of the teachers' movement regarding this plan, and specifically in contextual curriculum construction, as one of the necessary processes to reflect on in its spaces of co-creation between pedagogical elements and community knowledge.

We believe that the importance of an alternative education proposal arising from a teachers' movement lies in the communal approach and perspective of the indigenous peoples of Oaxaca. This is sustained by the context: its indigenous languages, its form of organization and normative systems, the territory, communal work and celebration, to mention some of the elements that give identity to Oaxaca. But it builds its own basis for the relevance of a communal education. However, in practice, it poses different challenges related to didactics, in the relationship with the community, in teacher education, and in its relationship with the state. In the face of this, PTEO is under constant analysis and construction, which has allowed the elaboration of concrete proposals to strengthen it.

What Do We Call the Autonomous Communal University of Oaxaca?

As we mentioned, in the 1980s different fields of social struggle and encounters were opened, allowing dialogue and thinking about how to incorporate, from the language and discourse of others, a conceptualization that would explain community life. As we mentioned in the previous section, there is a conceptual consensus in considering four fundamental pillars: shared territory; collective work for the common good (tequio); the Assembly as a horizontal space for collective decision-making; and celebration (rituals and collective festivities). Among some of its precursors are Jaime Martínez Luna, Floriberto Díaz and Juan José Rendón Monzón to mention a few. In the most recent dialogues on education in Oaxaca, we find reflections regarding a fifth pillar or element: *language*. This element language-communication incorporates incorporates the native language as an element that generates learning and community-school community dialogue. This fifth element or pillar, as mentioned by some contemporary thinkers, arises from the context and the identities of the territory of the native peoples and nations of Oaxaca, where the ways of thinking and of building community are made visible through their languages. These languages, in their use, are referred to as fundamental mechanisms of resistance and existence in addition to being a central element in the life of native communities, even before the learning of Spanish as the dominant language. Although this approach is not new, it is relevant because of its potential in the revitalization of the concept of language in the daily life of the peoples, as well as its occurrence in the reflections that emerge in the experience of communal education at the higher level.

In this framework – in 2009 – the conceptual idea of communality in the field of elementary education was managed and took force, giving way years later to the idea of a comprehensive project that could raise the concept and approach of PTEO to the professionalization of teachers as a first step; and so it was proposed from a horizontal dialogue between the Center for Studies and Educational Development of Section 22 (CEDES22–Section XXII) and the Academy of Communality AC. The design of a Master's degree program based on communal education – a project that stalled (as we mentioned) at the beginning due to the political repression of Oaxacan teachers, but which left a deep root in the project of professionalization from a critical and communal approach – years later materialized with teacher graduates in the Master's degree in Communal Education at the Benito Juárez Autonomous University of Oaxaca, a university that embraces the project without the collaboration agreement managed by CEDES22-Section XXII but, rather, autonomously with the Academy of Communality AC. Although this process was born in the midst of a high-profile political struggle against the teaching profession, the first generation Master's degree is a reference, which gives legitimacy to the education of graduates of the teaching profession and the initiators of the same program.

This experience was key in raising the perspective of a communal education for Higher Education. Some examples are the efforts made by the Ayuuk people, such as the Instituto Superior Intercultural Ayuuk

(ISIA), Universidad Intercultural de Cempoaltépetl (UNICEM), who reclaiming the principles of communality. There are also community efforts that have not received recognition in the public sphere, such as Santa María Yaviche and Capulálpam de Méndez, the initiators of the degree in communality, is the construct of communal education.

The management of the project of the Autonomous Communal University of Oaxaca (UACO), as we have explained, has as its background the teachers' pedagogical movement and the struggle of the indigenous peoples of Oaxaca, who have sought to exercise their right to their own education. These struggles, both at the institutional and community level, made possible not only the idea of UACO but also its possible scope, since its raison d'être is closely linked to the communities, peoples, and native nations. This is where its consolidation and reference to other public and autonomous universities in the country lies. Its sustainability as a proposal was made possible by the strength and close trajectory of struggle and construction of its founders and managers, as well as the collectives and projects of the 16 communities that joined and gave strength to this project. Its creation and institutionalization as a university was based on a permanent dialogue with the legislative body of government of the State of Oaxaca. The creation and definition of its leadership structure was a turning point, due to recognition of the assembly as part of the institutional level and the character of the university's governance system. In addition to the communal and historical trajectory of the founders of the university to be formed by Mtro. Jaime Martínez Luna (activist of Comunalidad), Erika Candelaria Hernández Aragón (Comunera and activist of communal education), Rigoberto Vásquez García (initiator of UNICEM) and Gustavo Ramírez Santiago (co-designer of the Master's degree program and activist of communal life), this was an unprecedented event in itself, leaving three representatives from Sierra Norte and one representative from Sierra Sur.

The UACO, in its autonomous character, would allow the university to build itself and its own governance system. Its creation and consolidation would be based on communal work in and for the most remote and historically denied communities. The ideal is to approach and build processes with young people and community that allow them to recognize their historical, political, philosophical, linguistic context, for reflection and construction of a life around their territory, their language, their self-government, their practices and celebrations. This vision reaffirms that the project does not propose to be of the people who represent it in a position in the university but, rather, it attempts to reclaim the place and participation of the communities, peoples, and native nations. This principle is manifest in its growth: today the university has 16 Community University Centers (CUC), and 16 Community Learning Units (UAC), which in their conception are endowed with the principles of communality and autonomy for their creation, organization, and consolidation. Both the centers and the learning units have elected by the communities where they were born, thus recognizing the communal principle and the governance system of the Communal University Assembly; composed by four main actors: the communal authorities (wise people, communal and/or municipal among others), facilitators, coordinators, and students. Therefore, this structure raises the decentralization of control and power, privileging the notion of shared authority in the organization of the university (Figure 4.1).

Cartografía Comunal, Bilingüe en Zapoteco del Sureste, realizada con jóvenes de la Unidad de Aprendizaje Comunal y sabios(as) de Candelaria Loxicha, Oaxaca, México. 2023-2024

Figure 4.1 Local knowledges. Communal knowledge as part of the organized daily activity in and from the communities. The image illustrates a curricular design: an 'activity calendar' from the collective teacher-work from Santa Cruz El Porvenir, Oaxaca, México

In this context, as this higher education project was being built, taking shape and content, within its three years of being established, it is not exempt from problems – such as the difficulty in its institutional creation, whereby it had to face the contextual, ideological, and political differences within how its centers should be governed. These differences had wide impact. Shortly after the organic creation of the UACO, its existence was challenged by the Supreme Court of Justice of the Nation (SCJN), calling into question the legality of the university as an institution of higher education. Many saw this as a legal contradiction since the need for the university emanated from the great majority of the communities and towns. To respond to the SCJN judgement and justify its legality, the leaders of UACO had to consult 11 forums. This made it difficult to manage the processes of recognition and budgetary classification necessary under the scheme of the State Public Universities (UPE), a reality that eroded the independence of the university and frames the precarious operation of the university to date.

The road to the Autonomous Communal University of Oaxaca was a long one. It is a communal and political project that expresses the idea, the aspiration and, in its creation, the concretion of a project which, as we have said, is cohesive with the epistemological and pedagogical advances of alternative experiences at different levels and modalities of education, and which at least coincide with two central elements: *autonomy* and *the communal*.

Final Thoughts

Communal education is proposed as an alternative to a hegemonic, colonialist, homogenizing model that has prevailed in the Mexican educational system and its national project. Under the latter, native peoples have been considered backward and an obstacle to the development of the country; not forgetting pretensions to implement neoliberal initiatives that attempt – in opposition to the labor rights of the teaching staff and with a disregard of the responsibility of the state – to guarantee a public education. Within this framework, the school became an instrument for the implementation of such educational policy at the same time as processes of resistance and struggle were developed.

In Oaxaca, both PTEO, as an elementary education program and UACO, as an effort for higher education, base their educational project on communality. By considering communality as the transforming horizon of institutional education, Martínez Luna (2015) poses the challenge of reflecting on who we are, how we are, what we have, and what we want. Formulations that lead us to look at ourselves from the community experience and to consider what is our own, sprout to guide from the teaching practice, adding the aspirations of social transformation that call for the building of build alternative projects.

As communal principles we find autonomy, the collective, horizontality, reciprocity, respect and work, to mention a few, which have allowed us to solve difficulties along the way as alternative projects to the hegemonic educational system that has contributed to colonial practices.

These experiences have allowed us to reflect on a number of tensions that are closely related in their origins and nature. Among these is the conception of autonomy in the institutional framework, on the one hand, while in PTEO, pedagogical, administrative and even political autonomy is proposed. The governing body is established from the project–collective in its levels, forms and principles, although this is a complex process to distinguish, since autonomy in one of its dimensions exposes additional work for certain vulnerable people in the education system in precarious conditions. This reality forces the project to create its own learning rhythm in a more social way, but at the same time it damages the collective work and the community.

UACO, for its part, builds a conception of autonomy on two levels, one institutional and the other as a system of governance. This has led to complex tensions that have disrupted the economic, administrative, political, and educational dimensions, considering on the one hand that public policies in Oaxaca and the country do not conceive or understand the type of university that is proposed. The reality is that these public policies do not establish procedures for a project that proposes an autonomy beyond the free professorship and system of governance. It is worth mentioning that communality, as an epistemological proposal in higher education learning, has found not only its natural space in diverse contexts but has exposed a faultline in the traditional reasoning, providing an opportunity for the communities to become visible in their own ways of thinking about education, in their own languages, and in their own ways of living in community.

In view of this, we consider that communal education is not a recipe to follow but, rather, a horizon of thought–action (being–doing) that allows us to weave with our own thoughts, words, and actions. Communities, peoples, nations and communal states are the basis for proposals, such as those shared, to take place and are sustained even with the same tensions that are found within the projects. We think that communal life will be the guide that directs the course of these and other proposals in education arising from the people. We walk in resistance in order to exist.

Note

(1) This article is part of the research approved by the Consejo Nacional de Humanidades, Ciencia y Tecnología (CONAHCyT) from Mèxico, in its call for Frontier Science 2023. It is numbered CF-2023-G-1068 and entitled 'Compartencia de haceres con la tierra, educativos y comunales como paradigma "otro" para la generación y aplicación colaborativa-comunitaria de conocimientos y solución de problemas comunes en la comunidad zapoteca de Candelaria Loxicha, en la Sierra Sur de Oaxaca, México.'

References

Arriaga, M.L. (1979) El magisterio en lucha. Informe. *Cuadernos Políticos* 27, 79–101.

CEDES22 (2013) Sistema de Formación Profesional de los Trabajadores de la Educación de Oaxaca. Seccion XXII.

CEDES22 (2021) Taller Estatal de Educación Alternativa (TEEA) 2021–2022. La educación propia como principio en la continuidad de la reorganización y transformación educativa ante la realidad social actual. Unpublished manuscript, Sección XII. Oaxaca, Mexico.

Hernández, L. (2019) Nochixtlán en las barricadas. In: Fabrizio Mejía, Diego Enrique Osorno and Luis Navarro Hernández. *Oaxaca, Tierra de Valientes* (pp. 86–133). Secretaría de Cultura Oaxaca.

Jiménez, Y. (2021) (Coord) *Compartencia de haceres campesinos, educativos y organizativos comunitarios para afrontar problemas comunes, Oaxaca*: Colectivo Editorial Casa de las Preguntas.

Martínez-Luna, J. (2015) *Educación comunal*. Casa de las preguntas.

Ortega, J. (2009) La crisis de la hegemonía en Oaxaca: El conflicto político de 2006. *La Bajo el Volcan* 14, 11–44.

Zibechi, R. (2006) Movimientos sociales: Nuevos escenarios y desafíos inéditos. *OSAL, Observatorio Social de América Latina* 7 (21), 221–230.

5 Experiences and Spaces of Opportunity for Work with the Ngigua Language

Teresa Damian Jara
Translated by Miguel Cervantes Aguilar
Revised by Ernesto Colín and José Antonio Flores Farfán

Tjse nánu bathu ku jaña tjse tangini, ngaxi'in thi tjaguni xruun ku kai are nche'eni xra ngai chujni rajna. Ngai rajna San Marcos Tlacoyalco yaa naa rajna nichjana Ngigua ku thu xra tjse ni uyeye ku ni dachrii ke nichjan tha ji'i; ku ixi mee ya xra kjini ji'i, tjangi xra kexrein thi kan nii nánu bathu ku kai kain thi kuen, tjangi xra ixi ni tjague chjan yaa tangini dathuna ixi xruin naa xruun jitaxin kexrein tjsaguna ku mexixnxi je'ena ndanda ku ndanda datsu'ena kexrein tjsaguna, inchi thinga tjsenkauna xan, inchi naa thinga tsuntakauna xan, inchi thinga tjaguna ku tangini. Xruun ji'i kai danjin xruun kexrein nchau kunixi suun chjan tangixan ku kai kexrein tangixan are nchiu ku nchiu tangini.

Kai dangi xruun kexrein tjse chujni ke taku'en nche'e xra ngai ni nichjana naa tha ku kexrein chujni jii thengijnana chujni rajna nchechjiana icha xruun ku kain tjaguna kexrein sechjian kain thu nu'e nii dachrii. Kain thi chru xruun ji'i yaa nchau kuen ixi tjse chujni baki'in naa raa kunixi thi nu'e ku kai bajun nchau'en. Xra ji'i kunchjian ixi naa nchri nchekuen chjan xraxaun kjen kexrein nchau xra tsangini kain thi nu'e ni rajna Ngigua ku jaña icha chujni ku icha rajna nchau sinchesuji xree ke jinche'e ku jaña ni i'cha nchau sikuna ke maski yau ku yau yaa siku'en.

Introduction

Historically, the Ngigua settled in the southern valley of Puebla, forming important city–states such as Tehuacán Viejo, Tepexi el Viejo, Cuthá and Tecamachalco, and creating a corridor that reached Coixtlahuaca, Oaxaca, where the Ngigua are currently unfortunately still known as 'Chochos' or 'Chocholtecos', pejorative terms that we struggle to substitute with our proper name: Ngigua. The Ngigua language belongs to the Otomanguean linguistic trunk, Popolocana family, which also includes Ixcatec and Mazatec. Other languages from the same stem, although more distant, are, among several others, Hñahñu/Otomi, Hñahtr/ Mazahua, Tu'un Savi/Mixtec, Dibaku, Cuicateco, Diixazá/Zapotec, and Me'phaa/Tlapanec.

The Ngigua are a dispersed people located in semi-arid areas of the southeast state of Puebla, and in the extreme north of the state of Oaxaca. In Puebla, Ngigua communities are found in the municipalities of Tepexi de Rodríguez, San Juan Ixcaquistla, Santa Inés Ahuatempan, Cuayuca, Zapotitlán Salinas, Tepanco de López, San Gabriel Chilac and Tlacotepec de Benito Juárez. This last municipality has a significant Ngigua population, which has allowed the creation of initial, preschool and primary education schools that integrate the teaching of the Ngigua (or Ngiwa) language, to which we refer in this contribution.

In terms of linguistic education and retention, at the Octavio Paz Indigenous Primary School, located on 6 South Street of Colonia Cuauhtémoc, San Marcos Tlacoyalco, municipality of Tlacotepec de Benito Juárez, Puebla, our educational experience has been implemented for two decades. Educational strategies have been developed in the Ngigua language, which is fundamental to the cultural identity of its speakers. Although some still mistakenly call the Ngigua language 'Popoloca,' a derogatory term imposed by the Mexica that means 'stutterers' or 'barbarians', as suggested, speakers prefer Ngigua, which means 'this is how we (really) speak' or 'what our people speak'.

The teacher's task is considered a constantly complex act and is developed in a multidimensional reality; and, like all social realities, a set of relationships is interwoven between the subjects and direct and indirect power contexts. Teachers' efforts first seek to create conditions where students know, interact with, appropriate and consolidate knowledge of their culture and language. Attention to these realities brings about a series of implications for the teacher, as formulated by Fierro *et al.* (1999: 29):

> The teaching practice contains multiple relationships, these relationships have been organized into six dimensions: personal, interpersonal, social, institutional, didactic and value-based; each of these dimensions highlights a particular set of teacher work relationships.

Likewise, teaching is holistic and allows personal and interpersonal relationships with various institutions. In these places, the speakers of the municipality of Tlacotepec de Benito Juárez, Puebla, Mexico, create spaces and connections leading to the formation of small communities and networks for working with the Ngigua mother tongue. This seeks to promote 'language revitalization from a *collaborative perspective*, with the objective of generating processes and activities that make it possible to recover or create spaces of communicative use for the language that is in a situation of displacement' (Flores Farfán *et al.*, 2020: 36, emphasis in the original). The relationships established between people have been achieved through co-participation, with small acts supporting the survival of the Ngigua language (which has been declared endangered by the UNESCO), as well as by the conservation, preservation, and strengthening of this language as a right. Also, the Mexican State recognizes Ngigua language, although more in rhetoric than in practice:

> The Constitution recognizes in its article 2, section A, Section IV, the right of Indigenous peoples to preserve and enrich their languages. The recognition of this right implies three elements: first, allowing and encouraging the use of languages; second, the recognition and respect of Indigenous languages as current languages and with the same validity as Spanish, especially in proceedings before institutions; and third, the promotion of these languages as an obligation on the Mexican State, from educational spaces to other institutional ones (Comisión Nacional de los Derechos Humanos. (CNDH, 2018: 5)

This chapter reflects upon the 25 years of service of Indigenous education, as a teacher of students ranging from 5 to 15 years of age. My service in the state of Puebla has allowed me to attend primarily to children in first and second grade, but also a handful of years were spent working with fifth and sixth graders. This is the time of reflection and analysis on this contribution, based on a set of planned, organized and systematized daily classroom activities. I also reflect on spaces in which teaching–learning situations were organized, understanding this activity as reflective praxis, since it goes beyond mechanized actions and requires cognitive work from the educators involved in the pedagogical process.

Challenges of Indigenous Education

Indigenous education is an official institution that faces various challenges, from political to financial, acceptance by the Secretary of Public Education, coverage at different levels after primary school, and with teaching practice. Teacher labor is the engine that moves and directs Indigenous education. In this sense, teaching is recognized as an activity configured and determined by the multiple interrelationships with subjects and institutions, in addition to the personal life history that contributes to the construction of being a teacher without losing oneself – that is, without ceasing to be Ngigua. Conversely, teacher training processes exist where individuals, far from being reinforced or recognized as an Indigenous being, are stripped of this identity in the school and in the community.

Speakers of Indigenous languages often occupy a status of economic, social and political inferiority, even if our languages *are* nationally recognized. By doing this exercise of reflexivity, I have come to realize projects have contributed to make small changes that have improved and transformed the work with what the National Institute for Indigenous Languages (INALI, in Spanish) has reckoned as national languages, especially given inequities stemming from discrimination, racism, stereotypes, stigmas, vertical relationships or, even, in the distribution and sharing of economic resources. This attempt to transform realities through alternative proposals of the Ngigua community does not neglect the official curriculum and educational reforms from the 1997 standards, the 2009 Educational Reform, Key Teachings of 2018, and the recent New Mexican School. In these two and half decades of teaching, the official state curriculum and Ngigua pedagogy have operated in tandem with federal policy. Yet, such constant changes in policy required permanent negotiation to reconcile the differing ideological and philosophical perspectives of communities and Western cultures. Ngigua teachers are given complex and challenging tasks since they are compelled to maintain this duality of language and culture. School days are extremely demanding due to two issues: the design of activities related to the official curriculum and some community practices, as well as the requirement of parents and supervisors to go out to spaces where they carry out teaching–learning practices that are more Ngigua oriented. Reconciling Ngigua culture and Western knowledge often becomes a utopian ideal because this practice is often hidden and contradictory, even conflictive, disguised as lesson plans and suggestions from the official standards. A clear example of working on Ngigua knowledge can be seen in the lesson we call 'Lo comemos aquí y allá' (We eat it here and there), a 2-week, 10-session lesson plan with a learning objective of students selecting informative texts on a topic of interest. The aforementioned lesson plan involves the collection of the texcal or kunthau. The texcal is an insect similar to the jumiles which live in cucharillas – flowers that grow in the mountains of the semi-arid zones of the region where the Ngiguas are currently dwell. The lesson plan includes the specific task of collecting oral traditions of the people who still carry out this practice. Students must learn the timing of the migration of these insects, their nutritional and medicinal value, and, of course, their sustainable collection technique, using the oral form of their language.

The work that has been carried out so far indicates movement towards an intercultural perspective, such as in school zone 408, headquartered in Tlacotepec de Benito Juárez, in Puebla, Mexico, where 68 teachers have the specific title of Indigenous elementary school educator. This conscripts them to conform to being Ngigua speakers, living in the community, engaging in extracurricular work promoting the use of the language at school and in the community, participating in the cultural and social activities of the community, and taking the Ngigua language as a focus of study. However, deeper examination reveals that only 8 teachers engaged in true Ngigua educational practice: the rest assume a teaching role limited to fulfilling a school-day schedule in which they address subjects dictated by the national curriculum but omit the Ngigua language and cultural practice content, as is unfortunately very common in many other Mexican Indigenous communities. That they are subject to influences outside the Ngigua community and are prone to adopting mew modes of living, dressing, speaking, being and acting within the community. These practices are not related to the Ngigua way of life, which affects teacher formation and, of course, students' education.

Therefore, teaching practices of Indigenous Ngigua-identified teachers differs largely from that of teachers who do not identify as Indigenous, despite being born and living in the same territorial space and working in the Indigenous primary schools of San Marcos Tlacoyalco. Contrasting these practices reveals factors that support or hinder the work of community knowledge. The beneficial factors include parallel work of the study programs and pedagogy, knowledge of the Ngigua language, participation of teachers in cultural and social activities inside and outside the school with students and parents, constant communication with parents, grandparents and relatives of the generations graduated from the elementary schools in which they have worked, and participation in community meetings and assemblies. The factors that hinder language and cultural reclamation are: neglecting and the lack of construction of a Ngigua identity, missing functions as a Ngigua teacher, lack of (Indigenous) language use, apathy, cultural assimilation, missing participation in cultural practices, and the way some consider these a waste of time since they prioritize all the content laid out by state study curricula, as many non-native teachers in other Mexican Indigenous communities do.

Thus, we face the following challenges for a multicultural perspective in Indigenous elementary settings:

(1) Finding teachers from the Octavio Paz elementary school who recognize themselves as Ngigua, that is, who speak the Indigenous national Ngigua language as well as practice their own knowledge, living according to the set of norms established by the Ngigua people of San Marcos Tlacoyalco, as recognized by the community.
(2) Using the Indigenous language inside and outside the classroom.
(3) Indigenous education teachers participating in cultural and social activities.
(4) Involving parents, students, and relatives in the teaching and learning process from a Ngigua pedagogy.
(5) Integrating Ngigua knowledge into lesson planning.

(6) Communicating consistently in Ngigua with the student population and community.
(7) Implementing district level Indigenous language formative evaluations for teachers and students.
(8) Implementing workshops in which materials are designed in the Ngigua language.

Reconciling the official curricula with the Ngigua knowledge system, language and pedagogy may seem utopian. However, personal experience and that of some teachers allows us to envision routes of possibility to reach a horizon in which there is harmony between our own knowledge, languages, cultures, equality amongst people, respect for diversity, and the training of functional bilinguals who can function freely inside and outside their community and in the academic and bureaucratic spheres. In this sense, utopia, far from being an unattainable and impossible imaginary, allows one to believe, walk, design, build and achieve the goals of Indigenous education. As Eduardo Galeano rightly says: 'utopia is good for walking' even if it is not likely achieved, but it allows one to visualize the horizon.

My 25 years of service have been full of constant challenges. The main challenge has been complying with the norms that govern the Mexican educational system, an official curriculum undergirded by the current studies and programs tied to each six-year presidential administration, Westernized studies which invalidate and minimize ancestral knowledge. This necessitates the construction of alternative education proposals that enable Ngigua knowledge, language and culture. Knowing that one serves a linguistic and culturally diverse population requires levels and modalities created for the care of this population. Even with constant changes and demands, materials and teaching–learning strategies have been designed for working with Ngigua as part of the curriculum of the elementary school level of the Indigenous environment.

Currently the new Mexican school curricula, corresponding to the 2022 study plan, allows for inclusion of local content, with land as a starting point, and the possibility of launching local projects. It is a proposal that requires breaking with old schooling paradigms and turning around the educational practices from pedagogy, methodology, and theoretical and philosophical approaches. However, it is a process that is under construction, going through appropriation and application processes, and it was recently established, during 2023–2024 school year. This proposal opens, at least rhetorically, a series of possibilities for a more locally defined and contextually located community education that allows integrating specific local contents into a horizontal dialogue with all the knowledge and languages of the country. It is only possible up to a certain point, since it can be truncated by the changing political and bureaucratic situation of the country.

In this period of work there has been an opportunity to transform and propose strategies for the subject called 'Indigenous language.' As suggested, in addition to new, enriching proposals, there is also a struggle to name correctly the native languages and nations of the country in accordance with self-determination. For example, the Ngigua culture is in the process of demanding it be recognized officially as Ngigua when it has been institutionally labeled as 'Popoloca', an inherited derogatory term applied long ago by the Aztecs or Mexica and which should be discarded.

Existing social relationships allow for the creation of small spaces that foster dialogue. This has helped establish a group of students and teachers who, according to their material and human resources, as well as a collective set of skills and abilities, are making materials such as board games, translations and composition of songs, recordings of advertisements, publicity materials in some businesses, as well as some handmade books with the help of students and parents. These promote the revitalization of the language, legitimize the reclamation efforts and questioning of language shift as well as the desire to expand these workshops to other institutions and in the community. New projects and networks expand and seek to revitalize the language and culture in other spaces and areas, including the care for the local native environment and land.

Elements of Ngigua Pedagogy

The complex task of Indigenous teachers who analyze their reality, requires proposing and tracing pedagogical routes for the inclusion of local knowledge and Ngigua language. This comes alongside defying the official curriculum. The focus on making this type of pedagogy possible gave rise to workshops and colloquiums that facilitated socialization of strategies and work modalities that aligned with Ngigua pedagogy. The meetings were conducted in Ngigua, an already revitalizing practice, and with this socialization it was possible for some teachers to systematize the set of pedagogical tasks to achieve strategies from a perspective they named, 'Experiencias pedagógicas de docentes Ngiguas poblanos' (Pedagogical experiences of Ngigua teachers from Puebla). These were presented in a book entitled *Pedagogía intercultural 2020 bilingüe desde la cultura Ngigua* (Bilingual and Intercultural Pedagogy from the Ngigua Culture), with a total of 12 contributors with different levels of bilingualism. Each chapter presents a series of activities for working with Indigenous language that is part of the curricular map of elementary education of the state of Puebla.

The volume 'combines a set of essays that come directly from the main actors who are working in front of the school groups, in this case, Indigenous primary level teachers from School Zone 408' (SEP, 2020: 8).

Included are strategies developed during the 2017–2018 school years, presented in three stages:

1) To prepare them, teachers were clearly presented with the goal of the meeting, so that in a creative and innovative way they will consider how to venture into this sharing of teaching practices and styles, under the specifications of the Curricular Framework for Indigenous Education that the General Directorate of Indigenous Education (DGEI) has provided to each school zone; 2) a series of visits to the schools was scheduled, so each teacher presented, in PowerPoint format, their progress in the strategy implemented for the teaching of the Ngigua language; and 3) Visits consisted of full day of work, where they presented the selected strategies in the school phase. (SEP, 2020: 16)

In the book, the following strategies are detailed: Nthaxruan, thian, nthachjiankutangi, I observe, listen, do and learn; Kexrein sayakuena nuntheana ku jaña sangina rukjena Ngigua, environmental practices leading to the production of texts in the Ngigua language; recovering the oral tradition in the production of texts in the Ngigua language and Spanish, such as 'Let's shell corn for planting'. Oral tradition as a strategy for writing in the Ngigua language, allows for the learning to read and write in the Ngigua language through texts such as 'the alphabetic clothesline', Thi tenda 'uni xroon; colors according to science that promote the teaching of Ngigua; the craft book as a strategy for teaching Ngigua; and community stories to develop reading and writing in Ngigua. In each, there are sections, moments, phases, evaluations, levels of bilingualism, information about territory, challenges, achievements, and the ways of teaching and learning Ngigua from distinct perspectives.

The culmination and presentation of these strategies have precedents in previous school cycles and the work each teacher carried out within their classrooms with their students and based on their needs. Thus, the essays presented in the volume come directly from the main individuals who are working in front of the school groups – in this case, Indigenous elementary school level teachers from school zone 408. In each one of the education strategies, a series of activities is included from the teaching experience of the authors for the development of reading and writing via the Ngigua language and culture.

In addition to strengthening the teaching community of zone 408, it makes a contribution so that the teachers of the other Indigenous groups are encouraged to design, provide feedback, and put into practice their education strategies promoting their languages. Other groups, of course, start with their own efforts and challenge the realities that each of them faces in the teaching of Indigenous languages with methodologies couched in the knowledge, culture and language spoken in each native community.

The Ngigua community of the north, from the state of Puebla, has acted on the suggestions of its inhabitants in their roles as translators, researchers, consultants, and altruistic citizens and have sought to conserve the language, with its multiple elements, which range from agriculture to the care of the social and natural environment that surrounds them. These records date from the year 1980, a period in which various printed materials were published. Among those that stand out is a book in which spellings for the Ngigua script are mentioned, as well as a book for first-grade students. For many years, no actions were taken to preserve and revitalize the Ngigua language. It was not until 2012 that workshops were organized with students of compulsory education, ranging from preschool to high school. Included in these workshops were topics such as writing in Ngigua, orality of the language, work by hand, fostering community via feasting, the process of claiming identity, the elaboration of some materials such as memorama (memory game) and lotería (lottery), as well as some stories, plus the creation of a Facebook profile to share the Ngigua language.

Networks in the Process of Revitalizing the Ngigua Language

The workshops that parents and teachers carried out with students were spaces that made it possible to identify some achievements and available resources, but also appreciate difficulties, deficiencies and needs that could not be addressed by teachers. This demanded the intervention of specialists in the areas of linguistics, anthropology, sociology and biology. Interdisciplinary networks collaborated in the revitalization of the Ngigua language, reflecting on processes of encounter and recognition of one's acentral language.

These meetings recognized that some resources necessary for safeguarding the Ngigua language were lacking. Likewise, it became clear that the good intentions of teachers, students and parents were not enough. The collaboration of a number of specialists was necessary in the recording and systematization of the numerous practices that the Ngigua community performs, but above all to ensure acceptance of strangers within this group. With the support of linguists focused on revitalization and conservation of language, the group recorded verbal arts. This was a 'creative' language act that appeals both to oral tradition and memory as well as the present and future of the original peoples. The formation of networks widened the field of practice, and this allowed the formation of a network of colleagues and students who documented the Ngigua language with the help of linguists expert in the recording of native languages. In San Marcos Tlacoyalco, a team was formed: Je'a je'u ngai jaana ku anseana sechjian thi nu'e ni juun (The knowledge of our grandparents persists in our minds and hearts).

The collaboration of the linguists helped to underscore the importance of safeguarding knowledge, language and culture in audio,

Figure 5.1 (left) Linguistic collaborations during workshop of language documentation.

Figure 5.2 (right) Dialogue with wise/knowledgable people about the preparation of temazcal (nchiachea)

video, and written records using electronic media for consultation, socialization, and dissemination, as well as stressing the importance of creating materials and contributing to the recognition of being and belonging to the Ngigua linguistic group.

Also fostered was more frequent interaction with elders, listening attentively to words in Ngigua that have scarcely been used, recording them in a notebook, using different applications and programs that help to classify the words and thereby create materials that can be used in the classroom.

Both local and external specialists helped the community in the recording and safeguarding of a considerable number of cultural practices that house knowledge, language and social relations between families, and between students and teachers. It is worth mentioning that the participation of external individuals, in their role as specialists, was not an easy element since Ngiguas, culturally and historically, hold that they have been dispossessed and looted throughout history. Therefore, opening spaces for meeting and dialogue between Ngiguas and outsiders implied a process of acceptance through practices that refer to action research and reciprocity in this collaborative construction (Figure 5.1).

Beyond the Classroom

Assuming the role of a teacher of Indigenous education requires the collaboration and participation of the Ngigua community and the design of a series of activities emerging from the needs that teachers have ascertained when being with Ngigua students. It also requires attempts to systematize practices emanating from classroom and community spaces, taking into account the life of the community manifested in the classroom and received by the teacher – such as community organization, mutual aid, food, celebrations, rituals and dances. In this way, the teacher promotes an Ngigua pedagogy, and the networks are expanded with the participation of grandparents, grandmothers, parents, neighbors and children, who participate by contributing their knowledge, and explaining natural and mystical phenomena in the classroom and in the community. The activities in each of the classes also arise linguistically from the monolingual Ngigua students, monolingual students in Spanish, and students with greater proficiency in one of the two languages.

The classroom and school space maintain a relationship with the community via the interactions established with the students, parents, adults, and those who know the life of the Ngigua. These interactions have been very helpful for the work with the Indigenous language project, in conjunction with corn agriculture, manual work, the narration of oral stories, the care and raising of children, the interpretation of time by the color of the sky, the song of birds, the sound of animals, and the position of the stars.

These elements have been taken in by the students for the appropriation and construction of Ngigua knowledge from the knowledge of the people of the community. From this perspective, language learning is seen as more than an appropriation of the language as a set of words that allows communication, since it is a goal that students know and want their language to be a part of the community context. It is about recognizing that it is a language that allows one to live respectfully and in equilibrium with all that surrounds us.

Thinking back on 25 years working in front of students, immersed in an Ngigua community, to which I am native, puts me in a unique role in complying with the norms of the institutions I am associated with, like to the Ministry of Public Education (Secretaría de Educación Pública, SEP) and the General Directorate of Intercultural and Bilingual Indigenous Education (Dirección General de Educación Indígena, Intercultural y Bilingüe, DGEIIB). I have not been impeded in a dialogue between school and community, since it has been a space that allowed me to investigate and systematize my knowledge of Spanish, artistic education, civic and ethical training, and exploration of nature and society. I hold together the lesson and study programs, the full-time curriculum together with the reading program of full-time schools, the calendar of standards proposed by the Ministry of Public Education (SEP) together with the Indigenous curriculum.

The work regarding Indigenous language content is made possible through situated learning and an inductive intercultural methodology, using transversality as a pedagogical proposal to link subjects at the primary level. This type of work was ongoing in school cycles prior to the COVID-19 pandemic. In the state of Puebla, Mexico, during forced isolation and remote instruction (and in the hybrid modality), situated learning methodologies were employed to prepare learning booklets for home schooling and lesson planning. Ironically, the pandemic encouraged a return to community education, since it involved making home visits, knowing and re-knowing one's land, and proposed activities were couched in the context and daily life of students. For example, the raising of the animals, the collection of seeds and seasonal fruits, the organization and the assigned tasks in the family, are all based on mutual help. Indeed, situated learning is based on lifelong learning, an opportune condition to cover both the needs of teachers and students. Following Diaz and Hernández (2015) this methodology utilizes the knowledge of the students as an everyday resource to construct teaching subjects, developing related abilities and good practices rooted in their positive community values and epistemologies, creating collaborative learning spaces, developing 'new' cognitive territories linked to the local contexts in practical ways.

During the isolation due to the SARS-CoV-2 virus, the causative agent of the COVID-19 disease, we had the opportunity to make some home visits in Ngigua rural communities, following health and safety measures. The interactions made it possible to recognize that some families resumed practices such as the use of hot plants for the remedy against COVID, as well as family manual labor, the care of backyard animals, and the cultivation of plants and native trees. Families shared their remedies through oral Ngigua, naming plants. Families knew how to prepare the steam bath – nchiachea (the temazcal steam bath) – with hot plants and they shared techniques of how to do it (Figure 5.2).

Pedagogical Alternatives from a Ngigua Perspective

Being a teacher of formal Indigenous education is a privilege that few truly understand. The work carried out in these bilingual contexts has many implications, from identifying as a person with a duality and at the same time as an individual who has the interest, commitment, and responsibility to design, propose, integrate, participate, collaborate, and apply schooling situations that contribute to the work of the Ngigua Indigenous language as a subject. Not having language teaching methods means that any interested teacher is in the precarious situation of not having an established curriculum for this subject and being placed in a dilemma whereby the teacher either innovates ways of working or the is forced to leave the subject on the margin.

Through trial and error, the following strategies have been implemented: Tsjen ku tangi (Sing and learn), or singing, as a means to cover school content regarding knowledge of the environment and Indigenous language, using the original language to compose and in some cases translate, songs. One example is Makun chinthju rua, kanxi ji'i techundana (Head, shoulders, knees and feet). In the 2016–2017 school years Nthaxruan, thian, nthachjian ku tangi (I observe, listen, do and learn) was developed from the activities of craft book, microteaching, oral tradition, the story, and collective writing. This approach is sometimes called constructive hyperfiction, or narratives written through collaboration between several authors (see https://es.wikipedia.org/wiki/Escritura_colaborativa). Ngigua students have built texts with the participation and collective contribution of ideas. Others have done individual writing or have adopted a chosen Ngigua name, which is later translated using an alphabet with the spellings of this language.

The aforementioned strategies have been developed during blocks of time in the different subjects of previous school cycles. In this process of reflection and construction, part of another strategy has been launched: Nthaxruan, thian, nthachjian ku tangi (I observe, lister, do, and learn) to develop oral proficiency in Ngigua. Nchichjaon tangi (I learn a little) activities of 'micro-teaching' are resumed, to develop orality. This is done from a sociocultural stance, where 5–8 words are taken in 20-minute sessions with students.

The Tsjen ku tangi (sing and learn) strategy composes short songs with the help of students who speak the Ngigua language. One of the songs they composed is Naa nthatjsachjan, naa nthatjsachjan, thinuu ri'i, thinuu ri'i, unda ndakjuyua, unda ndakjuyua, thinuu ri'i, thinuu ri'i (A mesquite, a mesquite, where are you?, where are you?, why are you green?, where are you?) (adopting the music of already existing songs).

Tsuntaaun ku tangi (play and learn) consists of repeating phrases for turns and indications, such as: jaan, na'i (Yes, No), thinga (Run, run), anchee ja'an, anchee ja'a, anchee je'e, anchee kaina (Now you, me, him, them and everyone).

Figure. 5.3 (left) Interactions in the context of the community project: 'cultivating food from a traditional field of cultivation (milpa)'

Figure 5.4 (right) Exploring natural territory con 1st graders, as part of the project 'Naming plants and trees in Ngigua language'

Figure 5.5 (left) Presentation of teaching material in Ngigua language with an enphasis on singing as a teching strategy

Figure 5.6 (right) Presentation of handmade books in Ngigua language from 1st grade students

The elaboration of craft books is another strategy. This approach consists of making three books per school year, working from a cultural practice, and later forming teams by affinity and programming sessions with the collaboration of parents and students. Three titles: produced were *Are xensa Elisa* (Elisa's Empacho), *Kunithjau* (The Crescent Moon), *Chijni tunkja jee* (Ngigua Spelling) and *A benu'ara ke kuchu'ka?* (Did You Know that the Ant?) (Figure 5.6).

The activities produced through the aforementioned strategies have been essential considering the local linguistic situation. The population is working in a context of Ngigua linguistic immersion (total or partial) since the use of the language in the family and the community is still present. In this context, the students are in contact with the Ngigua language. Although they might not speak it, they always listen to it with their grandparents and other people when interacting with them.

During my years working as an Indigenous education teacher, there have been opportunities to experiment through analysis and reflection. In this process of learning and re-learning we have gleaned that teachers have knowledge about teaching methodologies and learning styles, as well as knowledge about elements of official educational standards, but they have left aside mastery of the knowledge of the land in which they have to provide instruction. Being in a precarious situation to serve a population with specific needs, a population that makes use of Indigenous language in the family and community environment both orally and in representation of cultural practices, this process gave us a lens to recognize those elements necessary to consider and include on a daily basis. We acknowledge the intervention and support of Ngigua Indigenous knowledge experts in the execution of schooling projects proposed, by sharing the findings of their research and knowledge from the inquiry made by the Ngigua teacher. In the same way, the interaction that the teacher maintains with the community of parents is essential (Figure 5.5).

These more than two decades of work as a teacher from a Ngigua perspective have made it possible to approach the population and territory to learn, reaffirm, build and apply this knowledge immersed in the ways of life and the language of the Ngigua community. Similarly, it has been recognized that the participation and collaboration of the Ngigua community was necessary from its various roles. The collaborative participation of these agents contributes to giving credit, acceptance and recognition of belonging to an original community.

The relationship established between the school and the community has contributed to the construction of an Ngigua identity. In a recent academic year, we have given significant importance to designing materials for working with the Ngigua language, systemizing knowledge available to the community, the unification of spellings for Ngigua writing, a curriculum based on community knowledge, and the participation of the wise men of the community. In this way we get closer to the construction of Ngigua pedagogical alternatives.

Are chuuni ixi thenichani naa tha` (Siblings Standing the Fight for Native Languages)

Interaction with media (territory, community, language, worldview) and the people involved in revitalization, recognition, and strengthening of the native languages of Mexico has contributed to greater possibilities, such as guiding, forming, qualifying, training, informing, integrating, and promoting this language, which for many years received little attention. The role of experts in the recording of oral production has contributed to the documentation of the Ngigua language through audio and video resources compiled over the period 2019–2022. The care and dedication of these people protected cultural knowledge and practices, which would not be possible without the inputs provided by the Ngigua community.

Recognizing and taking up the knowledge of the experts allowed the community to participate in a call issued by the Ministry of Culture, through the National Fund for Culture and the Arts (FONCA) in collaboration with the National Institute of Indigenous Languages (INALI), which called for participation in the registry of 'Verbal Arts of National Indigenous Languages at Risk of Disappearing'. Until then, this resource which now contributes to the revitalization of the Ngigua language, was unknown. This opportunity was made available through the advice of linguists who, with their training and guidance, had the facility to be part of one more way of safeguarding the knowledge of the Ngigua community. This first project was named Je'a je'u ngai jaana ku anseana sechjian thi nu'e ni juun (The knowledge of our grandparents persists in our minds and hearts). The verbal record of this 2019 project guarantees its preservation.

Documenting is 'a complex task that directly involves the speakers, who act as teachers, collaborators, and many of them, linguists. For this reason, before beginning the recordings and the analysis of data, it is essential to subscribe to an ethical position of respect and recognition of the speakers who serve as a conduit to the knowledge of the language that is going to be documented' (CDI, 2012: 6).

Understanding that linguistic documentation is 'a discipline that within its functions addresses the extinction threat experienced by minority languages, data collection within this discipline is carried out with multidisciplinary tools that combine linguistic description with ethnography and information technologies' and its incorporation allows the 'study of structural, semantic, discursive, pragmatic, anthropological and sociolinguistic aspects of languages' (CDI, 2012: 5).

In the first usage of this resource, the only known concept was 'linguistic documentation,' understanding that this has its foundation in the linguistic practice of communities and therefore takes on a multipurpose character:

> that benefits both related public institutions with the Indigenous foci (but not only restricted to it), as well as researchers from various disciplines (e.g. linguistics, anthropology, oral history). It significantly benefits the language community itself in the strengthening, development, and revitalization of its tongues. (CDI, 2012: 3)

As a conclusion, the project was oriented towards the collaboration of people who join Indigenous struggles for linguistic revitalization and the dignity of national cultures and languages. It is worth noting the role played by Dr José Antonio Flores Farfán who, in his ethic of collaboration with the Ngigua (or Ngiva), opened spaces for meeting and dialogue with experts in linguistic recordings. In this work, Dr Maurice Pico de los Cobos and Dr Amanda Galván Delgado enriched the projects with their knowledge but above all with compassionate disposition for the process of safeguarding knowledge and the Ngigua language, thus becoming valuable allies and companions in the fight to preserve and retake what belongs to the community (Figure 5.8).

COVID-19 Isolation as a Space for Re-encounters

During this process of participation, analysis, and reflection as a teacher with a Ngigua identity, an intentional praxis emerges, carrying out multiple actions that on the one hand are accountable to the SEP and on the other encourage the use of language in its various manifestations, such as: how to cultivate crops, participate in community tasks,

Figure 5.7 Salida a la recolección de plantas para el baño de temazcal con la colaboración de la señora Angela Balderas Perez (An outing to collect plants for a temazcal sweat bath, with the collaboration of Mrs Angela Balderas Perez)

Figure 5.8 La grabacion de audio y video de lugares representativos de los Ngiguas, particularmente lugares donde habitaron los Ngiguas antes de la evangelización (The recording of audio and video of representative Ngigua sites, particularly sites where Ngigua lived before evangelism/conversion)

use traditional medicine, employ the power of speech, and create some materials for teaching Indigenous language. During the 2019–2020 school years, which included the teaching–learning processes of students in elementary education and the investigation of the social practices of the Ngigua community, the outbreak of coronavirus disease (COVID-19) happened. World governments mobilized and local organizations worked towards community health campaigns, with new rules of interaction, and with changes in hours and forms of care for the population in establishments such as banks, hospitals, churches and, of course, schools. The latter needed to change the modality of study throughout the Mexican Republic from the morning and evening face-to-face modality to a 'distance' modality.

This distance-learning modality allowed for the launch of the first project for the recording of verbal texts. These texts concerned with the following practices: permission for the use of the temazcal (kexrein danchiani juachaxin and xrein ndunda nchianchea); call of the spirit (Sayeena thi techunxina); cure for sickness (xruen chi'in chjan); and oral tradition (thi thekin ni dachrii), including (three legends): Xanchri binchian xe'en xi nchau'en jna tjsu (The girl who had a son of the guardian of the hill of the flower), Xru jithuxi (Rocked stone), and Xichjan kjuau kulantha (The boy who spoke with a lizard). The process of recording verbal art forms and oral tradition was complex, due to ignorance of the software and other resources. The support of linguists was essential due to their experience with the management of resources for the work that involved recording. Meanwhile, the Ngigua community had some strengths, such as the collaboration of people who are keepers of knowledge and the Ngigua language, and the unconditional support of parents, teachers, youth and students from this community.

These projects allowed time for investigation and application. In the first one referenced above (permission for the use of the nchianchea temazcal), time was allocated for the construction of the steam bath, in consideration of its shape, local building material, and the building permit which it was necessary to complete to be able to use it for the first time. The grandmothers and grandfathers had permission to perform this ritual. After a few days, the first steam bath was prepared, for which the following plants were obtained: kalanka, kaxranchuni, kanthachilaku, karomero jna, kanthatukuthe, kanthaka ku kanthaxruchau. These were for infusing into the water to be used in the nchianchea (temazcal) bath. During the bath there was the support and collaboration of people for preparation activities and the healing of women who took the bath to relieve cold symptoms they had accumulated (Figures 5.7 and 5.9).

The second practice was sayeena thi techunxina (call of the spirit). This process is made up of three parts. The first relates to the symptoms of the person who needs to call in the Ngigua spirits – for example, when a person is traumatized by having witnessed a violent act, such as a car crash, falling from somewhere, witnessing a murder, etc., or if they are a person who stops eating, is quiet, sobs, sleeps with their eyes half open, wakes up anguished with a high heart rate. People who have this gift are asked to go to the place where the trauma of the damaged person occurred, to call in a spirit using the following objects: a jug, a gourd with red flowers, four thin sweet-sticks or a broom to catch the spirit, and some chicken eggs. Once the person who has been asked to perform this ritual has arrived at the place, time is taken to lean on other people who take the sweet-sticks to bring the spirit until they reach the place where the trauma occurred. In this place the sick person stands together with the healer to catch the spirit. It manifests itself as a butterfly or moth. Finally, everyone returns home to leave the person with their spirit and the rods that were used are placed under the bed or petate (a bedroll, whose name comes from the Nahuatl language), for a few days.

The last practice is xrueen chi'in chjan (cure for epilepsy). This practice is recorded to keep the knowledge of healing white and purple epilepsy, as long as it is detected in time. It is an evil that afflicts children from infancy to six years. It is said that it is a disease that develops from gestation due to the condition experienced by the mother, ranging from the feeling in which she conceived, acts of physical violence and omission, and strong impressions experienced during gestation and child-rearing of infants. Small children present symptoms such as higher temperature only in the palms of the hands, crying and tantrums, bruised fingernails, toenails, as well as the lips, sobbing during naps, and in some cases pale skin tone. In newborns it is identified in two ways:

Figure 5.9 (left) La preparación del baño de vapor con plantas calientes en colaboración de las personas con este conocimiento (The preparation of the steam bath with hot plants in collaboration with people with this knowledge)

Figure 5.10 (right) La grabación del antes, durante y fin de la preparación del baño de temazcal (nchiachea) (The filming of the before, during, and after of the preparation of the temazcal (nchiachea) bath)

one is the skin tone and the other is that at times they spend their time biting their tongues and lips.

During the period of distance education, the project of recording the oral arts allowed the rethinking, reorienting, and design of a curriculum for an Ngigua Indigenous language (Figure 5.10). As resources, people had the videos and audio recordings of various cultural practices, rituals, and oral narratives, advice, and beliefs of the Ngigua. In the work carried out during 2019–2022, ancient words that many generations had forgotten were learned and recognized, such as Xrunchrin (deity who asks for rain) and Nchexruxin (thankfulness), as well as the practice of ways of life within the community that led us to make peace with the natural and social environment that surrounds us. Interaction in the physical and social environment that the land offered us allowed us to recognize the value of continuing to be Ngigua. The isolation of the pandemic era allowed us to return to the land, walk the old paths again, return to the use of medicinal plants, and experience the use of medicine through a re-encounter with wise people from the community.

Identity Configuration of the Ngigua Teacher

The teachers, who identify as Ngigua, even with multiple jobs, recognize that on occasion they had forgotten to live for and with the community, participating in its forms and manifestations of Ngigua culture. But, when carrying out the activities of the verbal arts recording, the teachers and other participants saw the need for going back to integrate themselves into community life and thus find a space for acceptance and collaboration in their community. Teachers encounter Ngigua oral and body language, the consumption of food, participation of ways of community governance, within the families and community, and the organization of activities in order to respect all of the ways of life.

The work carried out during the 2019–2020 school year continued with the recording of verbal arts for the 2021–2022 school year, starting the following project: Sechjian thi nu'e ni juun (The knowledge of our grandparents persists in our minds and hearts). Linguistic documentation is a resource that allows the protection of specialized parts in the Ngigua language that nowadays only grandparents have. In particular, two forms are involved: biographies and life stories (e.g. The life of a revolutionary Ngigua, the life of Felipe Peña and Tomasa Gómez Pérez), relevant for what each of the people represents. The first refers us to the participation that a man takes Ngigua in the movement of the Mexican revolution, the second refers to social control, from the discourse that the political groups of power used towards the Indigenous communities, and finally the Ngigua woman related to the submission or omission of the roles imposed by the same community and schooling (Figure 5.10).

This project also considered the following rituals: Cha'uen jna (Guardian of the hill), Sanchiagana nchiagana suuan jnayua (Prayer for the good harvest of chili peppers), Re thjexi tandani (The corn harvest), and Tsiatheni jinda (Let's tie the water). The recording of the prayers leaves us with great lessons about the ways each one should be done, and the recognition these had ceased for many years, and, of course, valuing the space that the community shared with us by allowing us to participate in these rituals. During informal talks prior to the interviews and organization for the recording of the aforementioned rituals, there was an opportunity to learn some words that had fallen out of use.

The oral tradition in which the recording was made (three legends) was also considered: Ni xintili (the xentiles or gentiles) is a story that refers to the history of the Ngiguas before the conquered. It mentions the forms organization within the family and community as well as their beliefs. Thjari'ue thuee jinda (El jaguey) is a story of the place where the Ngiguas communities collect rainwater to supply the community in times of drought. It is a space in the form of a lagoon and in it a ritual is carried out to conserve the water. The last story is Kunchechrin (Rain serpent referring to Quetzalcoatl), a wise god to whom the Indigenous cultures prayed before the conquest. They refer to it as a serpent that descends from heaven in the form of a water serpent.

An archive of Ngigua language is built. Reflection arises from the processes that are effectuated in spaces such as school and community. It is in the completion of the documentation projects that the language becomes active. It gratifies us, as teachers, to see all language forms and to continue promoting the ways of life of the Ngigua culture. Community documentation or self-documentation, in turn, becomes possible from the recognition and participation of the community, which is comprised of authorities, teachers, youth, children, parents, linguists and community scholars. By putting both documentation and culture as priorities, participants and Ngigua recognize both the school and the community as sources of knowledge that educate others, giving them prestige. Both offer means for the training of students who live in a dual reality offered by schools and aboriginal communities. Of course, this happens without forgetting that it starts from the needs of each one of the subjects who is positioned in the didactic triangle where the teacher is a mediator and manager of knowledge. For their part,

> the teacher exercises an important role of mediation between the student and knowledge. Among the central functions of the teacher are the orientation, promotion, and guidance of the constructive mental activity of his students, to whom he will provide pedagogical help adjusted to his competence. (Coll, 2001: 122)

What Directs the Course of the Teacher of Indigenous Education?

Indigenous language teaching as part of the Indigenous education curriculum of the state of Puebla, Mexico, has been complicated. It might be characterized as uncertain, because the course doesn't have its own study plan of the Ngigua language. There is no denying that it offers resources, such as guidelines in worksheets where teachers can design their didactic sequences and material from the linguistic documentation archive. It also includes the participation of the community—students and teachers – in knowing and performing communal tasks such as caring for the cornfield, tilling, caring for nature, and the intelligent use of natural resources. What is missing is a study plan and program for this subject, from the Ngigua philosophy and ideology itself, one that eventually moves across the entire curriculum.

The Indigenous language curriculum of basic education grades has printed material that has been organized according to grade level: first and second, third and fourth, and fifth and sixth grade. In each grade the material has been organized in the following areas: family and community life, oral tradition, literature and historical testimonies, intercommunity life, and the relationship with other peoples and the study and dissemination of knowledge. Each area presents possible projects that could be developed in the work with the language subject matter.

This is how two decades of working life have elapsed between one presidential 6-year term and another, governing the country's public education. For five decades, precarious conditions for Indigenous education in the state of Puebla have led its teachers to seek ways to intervene and ensure that it becomes real. With it, the goals of the subject matter of Indigenous language are fulfilled:

> Develop in children their self-esteem, autonomy, and ability to express opinions and points of view on matters that concern and affect them.

Appropriate the grammatical, rhetorical, and expressive resources of their mother tongues in accordance with the cultural principles that govern the various spheres of social life and reflect on the rules that govern the oral and written expression of Indigenous languages. (SEP, 2003: 14)

In my experience, the conditions in which the work with this subject matter has been developed in the last two decades have fomented uncertainty But they also provided opportunities that led me to interact with people who make small and large attempts to work on Indigenous language and the design of educational materials, teaching strategies, and audiovisual resources, as has been mentioned, including songs in Ngigua, stories, prayers, biographies, traditional medicine, and the care and germination of some plants and trees in the region.

This precariousness forces me to seek collaboration with, and the support of, people who can contribute to producing material and resources for the work of Indigenous languages. Support has been found in the networks formed by people who work in the advancement of Indigenous or native knowledge of ethnic groups in Mexico and other countries. The interaction and relationship established during this time has made it possible to discover other ways of recovering the knowledge of native communities to create conditions for appropriation, construction and promotion of what belongs to the community.

Conclusion

In conclusion, dialogue with people working with Indigenous knowledge and the manifestations of Indigenous culture of any place makes it possible to find ways of safeguarding the full range of knowledge and ways of life of Indigenous peoples who have preserved their languages and knowledge for thousands of years, despite the experience of so many types of invations (colonial, civil war, etc.) and so much looting. The Ngigua community displayed resistance to the evangelization that even today is shown in the dance of the *Toriteros*, in which a character named lantha in Ngigua and graciero in Spanish participates. This figure's movements reveal that it was not evangelized and is therefore prohibited from entrance to the atrium of the church. Since the Spanish invasion, the Ngigua community has resisted being evangelized. Likewise, it has resisted public policies in education and health – for example, the first public school was not established until 1945, and health centers were only accepted recently. Also, the community limited physical access to the Ngigua community in the case of programs such as those implemented by the federal government under the name of PROSPERA, a state social inclusion program.

The networks have fostered a determination for revitalizing Indigenous languages, as well as everything the language encapsulates, like all representations of social and natural environments. Being part of an Indigenous community has advantages, but it also implies responsibility: living within the community brings us closer to assuming the Ngigua identity role, which carries with it a responsibility to carry out, as far as possible, tasks that are carried out inside the community, based on what is dictated by community governance and norms. Likewise, people collaborate by participating in the tasks that correspond to assigned community work and its requirements or by representatives each family sends to help the community. According to people's skills and abilities, these range from the wax worker to Ngigua counselors and artisans.

This leads us to ask ourselves: What does it mean to be Ngigua? Being Ngigua means speaking the local language and living as the community dictates according to the education it has imparted to its people. This involves commitments, which are of two complementary types: one relates to oneself as a subject, i.e. assuming that it is in our hands to do more than just live outside culture. The second implies commitments to the group to which we belong, safeguarding this language with all its tangible and intangible representations. The pact with the group arises from the reciprocity of the participatory population in this language, which few value, as evidenced by its current status as a threatened language, but which also shows clear signs of resistance and vitality.

Another important point is the support of people outside the community, which, if well conceived, strengthens us, since their contribution helps us understand that we are not alone on this path. Communication established through dialogue in virtual and occasionally in-person meetings brings us closer to other means and resources that are particularly unknown, such as linguistic documentation. The language documentation from the Ngigua's own register brought us closer every day to the Ngigua community, resuming dialogue with parents, grandparents, elders and some family members who establish communication in the closest circle through daily work at school and outside it. Thus, the recording and documentation of the Ngigua language can be valued as a positive process, thanks to the support of the participants and the time invested. Documenting is a task with many benefits for safeguarding Indigenous knowledge, but it requires time to travel to the planned recording spaces and transcribe the recordings, a task that can become very demanding and even daunting.

The time provided by isolation during the COVID-19 pandemic allowed for the recording of the Ngigua language, working with community members in small groups not exceeding 10 people, including those who operated the camera and audio recorder, as well as those who shared your knowledge. This period, called 'Stay at home', benefited the group, as there was time and space to research, practice and reflect on planned practices and others that emerged as needs of the moment, such as the use of Ngigua medicinal plants for COVID-19 remedies, the recording of steam baths with hot plants and the technique of brushing feet with salt. This space and time allowed for deep discusions with the support and collaboration of the group members: Ntha'ana xra ixi jaña icha thi'ina thanana (It is our work that makes them listen to our language). All of whom are from the communities of San Marcos Tlacoyalco and San Jose Buenavista, both belonging to the Ngigua territory in the north of Puebla, where the need to carry out this work arises due to the points of coincidence and the desire to preserve and revitalize our mother language Ngigua. Despite the uncertainty of the pandemic, there were family situations that promoted teamwork and closeness between families to share knowledge that, in some way, could contribute to saving lives and with it the ancient ancestral knowledge kept by the native community. Ngigua, highlighting the value of communal education.

However, after the positive effects of the pandemic – in the sense of going back to one's own lands, pedagogies, and time – the new 'normal' conditions after COVID-19 led to a lower quality and quantity of records, as each member returned to their various occupations, fulfilling their different informal and formal roles. This situation led to little and, at times, no communication with community members. In general, the documentation experience shows that it is necessary to make linguistic documentation with simplified transcriptions adapted to the needs expressed by the community, with a local relevant meaning and focus where the community actively participates, highlighting its educational focus but without focusing exclusively on academic purposes. For us, each activity carried out in linguistic documentation and teaching work is linked to oneself, to others, and to the nature that surrounds each Ngigua individual. These practices result in a local archive that in the present and future will serve to know, value and understand the way of life of the Ngigua from their own ideology and philosophy of life.

Through the process of workshops and interaction with the linguists who joined the two aforementioned projects, the practical and theoretical elements of this resource were conceptualized as opportunities to learn, re-learn, value, document, record, know, collaborate, participate, revitalize and finally live within the framework of the ways of life dictated by the Ngigua community in terms of how to carry out research from the role that being Ngigua represents. These forms are manifested in family and community life in its diverse realities but with our own knowledge systems that make us part of this native group that few know. In this sense, the work of a Ngigua teacher places the rol of an educator in the position of actively listening to the students while they express their experiences in social and culturally sensitive tasks, relating them to the nature that surrounds them, their families, and informal conversations with elders and wise men of the Ngigua territory. The interaction with these agents creates spaces that will facilitate future projects. The review of the current study plans that govern official education in the Mexican Republic at the level of Indigenous education highlights the need for better documentation that directs our own local education. In this sense, the linguistic records provide an outline for a possible curriculum for the Ngigua Indigenous language subject, with audiovisual materials and the registration of various words that cover practices of the Ngigua community, composed by children, youth, adults, and elders together.

Climate change also impacts the socio-natural practices of the Ngiguas, since the activities proposed in the projects to register the Ngigua language did not coincide with the available time of the community members, delaying the execution of the project. In 2022, there was a record drought season, which prevented the carrying out of agricultural and social activities marked in the socio-natural calendar of the Ngigua community. During this agricultural year, the planting of rainfed corn, a practice registered in the project, was not carried out, nor was the collection of fruits, seeds, and plants for self-consumption and the healing of the population. Yet, this year of drought made it possible to document the behavior of endemic plants, mainly the harvest of pitaya (a cactus fruit), and the behavior of animals such as birds and insects. The behavior of the mesquite was also identified.

In conclusion, the time limitations on documentation for someone in the role of Ngigua teacher are complex, since being part of institutions such as SEP and DGEIIB implies a re-thinking of what to prioritize: address Westernized pedagogical issues or those of the community? The teacher is required to play more than one role, which at times is uncomfortable, since they are only taken to carry out procedures and protocols for validation and normalization of various public policies that have become law – not prioritizing the Ngigua own forms.

References

Coll, C. (2001) Constructivismo y educación: La concepción constructivista de la enseñanza y el aprendizaje. In C. Coll, J. Palacios and A. Marchesi (eds) *Desarrollo psicológico y educación II* (pp. 157–188). Alianza Editorial.

Comisión Nacional de los Derechos Humanos (2018) *Derechos lingüísticos de los pueblos indígenas* (2nd edn). CNDH.

Comisión Nacional para el Desarrollo de los Pueblos Indígenas (CDI) (2012) *Memoria Documental. Desarrollo con Identidad para los Pueblos y las Comunidades Indígenas 2006–2012*. CDI

Díaz, R and Hernández, J.L. (2015) *Aprendizaje Situado: Transformar la realidad educando*. Grupo Gráfico Editorial.

Fierro, C., Fourtoul, B. and Rosas, L. (1999) *Transformando la práctica docente*. Una propuesta basada en la investigación-acción. Paidós.

Flores Farfán, J.A., Córdova-Hernández, L. and Cru, J. (2020) *Guía de revitalización lingüística: Para una gestión formada e informada.* (2nd edn) (augmented and with corrections). Linguapax-Universidad Autónoma Benito Juárez de Oaxaca.

SEP (2003) *Lengua Indígena. Parámetros Curriculares. Educación primaria indígena y de la población migrante.* Secretaría de Educación Pública.

SEP (2020) *Pedagogía intercultural bilingüe desde la cultura Ngigua: experiencias pedagógicas de docentes Ngigua poblanos.* Secretaría de Educación Pública.

6 The Use of Indigenous Languages in Community-Based Indigenous Education in Oaxaca, Mx

Beatriz González and Cornelio Hernández Pérez
Translated by: Pamela Velázquez Camacho Velázquez
Revised by: Eulalia Gallegos Buitrón y Julieta Briseño-Roa

Ga rhui' didza' nhaka guka bidza' yu'u ga tusédabi' bido' len bi'i kuidi' bi'i yĕdzi xidza'

Ní kixjë'ëtu' nhaka rhuntu' chhin len bi'i kuidi' nu' yu'u ga rhizedigákabi', zía'ala güi'tu' didza' naka guka gulhaj chhinnhí rhuntu'. Zía'ala tika' guka balha le gunëzi'gake' bëni' gulha, bido' len bi'kuidi' biti' gului'gakebi' lhataj güi'gákabi' didza' xidza' nuyu'u ga tusédabi', buludëdizí'gakebi' kati' gului'bi' xtidza'gákabi', les ka' le gulunbée xhozigákabi' len *xhozigulhagákabi'*, bizedigékibi' le za' gayubla. Katíka'zi guka, xtsei guya gusló rhaka balha le de ke tu yëdzi xidza', kanhaka xtidza' gake' len le nhunbe'gake'. Zí'alha bengake' bayuchhi bido' güi'gákabi' didza' xtilha, le nha'nha' biti'gulúe lhataj güi'gakabi' xtidza'gákabi', ka'gukatíka'zi, nha' bichhin kati' bëni' tulhúinhe' nhakagake' bëni' xidza', nha' guslogake' ta'bëe banhiga nhaka gaka ki gidzá' kanha' rhakanha', butsaga luza'agake' gulúe didza' nhaka gilunhe', ka'guka gulhaj ikia'gake' ke ulugele' le tungake' len le nhunbe'gake' tuwaj yëdzi ke gila'zedi' bido' zi' tayu'ubi' tusédabi'. Zurhá lenhí gulunhe' guyazilhachhi' yëdzi ga gulunhe' ka', de nha' gulhaj ikiajgake' tanhe' ke de ke tsajka' len bi'i kuidi', ka' guka gulhaj yu'u useda ke bi'i kuidi' ganhi rhuntu' chhin na'a. Lenhí naka lisaka' na'a dza ke ti unhiti le nëzi' tuwaj yëdzi xidza', na'a zeajtíka'zi rhidza' le de ke tuwaj yëdzi lenha' rhun bayuchhi ugelagake' bëni' tusédinhe' bido' len bi'i kuidi'.

The Indigenous Community Middle Schools

In this text we want to introduce the experience of Indigenous Community Middle Schools (SECOIN), mainly in relation to the work of indigenous languages within the schools, but also their main characteristics. The SECOIN are in 12 small indigenous communities in the state of Oaxaca in Mexico and began working in September 2004. To better understand the characteristics of their pedagogical model, it is helpful to provide a brief overview of the educational policies that governments have implemented for indigenous peoples.

State education for Indigenous peoples in Mexico, across its various levels and modalities, has always been designed from an external perspective, often reflecting an ethnocentric view that overlooks the cultural diversity of our country. In the last two decades of the 20th century, efforts to develop a pertinent education for Indigenous communities began to take shape. This was driven by social and educational demands from Indigenous groups, social organizations, and academic professionals in the 1980s. During this period, there was a focus on incorporating Indigenous peoples' demands into educational policies, which was also a response to international agreements for indigenous rights. In the 1990s, the government's approach to Indigenous education went from being called 'Bilingual–Bicultural' to having an intercultural perspective, calling it Intercultural Bilingual Education (IBE). For us, assimilationism, acculturation, and the approach of a homogeneous curriculum to education for indigenous peoples continued to prevail.

In this period in Oaxaca, a group of Indigenous teachers gathered in the Coalition of Indigenous Teachers and Promoters (CMPIO), proposed alternative approaches to education in the indigenous context, beyond the framework of IBE. These proposals were put into practice in Indigenous bilingual elementary schools and, after wide acceptance by the communities, the idea of creating a secondary school that would give continuity to these alternative educational practices arose. It is in this scenario that the Indigenous Community Middle School was created: an educational model that was structured considering the characteristics of the Indigenous peoples, such as collective work, a pedagogy based on the natural, social and cultural environment, an education relevant to indigenous peoples.

This middle school modality offers a second cycle basic education (9th–12th grade of basic education) with cultural, historical, and linguistic relevance to the communities, Native peoples and Afro-Mexicans within the state of Oaxaca for the communitarian and intercultural formation of students, under the principles of communality. Communality is a counter-hegemonic category to explain the way of life (social and political organization) and thought of Indigenous peoples, proposed by Indigenous professionals, mainly

Floriberto Díaz and Jaime Martinez Luna (Aquino, 2010; Martínez Luna, 2015; Rendon, 2003; Robles & Cardoso, 2007). These schools are currently located in only 12 communities in the state and do not exist in any other part of the Mexican territory. They are in five regions of the state of Oaxaca: Sierra Norte, Sierra Sur, Papaloapan, Cañada and Mixteca.

These schools began operating in September 2004 and have fostered their own culture reclamation; the strengthening of community subjects; a reduction in migration, school dropout rates, and youth marriages, and they have promoted gender equity. As proposed in their founding principles, new generations have been able to complete their basic education and allow young people to continue their secondary and higher education in different educational modalities. Up to the 2022–2023 school year, 17 generations of students have graduated from the first 5 secondary schools where this educational model originated. We have served a total of 1,298 young people: 679 women and 619 men. In the 2022–2023 school year, a total of 276 students were enrolled, of which 128 are female and 148 are male.

When the SECOIN began their pedagogical work, there was a rejection – mainly by parents – of the use of Native languages and of working with local knowledges within the schools. Some of them stated that the use and learning of Spanish was a higher priority, as well as school subject knowledge. As time has gone by, the way these schools work has become better known and appreciated, and now there is more acceptance, especially in the area of Native language, both in oral and written expression. For example, parents pay special attention when young people present their research in the Native language (we will use Native language and Indigenous language interchangeably to refer to the languages spoken by the different indigenous peoples) since it is the language of communication in the community.

As educators, we have each navigated a similar journey of valuing and understanding deeply the pedagogical and community-oriented aspects of the model we employ. Our role as teachers of Indigenous education is not just a professional endeavor: it is intertwined with our personal identities, as many of us belong to Indigenous communities and speak Indigenous languages. The process of becoming educators within this model has significantly transformed our practices, altering our approaches to language and re-shaping the ways we engage with education in both personal and communal contexts. This transformation has not only affected how we teach but also how we learn and reflect upon our methods and interactions. We have come to recognize that the SECOIN pedagogical model is instrumental in facilitating our own learning, providing valuable insights both through its practical application and through the reflective process it encourages

The Paths

During 20 years of work, the proposal and the pedagogical model were consolidated in the first 5 communities where the work began and, currently, in the 12 communities where these secondary schools are located. The situation at present is that full recognition of this modality has not been achieved at the state and federal level. This means that there are no economic resources to function; only to pay the salaries of the community educators (teachers).

Throughout these years, we have faced different obstacles to the model's strengthening, since the educational and government authorities at both state and federal level considered that it was necessary to appear in the Laws. In this sense, in 2014, we educators, students, and parents participated in the different education forums that were established in the State of Oaxaca in order to influence state education law.

In the context of the Reform of the Education Laws, in 2019 we returned to again seek ways that would allow us to open the path of recognition of community education. We succeeded in gainined legal recognition of community secondary education

Despite having gained this legal recognition, we do not have the full recognition that this requires. This not only has a direct impact on the labor rights of community educators: it also jeopardizes the right to culturally and linguistically relevant education for the children of the Indigenous peoples of the State of Oaxaca and the country.

The implications of this modality require full-time work and accompaniment, in relation to the approaches of the learning projects and the times of the social life of the communities. For 20 years, the communities have supported the work and have also helped to sustain the schools. In this sense, we have searched for the conjunctural moments, the spaces, and the different actors in order to influence and achieve full recognition of Indigenous Community Middle Schools from the Teachers' Movement.

This modality represents an antecedent and a concrete proposal within the Plan for the Transformation of Education in the State of Oaxaca (PTEO). The pedagogical practices, the work undertaken by learning projects that are constructed from community knowledges, the experience and realities of each community, the link that is generated with the community, community authorities, parents, knowledge bearers, the use of language for the construction and development of learning projects, to name but a few elements that have been carried out since 2004, are a reference for current proposals and discussions in the educational and community environment.

How SECOIN Works

Sixteen years ago I, Beatriz, had the opportunity to begin as a teacher at the Indigenous Community Middle Schools. Like all my colleagues

I received a training course that allowed me to know in a general way what the work and the pedagogical model consisted of. Together with my experience with the Ikoots people, which lasted 10 years, this made it easier for me to start working in the Indigenous Community Middle Schools.

I recognize at this moment that I was very fortunate to arrive at the middle school, to work, and accompany the third-year group. They told me that in the first few days they needed to make agreements to continue – or not – with the learning project they had been working on, and they asked me to listen and said that, when the time came, I could intervene. What emotion I felt when I heard these words! It was my first moment of openness and from my experience it has been an important consideration in our work as educators or community educators. Those at the school had the experience and already knew the methodology with which we work; I did not have it because I was new to the model. Therefore, I had to listen, learn from the group, and facilitate the process with the elements I had taken from the training course. That is how I began my experience: I learned the importance of listening as part of the life of the communities and, therefore, the importance of community education, and of a consideration for the accompaniment of the educational processes.

The Indigenous Community Middle Schools seek that young people acquire not only academic but also community and intercultural knowledge. The schools aspire to form subjects who are aware of their reality, people who value the knowledge of their communities that were inherited from their ancestors, who value and strengthen their own language, as well as contribute to the development of their community. All this to flow from the educational work implemented by these school, through projects based on the concerns of the students themselves, of the parents, community authorities, and the community through their representatives in the school, who in the educational process of the students, and from which process, students conduct documentary research as well as community research through talks, interviews and activities with the bearers of community knowledges such as grandparents, farmers, artisans, healers. In this way, the school supports the transmission and strengthening of the language and local knowledges, an educational practice different from the state education approach by the Native peoples.

These schools construct spaces where the interest of the students, the concerns of the parents, of the community authorities, and of the community itself are listened to. They are also a space where we talk and recover the concerns of the situated and specific realities in order to organize them and carry out a process of inquiry within a learning project. And for this we resort to community, documentary, electronic and nature research.

The research carried out by the students allows them to deepen their knowledge of community life through learning projects that are approached from the interest of all those involved, projects which interrelate the cultural, language, local knowledge, cosmology, community values, and agricultural activities of the place. To achieve this aim, parents, community representatives and authorities participate, so that this educational process begins with a collective work, which allows the exchange of ideas among the participants and concludes with the achievement an apprenticeship project to be carried out by the students.

Once the project has been designed, the research outline is structured and then a plan is made together with the students. It is explained to the students – and they are asked about – what must be recorded in the planning to make possible the research on what is going to be investigated, the sources to be investigated. From there, what follows is the execution of the plan, whereby they begin the process of bibliographic, electronic and community research. Subsequently, the same participants meet again to learn about the students' progress and to make the necessary observations. At the end of the research projects, the parents, the representatives, and the authorities participate again to close the research project through the presentation of all the work done within the framework of the learning project.

The curricular organization by learning projects[1] enables the school to strengthen the use of the Indigenous language and community knowledge and practices, as well as access to other non-local knowledge such as scientific knowledge through bibliographic research and electronic media.

To carry out these educational practices, it has been necessary to train the teachers who work in them from the pedagogical and cultural approach of these schools. In so doing, this has allowed the first steps to be taken in this alternative and pertinent educational approach, for the original communities of Oaxaca where they operate. This training has been based on a revision of the pedagogical model of the Secoin, as well as the political-pedagogical foundations and the theoretical basis of communality.. And, in addition, reflection upon the personal experiences that each educator has undergone while acting as a guide for the generations of students who have studied in the secondary schools. In these 20 years, the training organized in semester workshops has gone through different stages. At the beginning they were more theoretical–methodological, so that we could understand and transform our practice. In recent years, and without economic resources, we have had to build other training strategies. We think that this adds to the situation we live in – that of a 'denied right' to our own education based on our own languages and community contexts, and which violates access to relevant training.

Experiences in the Use of the Indigenous Language at School

I, Cornelio, joined SECOIN in 2005, one year after the piloting of this educational model began. I joined to be able to guide the students using the pedagogical approach of these schools. I had to attend training courses given by some of the advisors who had created the pedagogical model. In these courses we were told that these schools allow the free circulation of the language for the interaction of the students, as well as the interaction between them and the carriers of knowledge. I observed, through the comments of other teachers who attended the intensive training courses during vacation periods and school breaks, that in most of the communities where these schools operate, the Native languages were preserved, so it was appropriate to allow students to express themselves in their language – contrary to my own school experience, where I was punished for speaking my language in the school space.

According to what I have learned, for SECOIN, language is of utmost importance for the transmission of knowledge, since it is through language that ancestral knowledge has been preserved and continues to be transmitted in the family and at school (Figure 6.1). The language contains the community's cosmology, the community's stories, and the values of the original communities.

In the Secoin I reviewed with the students the writing of the language using an alphabet created by Indigenous education teachers who were used to working in the Zapotec language of the northern highlands region of Oaxaca (Sierra Norte). The writing of the indigenous language is not very common in the communities – its most recurrent use is when writing agrarian documents to refer to the places that have the names in their own language, to make announcements, or in the names of streets.

Figure 6.1 Ga tabeje' panelha, chhinní tunke' lu yëdzi'/*Panela* production, one of the activities carried out in the community
Source: Cornelio Hernández.

However, for the Indigenous Community Middle Schools it is essential that students learn to write the indigenous language with the alphabets they have at hand (not all of them are standardized), that they do not write only in Spanish. The purpose of this is to break the hegemony of Spanish in school and to expand the written uses of Indigenous languages in the communities. These exercises also make it possible to recover words that the new generations no longer use. In addition, they also make it possible to shape materials as a type of community memory resource (testimony) and linguistic revitalization, and to encourage other types of practices with the Native language for the speakers themselves.

In the different learning projects in which I have advised students, both oral and written expression is always present: in the research, in the organization of the work, and in the writing of the final project papers. For example, in the community of San Pedro Yaneri, a community located in the northern highlands of Oaxaca, in the 'Cultivo de Maiz' project, once the students had learned to write in their language through the alphabet, they elaborated texts about the activities that are carried out in the community in relation to corn. The students wrote in Zapotec Xidza', as in the following example:

> Lu yëdziní tunke' chhin kanaka waza xhua', za, yëtaj, yaga yela' lenka' waza yagkafé Gixi' len yaga chhaka yëdziní ya'bidu', yaga giaj xhuxu'ba', yaga ya'wëlha, yaiba, yaga xuga, yaga la'wi, yamangu', ya'yërhi, len bipalha tua'. Lenka' ba'gixi' dzë'ba' nu gi'a ki yëdzi' bichhinha', bugupi', bëza', kuchi gixi', bixhidzu', chijedza', bichhi'a, bërhaj bëku', guxhibi, bëkiaj, biginido', bechhi yëtsi' lenka' ba'zian.

> [In this community, they are primarily dedicated to the planting of main crops are corn, beans, sugar cane, bananas and coffee. Among the community's flora trees such as the liquidambar, laurel, eaglewood, oaks, avocado trees, sapote trees, mango trees, pines, and others stand out. Regarding the community's fauna deer, armadillo, fox, wild boar, badger, opossum, partridge, chachalaca, roadrunner, crow, birds, porcupine, among others, stand out.]

> Tu tu tui'ke' didza' bëni' gulha, tanake' ki xuzi xto'rhu' zake' tu lu yu nazi'lei San Pedro La'dú, bichhinke' ga nazi'lei len didza' xidza' Lachi' zila', na' buga'nke' tu chi'i, ki ben bayechhi' tu ilawe' lenka rhun bali' ziaga na' buza'ke' buchhinke' ganazi'lei Gi'a ya'bago'; tuchi'zi guli'kua'ke' na' ki na' takaba'ba bela lenka' ben bayechi' ki nisa ka' guka ke butsa'ke' ga buchhinke' ga naka tu yu chhi'a.

> [According to the legends told by the grandparents, they say that our ancestors came from a place called San Pedro La'dú, they arrived to a place that they gave the Zapotec name of Lachi'zila', there they stayed for a short time, and due to food shortage and extreme cold, later they moved to Gi'a ya'bago', they also stayed for a very short time because

there were many snakes and there was no water nearby, so they continued in search of a suitable place.]

Buchhinke' tu lu yú ga nunbe'ke' natika nazi'lei Lachi' idoo', lu yuní gudëdikaba' bichhinha' tagichiba' buzuga' na' gunake' ki tibinaka ikua'ke' na', na' guli'za'ke' sjake' tsala'a ki rha'yëlha ga nazi'lei Lachi' xnuaxhi, na' dzë'ke' biyënkane' gurhëchhiba' tuba' jedrhuzi lenka' biyënkane' rdin gidi lenka' rbëchhi ya'gí, lake' guli'nake' ki na' kixajrhu' yëdzi kierhu'. Naya' tuní guka na' buli'za'ke', na' gudixajke' yëdzi'.

[They arrived to another place known as Lachi' idoo', in this place deer passed by and always left dung with worms, which they considered as a sign that this was not the place where they should stay, from there they went to Lachi' Xnuaxhi, while in this place they heard the crowing of a rooster, then they perceived the sound of a drum and a flute coming from the other side of where they were so they took it as a sign to go to populate that place, all this happened and they went to that place to inhabit the current community.]

Tu' tanake' bëni' gulha ki gati' bichhinke' lu yu na', budzëlake' tu yaga ya'yërhi rginaj nërhi, tua'na' be'ke'lei Yaneri, didza'ní za' tu nui'le' lei nërhi. Na' gului'ke' lei San Pedro, didza'ní gudela'ke' ki le' tu budo' le' San Pedro.

[The grandparents say that when they arrived to this place, they found an ocotal tree that threw turpentine and that is why they named the community 'Yaneri', which in Zapotec means 'yaga nërhi', that is, 'turpentine tree'. As for the patron saint of the community, they took the name of one of the twelve apostles of Jesus who was called Pedro, so the full name of the community is San Pedro Yaneri, this is the story that our grandparents left us.]

Lately, with the presence of communication technologies, I have witnessed that graduates have resorted to writing in the Native language, which they learned in middle school. They turn to writing in the Native language to communicate in media such as social networks. For example, among the Zapotec-speaking graduates of Sierra Norte, I have observed the systematic use of the Zapotec alphabet in writing (experience in San Pedro Yaneri, as well as in the community of Santa María Zoogochí, both belonging to the district of Ixtlán de Juárez, Oaxaca). In spite of this, there is still work to be done so that the writing of the language transcends the different spheres of community life, as happens with the Spanish language – that is to say, that there are printed materials in the language itself, in the community and in the families, and that the language is used in the communications that the community authorities use to contact the people, since I have observed that the second language is used more for these purposes.

One of the functions that I have performed as an educator is to guide the explanations that the students make in the Native language for the presentation of their research in their own language, the approach to take when preparing the interview scripts in their own language, as well as the execution of the interviews with the bearers of knowledge. That is why I consider it very important that the community educator knows – and above all speaks – the language or linguistic variant of the students, since this guarantees a greater use of the Indigenous language in the school, in the explanation of the research, and in the understanding of both what the knowledge bearers say and what the students explain. Also, the use of the spellings that have been established for the linguistic variants of the communities is guaranteed. However, this does not always happen, so our role as educators should be not to hinder the use of the language by the students, but to promote its written and oral use, and to learn the language of the community where we go.

Another aspect that I consider very important in the different stages of project work is the fluent communication, between the different actors, in the Native language, when a doubt arises on the part of a participant. Those involved often intervene to clarify and to argue or expand on some issue that arises as part of the processes that give rise to these stages, where language takes on a preponderant importance since it is the language of communication among the participants or the majority of the participants. This makes a lot of sense for everyone, both for the parents and for the students themselves, as these spaces (the public presentations) are another space for learning, for feedback on the research, as well as for deepening the research through the reflections, experiences, or anecdotes that arise in these spaces.

Another experience I had in the community realm of San Pedro Yaneri community, and which has to do with communicative skills in the Native language that the schools promote in the students, is to have observed a graduate of this school conducting a religious act in the Native language. I could witness the skills developed by this young woman to preside over an act in the Native language, based on a book written in the second language.

With these experiences I have been able to see that the graduates have made use of the different tools that the school has given them, and especially in the work that is done in the school's own language, by allowing and encouraging its use in the different processes involved in project work.

In all these practices that we community educators carry out through the Indigenous Community Middle Schools, we currently face new scenarios, which have to do with the introduction of technologies and media. This was especially so with the COVID-19 pandemic, which was experienced worldwide, and where the media played an important role in following up on education, where many children and especially young people began to have access to new technologies and media, as well as the introduction of cell phones in many communities after the pandemic. This has had repercussions, both in the excessive interest shown by young people and children towards these media, and in the lack of guidance from parents to their children regarding the use of these media. I have perceived through the dialogue of some people in the community that they have these concerns. Faced with these new scenarios, new challenges are arising for the Indigenous Community Middle Schools to guide and reorient young people, and also to work with parents and the community in general, for the proper use of media and technologies, so that these are means that contribute to the purposes of these schools and not means that denigrate the community culture. To meet these challenges, as educators we need to know more about these technologies, to focus on how they can benefit our educational practices, and how they can benefit the cultures of the Indigenous communities appropriating them.

SECOIN Achievements

Despite the current challenges and the lack of full recognition by the state and the national education authorities, we find that the original community pedagogical proposal of the Indigenous Community Middle Schools remains relevant. This is because the pedagogical model goes beyond Intercultural Bilingual Education, in which the indigenous culture is conceived as an object of learning and not as a way of learning. The IBE as a national educational policy addressed to the Indigenous peoples is organized on a curricular basis to Castilianize, and not to recognize the differences within the diversity that we signify.

In addition, from the axes of communality, local knowledge systems and ways of life are strengthened. For example, the communities, through the knowledge bearers, parents, and community authorities, have contributed with community experience, knowledges and know-how for the projects developed in the school, as well as in strengthening the continuity of the development of people with the values and knowledge of the Community. In this sense, the formation of the collective subject is recovered, as opposed to a formation that emphasizes education by competencies and individualism.

The bonds with the community and local authorities have been strengthened through the communication established with the Parents' Representative Council, who represent the school's governing body. In addition, the link is strengthened through public presentations of the results of the learning projects. Community residents not only listen, but also value and provide feedback on what the students have found in the process. In 20 years, parents and communities are aware of this exercise and when it is not carried out, it is the same authorities or parents who demand the importance of knowing the progress, the process and the results of the students.

The SECOIN model has enabled an education rooted in local knowledge systems, languages and practices, while also fostering learning processes that reflect the contexts and realities of each community. This right has been compromised by the lack of full recognition from state authorities. Nonetheless, educators, students, and communities continue to build an education that is relevant to their contexts and communal life within the school. As a result, Indigenous Community Middle Schools have become a space where communality is experienced and maintained.

Note

(1) The pedagogical model used by SECOIN does not align with the secondary school curriculum established by the Ministry of Public Education (Secretaría de Educación Pública, SEP). Despite being an independent educational model, SECOIN has developed methods to ensure that students receive a school certificate upon completion of their studies.

References

Aquino, A. (2010) La generación de la emergencia indígena y el comunalismo oaxaqueño. *Cuadernos del Sur* 15 (29), 7–21.
Martínez Luna, J. (2015) *Educación Comunal*. Casa de las Preguntas.
Rendón, J. (2003) *La comunalidad: modo de vida en los pueblos indios*. Conaculta.
Robles, S. and Cardoso, R. (eds) (2007) *Floriberto Díaz. Escrito*. UNAM.

7 Toward a Methodology of Urban Indigenous Youth Language Learning

Ernesto Colín

Omochihchi inin tekitl kwe tiknekih oksepa tiktlahtolkwepaskeh wan tikiskaliskeh inin tlakwikalmeh ika tlenon yopanok wan tlenon pawits, wan itewan ika intlanemilis inin nawatlatokeh, akin tlasalotikateh wan akin tlakwikamatinemih wan nawatlamatinimeh.

Ionka tekitl inon tlahtowah ika ini tlakwikalmeh wan inka iwehka xochitlakwikalmeh, maski, nochi inin tekitl amo yaweh asih inka akin oknoma tlahtowah, kwe san kinchihchiwiliah inon koyokaltlamachtilmeh maski amo tomasewalchantiliswan.

Inin tekitk inin axkan omochi otiknekeh oksepa tikintekipanoliskeh inin tlakwikalmeh maski ika inin kenin axkan titlahtowah nikan Kwentepek, Morelos; kiyon noihke, otekitkeh kenin tlawitekiskeh wan kenin mokwikatiskeh. Inin tekitl welihtika mochiwas kwe kimach ihtoti wits asi intech akinomeh moneki kixmatiskeh, kimach ihtoti kitlapowah inin ohtli itech innantlahtol.

The Soil and the Pavement

Tovangaar – the unceded ancestral territory of the Tongva people and neighboring nations, now called metropolitan Los Angeles – is home to the largest population of urban Indigenous people in the United States. Indigenous lifeways and cultural productions are part of the complex fabric of the region, woven into the landscape and fauna, art and festivals, cuisine and languages, churches and schools. More than 50 Indigenous languages from around the globe are spoken by families in the public schools of the second largest school district in the United States: the Los Angeles Unified School District (LAUSD). For some students and families, Spanish and English are second and third languages, requiring larger bridges connecting schools to homes. For decades, local schools have been widely indifferent or hostile to the linguistic and cultural needs of the Indigenous families they serve.

Educational outcomes of Indigenous students in the area are dismal. Overt bias, racism, and discrimination against Indigenous people, sometimes imported into the city from global theatres, occasionally rise to city-wide consciousness as with recent incidents embroiling the city council, or the federal complaint brought by the Office of Civil Rights against the school district for not funding and for mismanaging the federally protected rights of Indigenous students. Overall, this decay is deeply ingrained in cultural and civic institutions of the megalopolis. These are the habits of all colonial places, made exponentially complex in a place with the greatest urban Indigenous diversity in the country, a diversity comprised of Indigenous communities from across the hemisphere and beyond.

Pressure rises from the soil. Some schools, educators, and parents, supported by the inalienable rights outlined in the United Nations Declaration on the Rights of Indigenous Peoples, carve out spaces and build new relations, curricula, and projects for the revitalization of Indigenous language and culture. One vehicle for educational innovation is the charter school movement. Charter schools are publicly funded but independently operated schools that offer alternative educational approaches. They have been in place in California (and other states) for more than 25 years and have flexibility in curriculum and management, aiming to improve student achievement through innovation and choice within the public education system. Several Indigenous communities have taken advantage of these state laws which allow approved public schools autonomy over hiring, curriculum, and structure in an effort to reterritorialize (see Anthony-Stevens & Stevens, 2020) and revitalize language and identity (see for example, Anthony-Stevens, 2013; Fennimore-Smith, 2009; Goodyear-Ka'opua, 2013; Reeves, 2006, 2009). Over time, charter school law and movements have become intensely political, but have served to incubate successful innovations and compel traditional districts to change.

In this soil, out of this pavement, a unique school emerges: Anahuacalmecac International University Preparatory of North America (AIUPNA, also known as Anawakalmekak). Anawakalmekak is a Nahuatl compound made from the word for the North American continent and a house of learning. Like many of the contexts featured in this book, Anawakalmekak is a trilingual Indigenous-based charter school in Los Angeles established to foster Indigenous language and cultural reclamation. During its 20 year existence, the school refines approaches to make languages and other content areas meaningful to school-age youth.

This chapter documents an interdisciplinary curriculum project at Anawakalmekak. The project involves a series of student-led courses involving (re)interpretations of 16th-century Nahuatl poetry from the Florentine Codex and Cantares Mexicanos along with accompanying musical arrangements. I will refer to the series of courses as the Cantares Project in this chapter. Using an artist-in-residence model, middle- and high-school students both in the US and in a sister community in Mexico work with experts in 15th- and 16th- century codices to understand the original texts, with Nahuatl language instructors to interpret centuries-old lyrics into modern Nahuatl, with scholars of Indigenous music to co-compose music to accompany the pieces, and with a rap artist to learn music and video production en route to recorded performances. The collective of educators leading the project iterate a methodology for language autonomy, vibrance, and relevance. Among other things, the project asks: How do Indigenous youth revitalize ancestral languages in urban schools? and What methodologies can educators employ to foster Indigenous languages and language curriculum relevance to students and communities today?

Established in 2002 by community leaders with the permission of local Gabrielino Shoshone tribal leaders, Anawakalmekak is a school serving close to 300 students from pre-school to 12th grade. It is currently a charter school authorized under the Los Angeles Unified School District, after being authorized by the California State Board of Education. On top of a full curriculum that is accountable to the Common Core State Standards and the University of California A-G high school graduation requirements, Anawakalmekak is a model International Baccalaureate (IB) World School, with an *indigenized* curriculum that follows the requirements of the IB Primary Years Program (PYP) (K-5) and Middle Years Program (MYP) (6–10). For the 11th and 12th grades, the school delivers a curriculum of study called the IndigeNations program, which is the culmination of the culturally-rooted and community-based educational mission of the school. In all grades, there exists a focus on regenerative Indigenous language (Nahuatl in addition to English and Spanish) and Indigenous math, art, science, leadership and social and ethnic studies (see Figure 7.1). Nahuatl was chosen as an anchor language of the school due to a large population of Nahuatl-speaking individuals in Los Angeles, linkages to sister communities in Mexico, local and long-standing connections to Aztec dance communities, and because of the set of curricular materials available. Additionally, daily opening protocol ceremonies, weekly Aztec dance, and a cycle of ceremonies are embedded in the school calendar. The guiding metaphor of the school has always been the xinachtli, or seed, which is the vision for each of the students, who will grow to be skilled culture bearers, conscious descendants, and leaders for the good of the earth, the community, and future generations.

Through collaboration with students, educators and parents, Anawakalmekak established a compelling set of school-wide outcomes that guide the curriculum of all grades and extracurricular offerings. Students will graduate from Anawakalmekak as:

Figure 7.1 Classroom altar at Anawakalmekak school

- *Earth Guardians*: Empowered community leaders
- *Wind Talkers*: Multilingual students of mother tongue and Indigenous languages, stories, and laws
- *Fire Keepers:* Bearers of Indigenous wisdom
- *Water Protectors:* Culturally, socially and civically-engaged students
- *Star Walkers:* Students who are globally-engaged Indigenous learner–teachers

Through their program, students will be college and career ready, able to thrive in global contexts via a rigorous curriculum. They will have access to a curriculum rooted in the cultural, intellectual, and linguistic bodies of knowledge of Indigenous peoples. The school also fosters leadership, advocacy, civic and environmental engagement.

The global COVID-19 pandemic and the shutdown of all public schools (from March, 2020 to July, 2021) provided Anawakalmekak with an opportunity to pivot into temporary online instruction and thereby develop a paradigm that would guide the virtual school's operation and provide an approach that would be true to the school's vision, adaptive to family needs, and responsive to the lived reality of the health crisis acutely impacting the community and the need for a distance learning option. A consultative process between educators and parents produced educational priorities represented by the ideas of Life, Love, Learning and Liberation. The guiding documents developed by the school can be distilled into the ideas of a right to life and health, a context of socio-emotional support and healing, transformational, culturally-rooted and community-based distance learning, and a praxis of liberation through education.

Emerging from the period of this global pandemic, the school continued with in-person instruction and rejoined long-term curricular and pedagogical projects involving Mexican sister communities in Cuentepec, Morelos, and Acatlan, Guerrero (Mexico). Anawakalmekak has a long history of international collaboration and exchange.

The Sowing, the Gathering

Is The aforementioned elements provide the context for a project aimed at bridging ancestral ways of knowing and contemporary youth interests. This chapter focuses on the Cantares Project, one among many curriculum initiatives at the school. The school offered students in Los Angeles and Cuentepec courses layered with art history, linguistics, musicology, music production, video production, and more. The series of Nahuatl poetry/music courses utilizes a project-based learning approach and the artist-in-residence model at the school. In this chapter, I relay details of the initial phase of the ongoing work.

The Cantares Mexicanos Project

The Cantares Mexicanos is a 16th-century Indigenous Mexican codex and collection of 91 songs/poems written in classical Nahuatl. Early colonial settler–scholars were unable to clearly describe the poems as they did not possess enough context and familiarity with Indigenous cosmology and poetics to accurately understand the writings. Twentieth- and 21st-century scholars have also been challenged to translate, analyze, and characterize the songs in the codex, with only partial and uneven results. Bierhorst (1985), in his English translation of the Cantares Mexicanos, mis-characterized the cantares as verses meant to summon ancestors to join in a battle against colonizing forces, or nostalgic songs evoking a lost paradise. Bierhorst's hypotheses in the volume are based on a colonial lens and also conflict with evidence that many of the cantares had foundations in pre-invasion literary and narrative texts. Students in the Cantares Project also studied the translation of the Cantares Mexicanos undertaken by Miguel León Portilla. Additionally, and beyond translation, the students in the Cantares Project take up the question of the musical notation and theory that the aforementioned scholars have never taken up.

The Florentine Codex is another 16th-century text which contains accounts of Nahua cultural productions, encompassing diverse subjects such as religion, rituals, cosmology, natural history, societal organization and daily life. It combines Nahuatl texts with Spanish explanations with many accompanying illustrations, providing a cultural record that has become foundational in Mesoamerican studies after the destruction of thousands of native books during European invasion. Concerns about the commentary found in the Florentine Codex include cultural bias due to the European sponsorship of compilation, potential inaccuracies in translations, propaganda required by Christian evangelization, and selective presentation of Nahua culture, which might not fully represent pan-Indigenous perspectives or the complexity of the society. Nevertheless, important Nahuatl texts of the 16th century are captured in the volumes of the Florentine Codex.

Several scholars have provided an array of commentary and interpretation of the songs/poems found in the Cantares Mexicanos and the Florentine Codex. Most concur that the lyrics are both elegant and profound. As is customary with Nahua civic and ceremonial practice, music and dance accompany poetry and songs. The music that accompanied the poems/songs of the Cantares Mexicanos and the Florentine Codex has been disconnected from the texts, some of it lost to time.

In-depth study and interpretation of several poetry/songs is at the heart of the Cantares Project. This arises from a school priority for a curriculum led by native Nahuatl speakers and the study of classic texts and modern Nahuatl literature and music. Anawakalmekak educators in ancestral and migrant communities on both sides of the border have collaborated to study, translate, interpret, and arrange music en route to multimedia production and community performances.

The primary educators involved in this project and their (instructional) role is as follows:

- *Victorino Torres Nava* is the coordinator of Nahuatl language instruction at Anawakalmekak. He is a bi-national poet, author, linguist, and teacher–educator from and in Cuentepec, Morelos, Mexico, where his is a member of the national councils for Indigenous language instruction and the standardization of written Nahuatl. His role in the project is supporting students in the study of the original Nahuatl poetry, and their interpretation into Spanish and then English.
- *Kevin Terraciano* is Professor of History at UCLA, specializing in ancient Indigenous languages, writings, and cultures of central Mexico. He has published on, and translated, numerous ancient texts and has led research in ancient codices. He has worked with students on understanding the texts among other ancient codices and taught the history and context from which they emerge.
- *María Marisol Peñaloza* is a professional violinist, public school Mariachi educator, student of Nahuatl, and music instructor. She holds a Master's degree in music performance and leads music instruction for the students at Anawakalmekak.

- *Xiuhtezcatl Martínez* is a climate activist, actor, and Indigenous rapper and recording artist who taught about careers and technical aspects of the recording arts industry. He mentors students in the software and tools used in music production and in music video production as they make formal recordings of their performances.
- *Marcos Aguilar* is the co-founder and Executive Director of Anawakalmekak. He has more than 25 years public-school teaching experience and he oversees, with the Director of Education (Minnie Ferguson), the entire operation of the charter school, including partnerships with external organizations and communities. He has taught pieces, coordinated the instruction, composed music, and managed the project and subsequent dissemination campaigns.

Documenting the process of the study and media production of the Cantares Project assists educators in the refinement and characterization of a pedagogical methodology for culturally revitalizing language instruction. My research methodology was inspired by humanizing youth (Paris & Winn, 2013) and Indigenous research methodologies (Wilson, 2008), contemplating research as ceremony as well as a collective and mutually beneficial endeavor. Paris and Winn (2010) value the voices, experiences, and cultures of marginalized young individuals. They emphasize engaging in research that goes beyond academic analysis, fostering connections, empathy, and respect, and acknowledging the humanity and agency of the youth being studied. Wilson (2008) views research as a transformative and respectful process that parallels Indigenous ceremonial practices. Research as ceremony, to borrow Wilson's words, emphasizes building relationships, creating meaningful connections, and acknowledging the spiritual dimensions of research, as well as fostering understanding, empathy, and cultural appreciation.

Included in the study design were ethnographic data collection approaches such as classroom observation (witnessing), pedagogical interviews with the educators, and gathering the perspectives of participants (storytelling). The phase of the continuing Cantares Project outlined in this chapter took place in Summer 2023.

Calling in the Ancestors: Ideas that Help Us Understand the Dynamics

Organically and inductively, several conceptual frames emerged to help us understand and discuss the Cantares language revitalization project. Briefly, I refer to them here before describing project outcomes. Overall, the tradition of project-based learning characterizes the interdisciplinarity of the curriculum and products, which enhances an indigenized college- and career-ready comprehensive education.

As I contemplate the process and outcomes at Anawakalmekak, I find my own work on the concept of palimpsest to be relevant (Colín, 2014). I employ the metaphor of a manuscript, intentionally but incompletely erased, and re-authored in the present to characterize what these students and educators have done with the codices and music. Next, this project exemplifies McCarty and Lee's (2014) ideas around culturally sustaining and revitalizing pedagogy. These authors promote education that respects and nurtures diverse cultures, languages, and identities. They challenge educators in Indigenous contexts to sustain and empower via the integration of ancestral knowledge, languages, and traditions into the curriculum, fostering equity, authenticity and meaningful learning experiences. Vizenor's (1999) notion of survivance, which names the resilience, creativity, and adaptability of Indigenous peoples in the face of colonization and emphasizes their ability to not only survive but also thrive by asserting their cultural identity, stories, and traditions despite historical trauma and ongoing challenges, might serve to characterize the proposals and outcomes of this school project. The Cantares Project sees cultural survival, thriving, and persistence as central to Indigenous cultural productions, poetry, music, literature, etc. The linguistic dynamics of the project include students embodying translanguaging practices (García & Li, 2014; Vogel & García, 2017). In the classes, bi- and tri-lingual learners (poly if we include music as a language) are utilizing their full set of linguistic skills in multiple languages simultaneously, transcending narrow understanding of language production. Lastly, Hobot's (2017) work is helpful here when contemplating the characteristics of effective urban Indigenous schooling. He maintains that Indigenous resurgence is supported by learning that takes place in community, across generations, in redefined spaces, via Indigenous languages and cultural practices.

Ceremonies

The first Cantares project took place over six weeks at Anawakalmekak in the early summer of 2023. Middle-school students and Indigenous high-school students from across the county who enrolled in summer school at Anawakalmekak participated. Ms Peñalosa and Mr Aguilar selected a 16th-century poem (Chicomecoatl Icuic) re-published recently with new interpretations and context in Seler's (2016) *Los cantos religiosos de los antiguos mexicanos*. The poem is part of a set Sahagún recorded from Indigenous interlocutors between 1558 and 1561.

The course was interdisciplinary in the way it brought together history, language learning, literary criticism, music composition, agriculture, performance and music production software. Students and faculty members focused in the beginning weeks on the historical context and meaning behind the poem, which is a plea for the spirit of sacred corn to return to the people. Next, with the school's language instructors the students worked to transcribe the poem into modern Nahuatl (as spoken in Cuentepec, Morelos, Mexico). Students also discussed the meaning of the poem, which laments the loss of balance in the world and loss of the maternal spirit of the corn, connecting this to the colonial experiences of the original authors. Marcos Aguilar composed a drum beat to accompany the poem and act as a musical spine. María Peñaloza, as a music teacher, expressed that her goal was for students to develop melodies and compose music that incorporated other Indigenous instruments (e.g. slit drum, rattles, large drum). She spent several weeks delivering a curriculum focused on music theory and scales, and the concept of text painting (a.k.a. word painting), where musical elements like the melody mirror or illustrate the emotions, actions, or meanings of the lyrics. The text-painting lessons guided students to align sound with the text's content, creating vivid and evocative music. The weaving in and arranging of new instruments was student led and organic, undergoing several rounds of experimentation.

Students also decided to create a xilonen, or young corn, club during the Cantares Project. They embarked on a corn-planting project at a local park. They learned traditional planting and agricultural approaches as well as modern irrigation techniques with the Anawakalmekak's teachers.

As the summer session went on, faculty members and students decided their evolving musical interpretation of the poem was too dreary, with mourning vocals accompanied by minor chords. Collectively, students decided to change the tempo of the music and switch to major chords. Next, students learned music recording/editing software and used it to compose melodies and record their rehearsals.

At the end of the term, the students delivered performances to the school and to parents. Moving forward, students planned polished recordings and a music video. They also planned on selecting more poems for inclusion in the methodology developed by the school. María Peñaloza was satisfied with the evolution of student buy-in, which steadily increased during the summer session. She said, 'We [educators] can do more but it is important that this is student led. These students are young, many migrants, open, creative. With us as mentors, it [the methodology] will revitalize the language and culture' (personal communication, August 11, 2023).

Moving this process into the Fall of 2023, students selected both a second 16th-century poem to interpret as well as a poem that was written this year especially for Anawakalmekak by a senior school educator, spiritual leader, and Tecuane (jaguar) dancer, Vicente Seis, from the Acatlan, Guerrero in Mexico. The poem, commissioned by the school via Marcos Aguilar, honors the Tongva people (original caretakers of what is now the greater Los Angeles area) and centers on a famous and beloved mountain lion (tukuurot in Tongva, known as P-22) that recently died in what is now called Griffith Park. Nahuatl teachers Farías and Torres Nava assisted with translations, and Marcos Aguilar composed music for the poem. Students and educators will continue to work with Xiuhtezcatl Martínez on recording and production.

Meanwhile, in August 2023, the Cantares Project expanded to Mexico at the Xinachcalco center located in Cuentepec, Morelos. Educators designed an intensive one-week workshop entitled 'Cuentepec Xochitlakwikalli' and offered it to all local youth in the community, particularly those in the early secondary grades. Fifteen students joined Victorino Torres Nava with support from a local teacher, Arnulfo Calderón, and a pre-Columbian music scholar/musician, Nicolás García Lieberman, from Mexico City.

This team worked with two songs from the Cantares Mexicanos book: 'Itotokwik Totokiwatsin Tlakopan tlahtowani' (a song from a local council leader in ancient Tlacopan) and a second song called 'Tsokotekwikatl,' or song of the turtle dove. The team applied the same curricular methodology to the songs, where students discussed context, studied 'classical' Nahuatl, and revised the songs into modern Nahuatl and Spanish. Additionally, the group studied and developed the music, successfully following and re-creating the music of the era, which was recorded phonetically in the text (the Cantares Mexicanos songs have musical notations dating back to the 16th century). The students in Cuentepec also worked toward recording and community performance.

Part of the curriculum of the workshop included connection and comparison between the songs relating to birds in the Cantares Mexicanos and the bird songs that have been recovered and sung in ceremonies among transnational Indigenous communities, especially those from the Uto-Aztecan linguistic branch, including the bird songs of the Cahuilla people of Southern California. The workshop achieved Victorino Torres Nava's stated objectives of 'exposing students to ancient texts with which they were unfamiliar and, more importantly, placing them closer to their maternal language, to ancient epistemologies, and ancestral music' (personal communication, August 17, 2023).

Below is an example of the written work produced by the workshop.

Text in the original Nahuatl:

Ytotocuic Totoquihuatzin Tlacopan Tlatoani

Nictzotzona yan tohuehueuh
xahuiaca annicuihua
ma ihto huaya aya totototo
xochitl y huelic o ma ihtoa ichan yn Totoquihuatzi
tlalticpac ma ahuilihua ohua yye ayaoo
man tahuiacan ayio yiya

Chalchiuhtli noyollo
teocuitlatl noxochiuh yca ninapana ya
in nepapan xochitl i noxochiuh a niquitquitehuaz
quenmanian yyee
tlen cuicatl yyohuiya
Can oc moyolic a xoncuica ya toto
nican nicmana ya poyomaxochitla
amoxtlacuilohua

Song adapted by teachers and students to the modern variant of Nahuatl of central Mexico [Cuentepec]:

Itotokwik Totokiwatsin Tlakopan Tlatowani

Niktsotsona iwan towewe
Ahwiyakeh nikinkwiya
Ma mihtokan
Xochitl iweliyo ma mihtokan
ichan nin Totokiwatsin
tlaltikpak ma mahwili
owatl ma ye ayo o
Ma tahwiakan ayo o

Chalchiohtli noyolo
Teokwitlanoxochiyo
ika ninachiwa
nin nepa pan xochitl nin noxochiyo ya nikitstewas
Kemanian ye

San ika moyoli xmokwika ya
Nikan nikmana ya poyomaxochitla
Amoxtlacuilohua

Spanish-language interpretation:

El canto de Totokiwatsin del gobernante de Tlakopan

Toco sobre nuestro wewetl (tambor)
Tomo sus fragancias agradables
Que se pronuncien
Fragancia de flores que se pronuncien en la casa de Totokiwatsin en la tierra
Que se rieguen las cañas para que estén jugosas
Que nos llenemos de fragancia

Mi corazón de jade
Me lleno de flores de oro
Aquellas flores, mis flores que veré antes de partir
Algún día así sea la fragancia de los cantos
Sólo con tu corazón canta
Aquí ofrendo para que haya flores
Que se siga plasmando en los códices

English-language interpretation [author's translation]:

The song of Totokiwatsin of the Tlatowani of Tlakopan

I play our drum
I take in their pleasant fragrances
May they burst
May the fragrance of flowers surge in the house of Totokiwatsin
On the Earth
May the canes be watered so they be full
May we be imbued with fragrance

My jade heart
Flowers of gold fill me
Those flowers, my flowers, which I will see before departing
May the fragrance of the songs be similar one day
Sing only with your heart
I make an offering so there may be flowers
May it be recorded in our books

Sending Us Home

Through contemplation of the observed instruction and conversations with those involved, several components of the Cantares Project merit laudatory mention for the way they extend schoolwide learning outcomes (namely, students who are empowered, community leaders, multilingual bearers of Indigenous wisdom, culturally, socially, and civically engaged students, and globally-engaged Indigenous learner–teachers).

First is the advancement of a methodology that was established a decade ago for project-based student-centered language learning, which evolves presently. It is one which engages students in linguistic activity that fosters the richness of a culture from which the language emerges. Furthermore, the instruction featured in this project builds bridges, from past to present, nation to nation, students to co-teachers, diaspora to homelands, and the self to ancestors. As Victorino Torres Nava put it: 'we want students to walk toward what belongs to them' (personal communication, August 17, 2023). In other words, the project provides access to epistemologies, futurities, and cosmologies only available through a relationship with their ancestral language.

Next, as Marcos Aguillar relayed, the vision for the project centers around a decolonized education that is additive, healing, intergenerational, relevant and sustaining (personal communication, August 11, 2023). These examples of the work done at Anawakalmekak and sister schools represent education that propels students forward in contemporary contexts of schooling and career advancement. This approach to curriculum and instruction doesn't invite students to sacrifice any part of themselves and the heritage of knowledge guarded by their communities. Rather, the opposite occurs: this education honors educators, elders, knowledge keepers and future generations who struggle to revitalize and sustain heritage language, reclaiming their own identities.

Lastly, this project serves a long struggle for ethnic studies in schools. As such, it adds to the dynamic projects found in this volume and the countless ones that form the repertoire of schools and programs working on revitalizing language and culture from Aotearoa to Tawantisuyu to Anahuac.

References

Anthony-Stevens, V.E. (2013) Indigenous students, families and educators negotiating school choice and educational opportunity: A critical ethnographic case study of enduring struggle and educational survivance in a southwest charter school. The University of Arizona.

Anthony-Stevens, V. and Stevens, P. (2020) 'A space for you to be who you are': An ethnographic portrait of reterritorializing Indigenous student identities. In B. Pini, R. Mayes and L. Rodriguez Castro (eds) *Rurality and Education* (pp. 8–21). Routledge.

Bierhorst J. (1985) *Cantares Mexicanos: Songs of the Aztecs*. Stanford University Press.

Colín E. (2014) *Indigenous Education through Dance and Ceremony: A Mexica Palimpsest*. Postcolonial Studies in Education Series. Palgrave Macmillan.

Fenimore-Smith, J.K. (2009) The power of place: Creating an Indigenous charter school. *Journal of American Indian Education* 48 (2), 1–17.

García, O. and Li, W. (2014) *Translanguaging: Language, Bilingualism, and Education*. Palgrave MacMillan.

Goodyear-Ka'opua, N. (2013) *The Seeds We Planted: Portraits of a Native Hawaiian Charter School*. University of Minnesota Press.

Hobot, J. (2017) *Resurgence: Restructuring Urban American Indian Education*. National Urban Indian Family Coalition.

McCarty, T.L. and Lee, T.S. (2014) Critical culturally sustaining/revitalizing pedagogy and indigenous education sovereignty. *Harvard Educational Review* 84 (1), 101–124.

Paris, D. and Winn, M.T. (2014) *Humanizing Research: Decolonizing Qualitative Inquiry with Youth and Communities*. Sage.

Reeves, A.G. (2006) To us they are butterflies: A case study of the educational experience at an urban Indigenous-serving charter school. Doctoral thesis, University of Arizona.

Reeves, A. (2009) With or without reservation: An Indigenous community accesses charter school reform. *Vitae Scholasticae: The Journal of Educational Biography* 26 (2), 29–51.

Seler E. (2016) *Los cantos religiosos de los antiguos mexicanos* (1st edn). Universidad Nacional Autónoma de México.

Vizenor G.R. (1999) *Manifest Manners: Narratives on Postindian Survivance*. Bison Books (University of Nebraska Press).

Vogel, S. and García, O. (2017) Translanguaging. In G. Noblit and L. Moll (eds) *Oxford Research Encyclopedia of Education*. https://doi.org/10.1093/acrefore/9780190264093.013.181.

Wilson S. (2008) *Research Is Ceremony: Indigenous Research Methods*. Fernwood Publishing.

Poem: Gidro' Lihdxan/Placenta

Author: Felipe Ruiz Jiménez
Language: Zapotec
From: Valles Centrales Region of Oaxaca, Mexico
English Translation: Kelly Strachan

Gidro' Lihdxan
Kawin laadx gichlyuh
Giäl rwin kagui'ta.
Blähz rxioob bee.
Llia't ro' sa nisgieh kayaal
Ria yah ba kadxu na dahñ.
Nlas k aba rool ria bi's, rwin laadx gol; nad rak laadx gol subee gol.
Ba dzusnitlohn laa gak tuhñ, dzusnitlohn xtiidxn
Tsää tsää kanitlohn tuhñ. Ria skuel, dio, gobier ni'k reyuuna ni kayak liaadz re.
Ro'k ta lähz xuuy nad za na gak zi'k, nad za gak ba mnit te tuhñ.
Tuhñ ni nak behn re, ni nakn behn diidx zah, gihd ro' lihdx ni gokn ptoo ni'k rsnaa na laadxdn nakn behn diidx zah, rgeedxa tuhñ, laa na ruun ni mbahñ, laa na ruun ni zädnaa xtiidxn.
Xtiidxn nak tuhñ, xtiidxn nak xkiäl mbahñn, giäl mbahñ nak xtiidxn
Nde nak tuhñ, xteedxn nak tuhñ, nadn tuuy ni nak behn ni gokxeh dahñ re.
Xtiidxn naka zi'k ni rool ria bi's.
Xtiidxn rsiaa na loh bedox.
Xtiidxn naka zi'k ni rkobee lad ni loob nis.
Xtiidxn naka zi'k nak rehn ni un tuhñ.
Zeka naa dionchin Xtiidxn zi'k ni rdionchin tohb ptoo bäz, zi'k ni rdionchin tuhñ, zi'k ni rdionchin
Tsonal xkiäl riehn lluis: "Luuy, doo, be xtiidxn zek nak gäita, zek nak lool gichlyuh".
Naka gui'tn xtiidxn, naka gui'tn tuhñ
Ria ten gakmn tohb sa. Gak tuhn zi'k nak gihd ro' lihdxn, rgeedxa tuhñ, ranchi na tuhñ. Zi'k dionchin xtiidxn zek chienaa na, zek ria benin nii na, goola, chie zaa ra diidx zah.
Zek mase gäit tuhñ, xtiidx ni'k lal tas chiezaa na.

Placenta

The Earth is sad
Sadness drains Her
The wind no longer blows
Very little rain falls
The forests are wilting
The flowers have lost their scent
The birds no longer sing or fly the same way
Our origins, our tongues cry, we slowly die
School, church and government conspire to extinguish us
But wait a moment: there is a ray of hope
A hope that indigenous communities become the placenta that embraces, feeds and nurtures us, lifting up our languages
Our language is our core being, so we can show with pride how we emerged from Mother Earth
Because language is the birdsong, the sound of the wind and of the water
The blood running in our veins is that same life blood
So today we murmur love, a murmur of knowledge and wisdom that infuses schools, churches and government, making our world whole
As Grandmother would say – speak our tongue and our wisdom so that our world survives
Let's not kill our languages
We must be the placenta that embraces, that cares, that nourishes our indigenous languages so they flourish
Then we can die together when Earth expires gazing upon the Sun

Part 3
Redefining Language Learning in Diverse Spaces and Modes

8 Nłt'éégo bénáłdiih: The Dissemination of Ndee Epistemology in Contemporary Times

Louie Lorenzo and Philip Stevens

> Shichoo dohwanowhinii bitiis chinaa'ndaa'da nnee lihi łahi haadi'nahnihi hike hayudinyahi benanłni le'.[1,2]

Shiwohe shiłi'oozhê. There is an appreciation for others than yourself that precedes any attempt to impact events and struggles within your own life. This appreciation, or love, is sculpted and shaped and added to in order both to come to the realization that you are responsible to others and (thus) that you must be respectful to others. At the end of this realization there shape is given to your life that has at the center values accessed through language and culture. These values – humility, respect, love, clear and intentional thought, resistance to fear, anxiety and shame, and the discipline to resist emotions born of hostility, jealousy, and pride – become the objective of your actions and wishes. N'daa, the negative things associated with life, can become superfluous if nnee bi'at'e'ihii nłdziłgo ádanłzih. Avoidance of n'daa should not be the focus of your life. Actions that are designed to purposely avoid n'daa should not supplant actions that have values as the objective. Through an Apache lens, preventative actions are low and useless objectives. Preventative actions serve only to shift the goal to incidental achievements rather than values. This chapter will attempt to put into a Eurocentric framework (written words meant to be spoken to an unknown audience) Apache ontological perspectives. As such a translation is attempted, Apache ontological and epistemological perspectives will impact how a non-Apache grant provides funding for a drug and alcohol prevention program.

Nnee, or Apache people, were defined by Europeans as simply 'had resisted Spanish rule and was therefore an "enemy" to colonial society' (Conrad, 2021: 5). Apache people were highly mobile people who lived in groups corresponding to what the environment could sustain. Apaches in the plains had larger groups than the Apaches of the mountains. Territory used by Apaches ranged from Kansas and Colorado to Central Mexico. Eurocentric people define San Carlos Apaches as a mixture of Chiricahua, Eastern White Mountain, Western White Mountain, San Carlos, and Tonto people (Opler, 1973). Currently there are eight federally recognized Apache tribes in the US (Bureau of Indian Affairs, n.d.). The San Carlos Apache tribe is one of these recognized tribes. This acute Eurocentric classification of Nnee belies the understanding that we are simply the people. As a people, we consider ourselves to be children of the earth, with all other living beings that exist within our homeland as our co-equal; our origin of being is our homeland.

The Difference between Apache and Nnee

The Apache Youth Mentorship (AYM) program grew out of a Substance Abuse and Mental Health Services Administration Native Connections grant with the San Carlos Wellness Center. This grant was designed to address the high rates of underage substance misuse, addiction, and loss of hope on the San Carlos Apache Reservation in central Arizona and its audience is young children at risk of substance abuse. There are many reports and studies that document a deficit perspective of the San Carlos Apache Reservation (Stevens, 2021), like many other reservations. These reports document the failure of our tribe in assimilating to colonial society, in high substance abuse, high poverty rates, high suicide rates and general sadness associated with not being assimilated. Nnee perspectives differ. N'daa, the negative things of life, proliferate when we forget what we were taught and lose sight of the goals of gozhooné. The AYM program was designed to focus not on substance abuse, which would be in opposition to traditional Nnee methodologies, but rather to focus on language and the culture. The objective of AYM was to teach in a traditional Nnee way.

This difference of methodology tends to have similar objectives. Whereas the Eurocentric grant objective has as its methodology the recognition, classification and subsequent steps that delineate how to avoid alcohol and drug addiction, the traditional Ndee methodology instead focuses on what it means to be a good person, with the understanding that a good person does not engage in disrespect to others. Addiction is a forfeiture of your obligations to others and therefore disrespectful. Addiction is in opposition to clear and intentional thought. When an Apache girl begins the Na'i'ess ceremony she is told that she needs to be especially aware that her clear and intentional thoughts guide her actions even more so in this sacred time. In the course of the work she is doing for the community, she is reminded that gozhooné thoughts create gozhooné actions. It is often unsaid but understood that n'daa thoughts will breed n'daa actions. This Nnee understanding of the relationship between thoughts, voice, and action historically has been undermined within interactions with Eurocentric ontologies; such as the Na'i'ess ceremony being seen as a superstitious belief in anthropomorphic spirits.

Within the course of intergenerational dissemination of language and values (storytelling) the aforementioned values are verbally earmarked in ways that can become parables. Coyote stories often are emblematic of this earmarking. Within these stories nearly every aspect — from the place, voice, thoughts, characters, and time — is a reification of an embedded cultural value. In order to access many of these values it is imperative to be familiar with the *Apache language and culture*. While I, Philip, am a learning Nnee speaker, I am often reminded that language is also a cultural practice (Gao, 2006; Nicholas, 2009), the maintaining of obligated individual autonomy (you are free to choose how to be respectful to others) framed in stories from local radio stations to ceremonies. When Nnee stories are translated into the English language and culture, there are many opportunities to misunderstand the earmarking. Traditionally, stories were shared during the season when 'the snakes were asleep'. When this earmarking is shared with non-Apache people, there can be a number of interpretations. The most common interpretations are: (1) a respectful understanding that there is a different belief system being shared, which can precede the desire to ask questions why; (2) an attempt to give meaning derived from their own cultural understandings; or (3) the simple relegation of Apache culture as ignorant and superstitious. However, what can be understood from an Apache perspective is that the thoughts preceding the sharing of the stories, the subsequent exhalation of breath to make voice, and the actions of the hearers, all are sources of personal power. This power can be understood to share language and values that are essential to Apache culture. It is the power of the people. Suffice to say, that the theft of this power is one of the greatest n'daa in existence. Some of those who wish to steal this power can be known as snakes. Snakes can make you feel ignorant or superstitious or make you question your power so that it does not compete with their power.

Nnee Bi'at'e'ihii Nłdziłgo Ádanłzih

Louie Lorenzo is a project director for the Native Connections in the Apache Youth Mentorship program and a spiritual leader of the community. Louie works with adolescent boys of at least 8 years of age in the AYM program. The AYM program has a partnership with neighboring schools to form a type of after-school club. There are roughly a dozen boys involved. While hired to address the goals of the grant (prevention of substance abuse), he decidedly implements traditional Apache methodologies with Apache culture and values as the objective. Oftentimes this methodology entails the utilization of language, culture, season, and place. With the language and culture component in mind, he uses the term shiwohe shiłi'oozhê, 'I appreciate' or 'I love my grandmother', as the catalyst to reintroduce the boys to Apache values. Using his voice and later writing the words down, Louie starts to talk about family with the boys. The boys begin to understand the meaning by using correct pronunciation of the words. The full enunciation of the words allows the novice speaker to hear what was written down, as Apache is a verb-based language that prioritizes action with direct and indirect objects referenced within the spoken words. For example, the word grandmother in English is presented as a stand-alone noun that can be decontextualized. In effect, the English word grandmother can remove the idea of 'grandmotherness' from the community that defines a grandmother. Shiwohe, as an Apache noun, is embedded in a relational aspect. Shi (I, me or my) -wohe (maternal grandmother) presents the relational aspect of the word so that -wohe does not make any sense without relational in/pre/postfix on its own, as a grandmother is always grandmother to someone. Much like the Berlin–Kay (Berlin & Kay,1969) color theory created the perception of linguistic hierarchy (level 1–7) in regard to colors, the linguistic idea of 'grandmotherness' needing to be connected to a subject is often thought of as the absence of intellectual capabilities to distinguish. This desert is replete with snakes.

Having introduced the initial phrase, shiwohe shiłi'oozhê, Louie works the language and culture like clay to introduce shimaa, shitaa and other community members. This inclusion of the mother and father serves to again reinforce the shiłi'oozhê, the appreciation or love for others. Another aspect of this appreciation for others manifests itself through the understanding that others are intelligent beings. As intelligent beings, actions by these beings that differ from common actions are initially met with the understanding that new knowledge must guide these new actions. It is understood that every being, as they are intelligent, must have new knowledge that causes them to create new actions that differ from those without access to the new knowledge. This new knowledge/new actions gives/give rise to innovation: new ways to do old things. This innovation is valued by Apache communities. However, it is important to know that not all new actions are formed by new knowledge. Sometimes the new action is simply an imperfect attempt at replication. As such, instructive actions are taken to inform the being. Another way to understand this is that you are thought of as intelligent until you prove that you are not; and we all at one time or another prove that we are not.

A corollary Apache tenet is that some beings have access to some knowledge that others may not. As such, an individual should not try to possess this knowledge but, rather, create a respectful relationship with those who have that knowledge. In effect, it means that knowledge can be gendered. Apache men do not possess Apache women knowledge, so rather than attempting to gain this knowledge, it is imperative to men and women maintain respectful relations so that both men and women may benefit from each other's knowledge. Louie shares this knowledge as an Apache man with the boys but is explicit in his inclusion of their family, in particular the female members of the boys' family, to share their own different understandings of shiwohe shiłi'oozhê.

It is uncommon to hear the word love in Apache culture. Popular culture often states that there is no word for love in Apache (Didier, 2008; L'Amour, 1983). Again, it should be noted that the perceived absence of love does not denote an absence of love but more that the separation of gozhooné in isolation is peculiar from an Apache perspective. As an analogy, the English word for chair, in the essence of old French 'chaiere' a seat of power, is firmly seated in a Eurocentric linguistic relation between where you sit and power. Apache does not necessarily designate where one is to sit as any source of power. It could be misunderstood that the concept of a sitting place does not exist in Apache intellect. However, this denies the aforementioned Eurocentric etymology and linguistic relativity for the current understanding of the word chair. This is similar to the Apache concept of love: gozhooné is understood to be always the objective.

Conversations with the family of the boys in AYM often explicitly utilize the concept of gozhoone in particular, since the historical legacy of schools and churches has had the effect of negating the Apache concept of gozhoone. Grandparents retain the stories of the Apache wars, boarding schools and the outlawing of Apache spirituality. These stories often have little gozhoone and plenty of n'daa. As partners of AYM, grandparents are reminded to share stories of gozhoone as the boys often are already familiar with n'daa.

The boys involved within the AYM program are treated with the understanding that not only are they intelligent but they also embody gozhoone. Instructors and parents are reminded that gozhoone is in the boys. This can be seen as in opposition to Eurocentric pedagogical models that treat students as 'blank slates' or 'empty vessels' that are meant to be filled with the knowledge of the teacher (Rahman & Cochrane, 2023). Apache pedagogy is co-constructed. As such it would be an insult to the imaginative and intellectual capabilities of the students to negate the knowledge that they possess. Apache lessons are often presented as an opportunity for the student to demonstrate or share the knowledge they understand. Parents of students involved with AYM are encouraged to share their knowledge of language and culture not in the manner of teaching but rather as an invitation to bring out the knowledge that is within the students. This can mean not replicating 'flashcard' learning but, rather, using the language and culture in the simple dynamic ways that occur within the family day.

AYM lessons also reflect the traditional Apache utilization of the strengths of the seasons. Depending on the season, if góshdii is active, short stories are shared about him. These stories are first shared in Apache then later talked about in English. As these stories are told outside, there is a chance that the students may see a roadrunner. Later, when the students are driven toward other places on their homeland, Louie will start a game where the first student who sees and calls out the name, góshdii, will receive a small reward. Students are often attentive rather than passive as they are traveling in their homeland. This simple exercise or lesson accesses and utilizes a few Apache cultural goals and concepts.

Apache Cultural Goals and Concepts

Language and culture become more than words on pages but, rather, potential daily events that can be recognized by the student. Attentive, and actively looking for animals, shifts the student mindset from a passive educational format to students reinitiating the previous lessons in a new time and place. In effect, the boys are re-teaching the lesson to themselves and the instructor. By recognizing and rewarding the student's re-teaching of the initial lesson shared by the AYM instructor, language and culture have the chance to be recognized as relevant to today. This echoes the Apache understanding that the lessons in and of themselves can and are in the students, just waiting to be drawn out. Granted, it could be understood that the students are simply regurgitating what they have heard, but the identification of the concept of 'góshdii-ness' as potentially behind every bush allows the students to appreciate the malleability of the concept of 'góshdii-ness' as being available to them if only they are attentive. This recognizes their own power of knowledge.

The recognition of the imaginative and creative power of the students allows community teachers (i.e. family members, AYM instructor, and other community members) to share their own imaginative and creative understandings of Apache culture and language. AYM instructors re-activate dormant knowledge of the community by asking how things were when the older members were young. As an example, questions were asked about the thoughts regarding hashbidi. Quails are a source of food. Regarding the harvesting of hashbidi, elders recount that you only took what you could use rather than taking all the quail in a covey. Elders explained that you did not need to kill all of them. It was important to let some of the hashbidi rejoin their own family. This recollection reaffirms the Apache tenet that respect and appreciation for others is the objective. There is also the recognition that respect and appreciation are not limited to humans and that a community includes more than humans. Another aspect is that food is understood to be energy and not

Figure 8.1 Apache boys singing
(Photo credit: Louie Lorenzo).

an indulgence: you eat until you have had enough, not until you are full. Recognizing these lessons allows the AYM program to bring traditional Apache lessons to address issues of indulgence (i.e. obesity, diabetes, addiction).

As these traditional Apache lessons are dynamic and gain power when they are personalized, it is important to recognize that everyone has power or knowledge to share and that over-reliance on one source leaves you vulnerable to the weaknesses of that source. Empathy is an Apache value that becomes apparent as it becomes important and respectful to consider what others see as important so that their goals and objectives can be assessed with your own goals and objectives. Community, then, is recognized as a source of power only limited by the other community members. Students become aware that they are powerful community members also. Empathetic lessons can situate their own understanding of reliance on the community where they, as community members themselves, are being relied upon. Therefore, there is an obligation to others that one must better oneself also.

Expergiscimini ac Recordabor

AYM attempts to reawaken cultural understanding within the Apache community through the younger members. The students are made aware that Apache is at the core of their identity. Immersive lessons that purposely blur the barriers of education – either the mental barrier excluding student knowledge, or the physical walls of schoolrooms excluding the reality of the students – allow the students to begin to recognize their own life journey and purpose for coming to this planet. AYM lessons are designed to recognize pre-reservation times as being guided by processes apart from Eurocentric ontologies. Apache language allows us to access these processes so that we can bring them out again.

Louie Lorenzo often speaks Apache on the community radio station, KYAY (itself an Apache word akin to, 'Wow'). His work with AYM brought him to a local school where a fluent Apache speaker approached him. The fluent speaker, who was also a student, expressed a desire to see the Apache man whom he had heard often on the radio. The student then decided to participate in the AYM program outside school. As the other students in AYM have a range of Apache language proficiency, it could be understandable to see the fluent student as another language teacher. In effect, AYM could make him a language teacher. However, this is not what happened. The fluent speaker participated with the other students in the culture and language lessons. The fluent speaker was not put on the spot and 'made' a leader: rather, the fluent speaker was given the space to recognize for himself his respect, appreciation, and obligations to the community. Empathy should be what makes him a leader.

Dló łitsogé begins to appear in the spring. This bird used to stay around for about two months but now stays until the beginning of fall. AYM students are given time and space to turn their thoughts to dló łitsogé; to be empathetic to the bird as a community member. Perhaps dló łitsogé has thoughts of old (not new) Mexico where it becomes heavy with eggs or thoughts of the ocean where babies hatch or perhaps what caused it to be seen by the student? Students may wonder what the bird knows of stars, magnetic fields, and navigation.

AYM is an example of everyday efforts to re-center Nnee language and culture. Aspects of community, obligations, respect and self-discipline are utilized within the framework of reminding students of Nnee ontologies that are still evident within the expansive, traditional Apache homelands: Apacheria. This constant reminder to 'pay attention' not only with your eyes and ears but with your whole self to your surroundings while also understanding that lessons are also taught by the environment, creates a world full of reminders. As even a non-Apache person realized, wisdom sits in places (Basso, 1996). Nature entails so much community involvement. There are so many lessons to be brought forth and realized. When the first thunder comes, so does the acorn. The sound reverberates now as it did many years ago. Chíchn'il reverberates. The Apache language is a soundwave that stretches from the past into the future. AYM students are reminded that the soundwave envelops them completely. Students are reminded that they only need to hear it and recognize it to begin to make sense of it and to appreciate it so that they will come to understand shiatii shiloozho.

Notes

(1) This statement comes from a grandmother to her grandson (maternal life patterns). It reflects identity, appreciation of knowledge received from family/larger community, and purpose of life, gifts and achievement.
(2) There will be an attempt to value Apache thought and language throughout this chapter. As such, Eurocentric ontologies (including writing styles) may be challenged.

References

Basso, K.H. (1996) *Wisdom Sits in Places: Landscape and Language Among the Western Apache*. University of New Mexico Press.
Berlin, B. and Kay, P. (1969) *Basic Color Terms: Their Universality and Evolution*. University of California Press.
Bureau of Indian Affairs (n.d.) https://www.bia.gov/frequently-asked-questions#:~:text= A%20federally%20recognized%20tribe%20is,funding%20and%20services%20 from%20the.
Conrad, P. (2021) *The Apache Diaspora: Four Centuries of Displacement and Survival*. University of Pennsylvania Press.
Didier, C.A. (2008) *Apache Warrior*. Zebra Books.
Gao, F. (2006) Language is culture: On intercultural communication. *Journal of Language and Linguistics* 5 (1), 58–67.
L'Amour, L. (1983) *Hondo*. Bantam.
Nicholas, S.E. (2009) 'I live Hopi, I just don't speak it': The critical intersection of language, culture, and identity in the lives of contemporary Hopi youth. *Journal of Language, Identity, and Education* 8 (5), 321–334.
Opler, M.E. (ed.) (1973) *Grenville Goodwin Among the Western Apache: Letters from the Field*. University of Arizona Press. Available at ttps://doi.org/10.2307/j.ctvss3xx8.
Rahman, A.E. and Cochrane, T. (2023) Pedagogy and Indigenous knowing and learning. *Oxford Review of Education* 49 (4), 429–445.
Stevens, P.J. (2021) A woodcutter's story: Perceptions and uses of mathematics on the San Carlos Apache Reservation. *Anthropology & Education Quarterly* 52 (4), 430–450.

9 Reconnecting to Homelands through Digital Storywork

Jessica Matsaw and Sammy Matsaw

Nanisundehai demme tsasuakande' deas dewazia deas nahii'wi. Demme tsand'e nanangha.[1]

Introduction

A component of nation-building through River Newe – an Indigenous-owned not-for-profit (non-profit) organization – has its challenges, as well as opportunities to become a way to reconnect to homelands. Newe is the Shoshone word for people, Shoshone People. The very name River Newe holds considerable meaning, not just in the direct translation but also as a reminder of the culturally sustaining and revitalizing pedagogy (McCarty & Lee, 2014) grounded in hope with our community and Newenne. The decision to name our work River Newe came from the request of a Tribal Elder known for her expertise as the Shoshone–Bannock tribal interpreter on the Middle Fork of the Salmon River. This elder had seen us do our river work over the years as a family, even accompanying us on many of our initial rafting trips. River Newe is a response to that listening, and grounded initiatives through our mission statement, vision and goals, which you can find at rivernewe.org. Writing this chapter, we respectfully acknowledge our elder, Diana Yupe naap, who gave us our name and has since passed on to the spirit world, hence the Shoshone word naap.

Community-based, Family Run Non-profit

Before River Newe was founded, we navigated academia as a family. Our children were our center. As parents, we pushed back on institutional spaces, making it clear we moved as a family needing to approach academia in a culturally relevant way. We rejected Eurocentric ideologies within education based on harmful assumptions of individualism and anthropocentrism (Grande, 2007) that make succeeding as a family nearly impossible. Not an easy task for us when first moving from our home on the reservation into family housing on a university campus. How our family moved across the land to Tygi was how we moved within our education, to remember and protect who (to hunt) we are as Newenne. Our children moved fluidly with us, mimicking our hunting trips or gathering medicine as they sat in observation within massive lecture halls, still gathering teachings but in a different way. We would bring little brown faces to academic events that were not inviting for our children. We knew the importance of traditional parenting in these moments of disrupting institutional norms were opportunities for folks in academia to take pause. For our children to feel secure regardless of being away from our tribal community and culture, we had to model to the best of our ability what it meant to be Shoshone–Bannock.

From the parents' example, our children understood when they were not being represented in their own education to fully be themselves. Our son, Luzahan, would get so frustrated at his new school when the teacher would pull down the books about Native Americans only for the month of November – Native American Heritage Month – the teacher telling Luzahan, 'these books are only for special times'. Special times were juxtaposed with the inherent heritage our children had creating their own place of learning in student housing, finding the traditional plants that grew around our gray-colored apartments, or mimicking the setup of snares around their favorite bushes that surrounded the student housing parking lots. Little moments, quiet, almost secretive moments, our children could express who they are as Newenne. We engaged in the everyday practice of being Indigenous, so that our children would have moments of learning, *regeneration and renewing of relationships* for guidance and direction (San Pedro, 2021). Our children never asked why they had to go to this event or that, just like they never questioned when it was time to harvest tsiina (wild carrots) or hunt Baadeheya (elk). Our children understood they had to pay attention, listen, and be observant if we were in a lecture or hunting elk. Their early teachings of how to be like Bonai (mouse), to nanga (listen) with all their senses helped them adapt from outdoor to indoor learning events. This is how our family moved.

Before River Newe, we purposefully sought out our education with the intent of giving back to our tribe. We had elders tell us: 'Go to school, learn, get knowledge and bring it back to our people'. These words, and many like them, were guides for both Sam and I as we made decisions on where to direct our studies. Our children were the young ones also driving us to contribute to a future of healing. Progressing through our learning, the words of Sandy Grande, Linda T. Smith and Bryan M. J. Brayboy empowered what naturally pulled us towards community-based research and the importance of amplifying our unique lived experiences as Shoshone–Bannocks. We situated our education to be scouts: to reclaim space, voice, identity, power, while gathering tools to fight for social and environmental justice. We found our paths in water ecology and traditional first foods while challenging the education system as Indigenous educators. Early moments that would contribute to our seeking out what is Shoshone–Bannock pedagogy.

River Newe: Our Origin Story

When we first traveled down the Middle Fork of the Salmon River as a family our children were babies. We were apprehensive about taking our 3-year-old daughter down the white waters of our traditional homelands. We thought about how our people traveled down these sacred waters since time immemorial and trusted that we could get down the river just as our ancestors had done. Our children were natural on the water as we simultaneously engaged in research methodologies and praxis of being Shoshone–Bannock (Figure 9.1). Our children assisted in gathering mussels for harvest, giving thanks, preparing the mussels, and cooking with their bia (mother), which would end in feeding our community on the river that simultaneously served as their apa (father's) doctoral study on mussel ecology. This is what our children

Figure 9.1 Abrianna Matsaw (3 years old) with her bia (mom), Jessica Matsaw, visiting a cultural site on the Middle Fork of the Salmon River (Summer 2017)
Photo credit: Sammy Matsaw Jr.

had come to know to be research. The Introduction to *Decolonizing Methodologies* states, 'research is the dirtiest word' (Smith, 2012). River Newe can follow with 'however, when we make it ours, this is where we heal'. Returning to the Middle Fork of the Salmon River, a place our people had been forcibly removed from, to the reservation where we live amongst intergenerational trauma was painful. Watching our four children connect to our homelands so naturally, as if we had never left, was healing and we knew River Newe was conducting acts of resistance just being on the water.

The early years getting our family on the water was an essential learning curve in understanding what our community would need for reconnection and revitalization. The Middle Fork, and returning to our Shoshone–Bannock homeland, became the catalyst for what is now River Newe. Returning to a place still mostly intact with pit-house depressions that holds stories of a time before colonization has been overwhelming. Our happiness at a beautiful homecoming, and sorrow realizing how long we had been away, bring hope for our children to always be here, are the beginnings of our own self-awareness. Deep feelings holding hands with the realization of a time before forcible removal and the juncture of harm that has followed. Where 'the most vulnerable populations remain vulnerable to a society that is poised, at best, to assimilate them into dominant cultural practices' (Patel, 2015: 23). Coming to terms with the cognitive dissonance and struggle of an imposed narrative that Indians stay within reservation boundaries. When we know that our reservation borders were drawn without any correlation to historical usage or occupancy, like other reservations (Grande, 2007). Because of this we often ask: Where else, then, do we belong? This is not uncommon to hear among our community and tribal youth back on the Fort Hall Reservation, among community gatherings, within the classroom, reminiscing of places we used to and seasonally occupy.

As River Newe began to grow roots, we could see expression of culture and self-identity blooming with every summer we returned to the Middle Fork of the Salmon River. Our time on the river, our children, and later tribal youth were able to just be who they are, forming deep connections to the land, water, our community, and themselves. Each day we traveled down the river – the closer we moved to our cultural sites – we felt belonging to places and people. Examining the pictographs left by our ancestors to tell us: 'You! You are still here'. We saw and felt our survivance (Vizenor, 2008) – our continued existence, persistence and creation – as we stood next to our sacred places, as if they were living, breathing relatives, arms wide open. There was overwhelming reciprocity between us and the land, and we saw right away that self-determination and community empowerment could be carried within us regardless of being on a reservation or not.

Figure 9.2 The Matsaw family tygi (hunt/harvest) medicines in Mount Putnam, fall 2023, with our isha-saade (wolf-dog) Smokey. Kids listen to their apa (dad) tell stories of his childhood harvesting in the mountains with his family. Malia demonstrates her developing skills to identify medicinal plants
Photo credit: Jessica Matsaw.

A foundational teaching of River Newe has been situated in community-based learning and relationship-building. River Newe has become what it is today because of what our community made it to be, braided with the efforts and support of cultivated alliances built along the way (Anthony-Stevens, 2017). We did not know what River Newe would become but we knew that learning together would simultaneously help us heal together. Our people, the Shoshone–Bannocks, still exist. The love and transmission of knowledge to tygi, to care for one another, to think beyond an individualistic ideology, are all acts of survivance and protection of us as a people. This is a form of Shoshone–Bannock pedagogy (Figure 9.2).

A Shoshone–Bannock Pedagogy

We have found points of pause and reflection on the importance of Indigenous pedagogy. Now more than ever we are coming to understand there cannot be institutional change until there is understanding of the 'why' and 'how' we learn and transmit Indigenous Knowledge (IK) as Shoshone–Bannock people. By stepping back to pause and understand the pedagogy of how our community learns, teaches, and engages in relationality, then can we engage in research, teach and learn in a way that does not cause further harm.

Respectfully, we acknowledge there are different Shoshone bands, dialects and traditions, family groups, and more than 6,000 people making up the population of the Shoshone–Bannock tribes. The suggestions, organization and recommendations provided here are merely the perspective of one Shoshone–Bannock tribal family utilizing the application of our lived experiences and what it means to be a part of our Newene (Shoshone people). Further, we acknowledge and deeply respect that there are teachings, and certain traditional knowledges, not meant to be shared with those outside our community and it is a fine line we must walk to discern and continue to check in with our community for accountability.

The theoretical outline of the early emergence of Shoshone–Bannock pedagogy that informs our reclamation work provides a guide to what community-based work can look like considering the unique lived experiences of Shoshone–Bannock people centering our identities as a sovereign nation. An outline of the initial guiding precepts is:

(1) Shoshone–Bannock pedagogy is unique to the lived experiences, traditional knowledge, and cultural lifeways in connection to language, land, and us as Indigenous people.
(2) Shoshone–Bannock pedagogy is the active praxis of exercising treaty rights.
(3) Shoshone–Bannock pedagogy refuses damage-centered research.
(4) Shoshone–Bannock pedagogy has a direct connection to land and place.
(5) Shoshone–Bannock pedagogy is situated in community-based power.
(6) Sharing of narratives is central to the transmission of intellectual knowledge and what is Shoshone–Bannock pedagogy.
(7) Shoshone–Bannock pedagogy is a call to action for social justice.

Shoshone–Bannock pedagogy is directly inspired from the theoretical framework of Red Pedagogy (2000), tenants that we could see actively living and breathing within our community. A way of engagement and relationality that situates Shoshone–Bannock pedagogy in sovereignty and self-determination. From these tenants our understanding is that if Shoshone–Bannock pedagogy does not put tribal sovereignty at the forefront, then the educational endeavors of tribal communities will be undermined. Our Indigenous intellect situates us in 'community-based power', to live in an active state of survivance and not as victims of settler colonialism. We reclaim our indigeneity as peoples of a sovereign nation.

The tenants learning while on the land is imperative for considering power inequities when thinking about a Shoshone–Bannock pedagogy and the very essence of the work that River Newe engages in. To be forcibly removed from our homelands, disconnected from our teachings, was and is a violent disruption to intergenerational learning that will take generations to heal. Tuck and Yang (2012: 5) describe settler colonialism as separate from other methods of colonialism, as 'settlers come in with the intention of making a new home on the land, a homemaking that insists on settler sovereignty over all things in their new domain'. There is no lack of settler colonial racism within educational institutions, where Stevens *et al.* (2021) describe higher education as a 'battle of sovereigns' that is overtly present in all levels of education, including spaces and places of learning occurring on Indigenous homelands.

River Newe is not limited to one place (as Shoshone–Bannock homelands are vast). However, we chose the Middle Fork of the Salmon River as a significant location of self-determined space for American Indian intellectualism (Grande, 2004). As a historical place of forcible removal of our people, it is also a space where we can expand the exercise of our treaty rights, thus actively engaging in social justice. This serves as a reminder to settler colonial America, specifically Idaho residents, that not only were Shoshone peoples forcibly removed from our homelands but that forcible removal resulted in a treaty that must be honored. This expression of social justice is not unique to River Newe: we are simply following the many examples from our community to bring awareness of our status as a treaty tribe and the unjust means by which lands were taken, and our refusal to let history be forgotten.

The hope of Shoshone–Bannock pedagogy is to 'provoke change' and reignite knowledge and cultural transmission by and for the people. One of the objectives of Shoshone–Bannock pedagogy is to provoke change while also disrupting settler colonial racism and engage in community-based power. Through the development of a Shoshone–Bannock pedagogy we can then begin to look at institutional change which has historically and presently been a place of violence. Through a Shoshone–Bannock pedagogy it is our hope that we can move away from education as a 'battle of sovereigns' and move towards education situated in tribal self-determination.

Shoshone–Bannock Pedagogy through Digital Storywork

Tribal self-determination calls on a need for independence from outside influence because Indigenous forms of learning are both complex and simple at the same time. We do as we are taught through mimicking, guiding, mentoring, and then stepping into age-appropriate roles after we show we've adhered to the customs and protocols. When coming back to places of removal and working back through reconnection, we were trying to do too much. Our shoestring budget was based on STEM and youth initiatives while we knew we were in a place that was the home of our ancestors. And we wanted to honor them, acknowledge them, so we were remembering to remember through protocols and customary acts of honoring. We also had to check the STEM youth initiative box for the funding undergirding our trips. Through a lot of hard work, onboarding to white water rafting expertise, and backcountry food menu designing, we were doing it all and doing it all at once. Then came our film.

The name *River of Return* was a play on the Frank Church River of No Return wilderness, where we were returning on our terms, in our own way. The film helped us in lots of ways but mostly to bring together the many themes of honoring and the work we were doing, all at once – in other words, a nice way to say we made a mess look fancy. The filming process with director Skip Armstrong was both frustrating and rewarding, to tell the story of the work we had on film. We couldn't ignore the fact of what we had on film, and we faced it head on. When we see the film there are so many emotions, and we're so proud of how it came out.

Off the river, we have our community still learning together. This past summer (2022) River Newe held a salmon camp, and the community hunters and fishermen showed up in full force, ready to share their knowledge with the next generation. Tribal members, rough and tough men who might be perceived as intimidating, were kind and patient, open to youth asking questions, taking pictures, and even recording them. Throughout our learning there is humor. As an example, a skilled fisherman was showing the tribal kids how to fix a salmon hook but he had accidently tied the hook backwards. Our daughter Malia (almost 11 years old) had recorded the tribal fisherman. She made a short film with an iPad that had been handed out to the kids. Her film was titled *The Wrong Way to Tie a Hook*. Both our daughter and the tribal fisherman had a good laugh.

Isha, the wolf, has many foundational teachings for us that we must remember to remember if the stories of our ancestors are to live on, in this we pray. Tying hooks and hunting salmon mimic a teaching from learning alongside Isha to feed our families. From this we mimicked, guided, and learned from the land together.

Isha Teachings and the Transmission of Family Dialects

River Newe is grounded in Isha (wolf) teachings, and storytelling of muskrat's creation of Turtle Island aka North America, to name a few of how our young people are learning to be on and along rivers. Our greatest classrooms are tribal youth night spearfishing/hunting for Agai (salmon) along the Salmon River tributaries, emulating how Isha hunts salmon and passing of this precious Indigenous Knowledge (IK) generation after generation. By night the fish don't need to hide from predators, so Agai will use the whole stream, preferring the deepest part in the thalweg where it's the coolest, and behind rocks to conserve energy. Night fishing provides us with opportunities to teach our youth about fish behavior, ecology, interactions with our IK, and teachings. Engaging in Shoshone–Bannock teaching directly rejects and dispels myths of Indian students being one-dimensional learners (Lomawaima & McCarty, 2025). The tygi (hunt) is central to Shoshone–Bannock ways of knowing, that is multi-dimensional, where tribal youth become young teachers themselves reaching expert level, able to transmute teachings and learning in direct response to present-day life. Professors from surrounding universities in the fish ecology world will approach Shoshone–Bannocks with the profound enlightenment of night-fishing juveniles wanting to publish this new method to name it and claim it as their own. Shoshone–Bannock members and tribal scientists themselves will humbly share that this method of fishing 'is not new'. Shoshone–Bannock scientists will point their non-Native colleagues to Lewis and Clark documentation of Shoshones night fishing dating back to 1805. For us and our youth, to know that our IK systems are still being 'discovered' (Schmitke *et al.*, 2020) speaks to the challenges faced in disrupting dominant settler colonial narratives, at the same time engaging in the relentless struggle of validating our IK systems as meaningful. Through our Isha teachings we are not discovering anything but looking through the lens of observation and relationality to language, land, and community, asking ourselves 'Are we being good listeners?' and 'Are we being a good relative?'

The language we share here is Shoshone, and there are dialect differences within it, also different from Bannock. They are the same root language group: Numic from the Uto-Aztecan family. We are not, however, linguists, and the phylo-linguistic references could differ from expert knowledge. Instead, we are demonstrating the praxis of the everyday actions of living as Shoshone–Bannock people, using the linguistic dialect transmitted from family member to family member, and the act of living with the land in reciprocity and relationality. We teach our children how to survive utilizing and valuing IK transmitted between relatives (San Pedro, 2021) learning and remembering what Linda Tuhiwai Smith calls a 'collective memory and critical conscience of past experiences' (Smith 2012: 145). Our teachings are family oriented, and communal; however, they are misunderstood as informal methods of learning, and are diminished when not written down or taught from a book. On the contrary, there is an abundance of protocols and traditional formalities that are in many ways returning to the very teachings we received long ago from Isha. These teachings and protocols are multifaceted, as our children must learn in their early years of life how to survive as dual citizens of nations with conflicting ideologies. We, as Shoshone–Bannock people, are still learning how to survive while simultaneously exemplifying survivance and the act of preserving our identity and resistance to colonialism (Smith, 2012) in these complex contemporary lifeways. To escape the contemporary, we seek learning in the backcountry.

Equity in Accessing Traditional Homelands

The Middle Fork of the Salmon River (Figure 9.3) is a beautiful winding waterway with the landscape transitioning from mountains and pines to massive canyons and pictographs. We stop at places to eat lunch and swim, surrounded by sand and wild rose bushes, ponderosa pines and giant sleeping dimbi (rock) relatives. Our evening campsites are always a welcome end to the day. Our elders and youth are happy, as we try to pick the camps close to hot springs so they can soak their old bones and play. The days we travel down the water are long, with moments of self-reflection, excitement, with lots of teasing and laughter. As River Newe our camp setup is family style. Every morning and evening you will see a row of rafts adorned with sage and tobacco, a huge circle of camp chairs, our crew moving on a different timeline than what one is accustomed to with the industrial recreational companies. Shoshone–Bannock kids unloading rafts, setting up their tents, big smiles, grazing chips and salsa while engaging with the art box and prompts to remember the highlight of their day, or gift-making.

We like to say that River Newe started on a shoestring budget. Originally, the rafts were borrowed from a tribal department and brought in by volunteers who owned rafts. Additionally, the food, equipment, groover, kitchen, and handwashing station were all pulled together by us and volunteers, and by people who believe in the work we do: rowers, professional guides, volunteering their expertise to support River Newe as Shoshone–Bannocks return home.

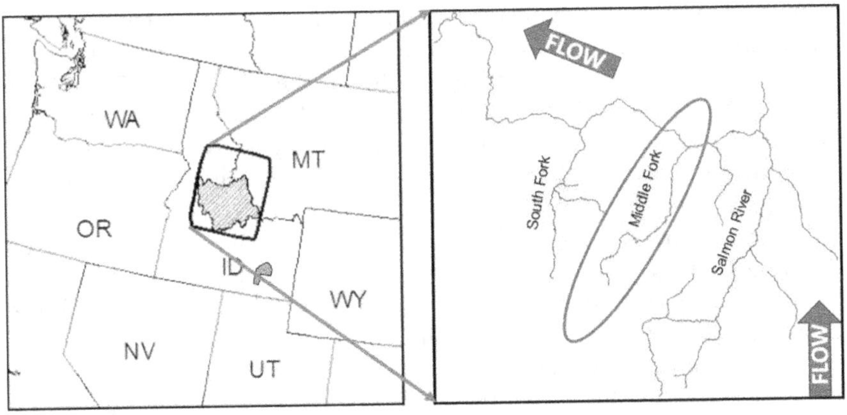

Figure 9.3 The Middle Fork of the Salmon River flows to the Columbia River into the Pacific Ocean. We put in at the top, traveling 99 miles of wild and scenic river surrounded by wilderness over a week, breaking down and setting up camp every day

A limitation we identified early on was the amount of funding needed to travel through the Middle Fork and the financial limitations our tribal community faced merely accessing our traditional waterways. As River Newe we have come to understand threats of commodification and consumerist culture impacting tribal access to our homelands, especially into the Middle Fork of the Salmon River. In the past, the lack of Shoshone–Bannock representation on the river was not because our people did not want to be there: it was largely due to lack of money, resources, experience, etc. The main participants traveling the Middle Fork of the Salmon are individuals who have large amounts of disposable income, time and resources. Celebrities, tourists from other countries, public figures, and individuals well above the poverty line attaining first access to our traditional homelands. The commodification of wild and scenic waters surrounded by the physical limits of navigating protected wilderness and the inaccessibility for our tribal people was something we wanted to change. Not only did we want to address the inequity of Shoshone–Bannocks having access, but we also wanted to address the needs of our oldest and youngest relatives. Another limitation was finding gear that fit our small children and larger tribal members. When we revisit years preceding River Newe we can see our youngest daughter wearing a sturdy bike helmet proudly sitting on a raft with her apa (dad). As River Newe continues to grow, we now have five fully geared rafts to our name, and our goal is the same: to fill the rafts with as many tribal members as we can.

From our first River Newe trip to the present, we cover all costs and expenses on each trip, which is equal to what is provided on a chartered trip with no additional expense of a cultural STEAM experience, and we include an additional day. Commercial trips are approximately $3,500 per person for 6 days or private trips that are bring-your-own-raft, food, camping and rafting gear, coolers, and ice, scheduling shuttles, and all the logistics on your own. More than 11,000 people take this trip through the permit season from May 28th to September 3rd, with 7 launches per day. We provide all of this cost-free for Shoshone–Bannock tribal members, made possible by small donations, grants, a reliable network of volunteers, and support from organizations such as OARS–Idaho (Curt Chang, owner), and Northwest River Supply (NRS) as Leaders in Environment, Access, and Diversity–LEAD ambassadors, and the Shoshone–Bannock Tribes, our formal government entity.

We looked at the natural development of River Newe and the reciprocity of our tribal people learning from the land, and we looked on the land as transformational. Once we addressed the barrier of accessing our traditional homelands of the Middle Fork of the Salmon River, we began to see other inequities needing attention among our youth. For example, for most of our young people committing to traveling down the river with us it would be their first experience with the outdoors.

Figure 9.4 River Newe trip, Middle Fork of the Salmon, 2023. Shoshone–Bannock community members hike up to Veil Falls. A Chief Tahgee Elementary Academy Language teacher with drum in hand shares songs with the tribal youth. For some, this is their first time returning to the Middle Fork since forcible removal
Photo credit: Brant Miller.

Additionally, many of our youth had not had the opportunity to engage in outdoor learning within the reservation largely surrounded by farming. As a result, tribal students responded positively to the opportunity for our youth to go camping for a week, not even knowing exactly what that meant. Furthermore, there was a strong response to our approach of culturally relevant and culturally competent education, creating a new way of looking at learning through a Shoshone–Bannock pedagogy. For some, our trip is the only experience a tribal member has had to see how our ancestors lived, experiencing firsthand the house depressions, pictographs, mussel beds, cambium peels, etc. When we visit our relatives' past homes and ways of life, we do not see them as relics but as living, breathing entities that transcend through us as Shoshone–Bannocks. Further, some of our youth returning to the Middle Fork are the first of their family unit coming home since forcible removal more than a century ago (Figure 9.4).

Conclusion

The doing of activities related to living through a seasonal round in our homelands and returning to places is important to language revitalization. As we are learning, language comes from land, from the plants and animals that are our relatives. When we are back in those places disconnected from the outside world, we are there to hear our language, and the beauty represented by the tongue of the peoples and the land we call home. Coming from verb-based languages, moving across land, packing and unpacking like our people still do, and have always done, are how Indigenous languages like Shoshone–Bannock live on. River Newe is one example of one way, among many ways, to pursue language and cultural revitalization.

Note

(1) Shoshone translation 'we are listening well'.

References

Anthony-Stevens, V. (2017) Cultivating alliances: Reflections on the role of non-Indigenous collaborators in Indigenous educational sovereignty. *Journal of American Indian Education* 56 (1), 81–104.
Brayboy, B.M.J. (2005) Toward a tribal critical race theory in education. *Urban Review* 37 (5), 425–446.
Grande, S. (2000) American Indian identity and intellectualism: The quest for a new red pedagogy. *International Journal of Qualitative Studies in Education* 13 (4), 343–359.
Grande, S. (2004) Whitestream feminism and the Colonialist Project: Toward a theory of indigenista. *Red Pedagogy: Native American Social and Political Thought*, 123–157.
Grande, S. (2007) Red Lake Woebegone: Pedagogy, decolonization, and the Critical Project. In P. McLaren and J.L. Kincheloe (eds) *Critical Pedagogy: Where Are We Now?* (pp. 315–336). Peter Lang.
Grande, S. (2008) Red pedagogy: The un-methodology. In N.K. Denzin, Y.S. Lincoln and L.T. Smith (eds) *Handbook of Critical and Indigenous Methodologies* (pp. 233–254). Sage.
Lomawaima, K.T. and McCarty, T.L. (2025) *'To remain an Indian': Lessons in Democracy from a Century of Native American Education*. Teachers College Press.
McCarty, T.L. and Lee, T.S. (2014) Critical culturally sustaining/revitalizing pedagogy and indigenous education sovereignty. *Harvard Educational Review* 84 (1), 101–124.
Patel, L. (2015) *Decolonizing Educational Research: From Ownership to Responsibility*. Routledge.
San Pedro, T. (2021) *Protecting the Promise: Indigenous Education Between Mothers and their Children*. Teachers College Press.
Stevens, P.J. (2021) A woodcutter's story: Perceptions and uses of mathematics on the San Carlos Apache Reservation. *Anthropology & Education Quarterly* 52 (4), 430–450.
Stevens, P.J., Anthony-Stevens, V., Hedden-Nicely, D.R. and Hamilton, C.A. (2021) Tribal nation building and the role of faculty: Paying the debt on Indigenous well-being in higher education. *Journal of American Indian Education* 60 (3), 13–43.
Tuck, E. (2009) Suspending damage: A letter to communities. *Harvard Educational Review* 79 (3), 409–428.
Tuck, E. and Yang, K.W. (2014) Decolonization is not a metaphor. *Tabula Rasa* (38), 61–111.
Tuhiwai Smith, L. (2012) *Decolonizing Methodologies: Research and Indigenous Peoples*. Zed Books.
Vizenor, G. (ed.) (2008) *Survivance: Narratives of Native Presence*. University of Nebraska Press.

10 Learning from Narratives: Life Stories of Indigenous Students in Chilean Graduate Science Programs as Voices of Advocacy for University Space Reclamation

Marta Silva Fernández, Jennifer Brito Pacheco and Paulina Griñó

First, we present some characteristics of indigenous education in Chile. Second, we demonstrate how, through a biographical–reflective process, these narratives emerge as voices advocating for culturally relevant university spaces. These spaces serve as platforms for the preservation and reclamation of ethnic identity.

The stories presented invite us to consider that an indigenous person entering university to study science may, in itself, be an act of insurgency against the capitalist logic prevailing in most universities today. Therefore, we believe that for the indigenous youth who participated in these interviews, completing their graduate studies is, in essence, an act of advocacy that equips them with the necessary tools to fight for justice, equality and the preservation of their cultures.

Indigenous Education in Chile

The Socioeconomic Characterization Survey of Chile (CASEN), conducted by the Ministry of Social Development and Family, aims to gather information on households across the country and evaluate the impact of social policies. Concerning Indigenous people in higher education, their participation is notably lower compared to non-Indigenous students. The proportion of the Indigenous population enrolled in higher education is smaller than that of the non-Indigenous population (Ministry of Social Development, 2017). This disparity can be explained by various factors, including economic challenges, hegemonic and monocultural teaching practices that fail to recognize Indigenous knowledge and cultural diversity, the assumption that all students learn uniformly, the lack of intercultural pedagogy, and the difficulties that Indigenous students face in a university environment that prioritizes Western Eurocentric knowledge over their own cultural perspectives. These difficulties are related not only to the ethnic variable but also to the multidimensional inequalities faced by the country's inhabitants (United Nations Development Programme, 2017). Additionally, the disparity could reflect the personal choices of members of Indigenous communities, who may opt not to access higher education institutions and their hegemonic Eurocentric models, which often impose normative frameworks on students (Arias-Ortega et al., 2022).

During the period 2006–2017, however, there was a noticeable increase of 69% in the number of students belonging to Indigenous peoples who enrolled in universities, according to data from the National Council of Education (Consejo Nacional de Educación, CNED) in 2017. The CASEN survey (Ministry of Social Development, 2017) also revealed a steady growth in the indigenous population accessing higher education. In 2006, it represented 16.5% of all young people aged 18–24, while in 2017 that figure increased significantly to 32.7%. During the same period, the proportion of the non-Indigenous population attending higher education rose from 28.1% in 2006 to 38.1% in 2017. To support Indigenous students with good academic performance and unfavorable economic situations, the National Corporation for Indigenous Development (CONADI) established a scholarship program in 1992 that allows them to continue in the educational system.

Many of these initiatives have, however, been criticized for their focus on economic aspects while neglecting other fundamental aspects, such as school segregation, lack of dialogue between policies, institutions and actors (Webb et al., 2017), socio-emotional dimensions, sense of belonging with universities (Arias-Ortega et al., 2022), parents' level of education, and family position upon entering university (Segovia-González & Flanagan-Bórquez, 2019), among others.

In this regard, Chilean universities face significant challenges that must be addressed. If we focus on the exact or natural sciences, there is a knowledge gap regarding the continuity of undergraduate and postgraduate studies of Indigenous students and how they choose their fields of study in these disciplines. Therefore, it is essential to understand their experiences regarding their Indigenous knowledge and their interaction with the sciences in the university environment.

Life Stories in the Trajectories of Indigenous University Students in Chile

Over the past two decades, access to university education and the attainment of academic degrees have become a reality and an aspiration for many people, associated with promises of social mobility and personal success. However, institutions of higher education, from their inception, have maintained elitist foundations hidden behind a supposed individualistic meritocracy. This, together with the capitalist and colonialist system, has perpetuated processes of exclusion and discrimination (Arias-Ortega *et al.*, 2022). In this context, access to university does not guarantee the right to an education that respects the particularities, characteristics, identities, and cultures of each individual.

This issue has been explored previously (Silva *et al.*, 2020), examining the tensions between the promises of educational inclusion in higher education and the experiences of Indigenous students in the fields of exact sciences and natural sciences. These tensions originate from Eurocentric curricula and teaching–learning approaches that are disconnected from ethnic knowledge and ultimately impact the identity of these community members. Despite these difficulties, various initiatives have emerged to try to incorporate these elements and the worldviews of Indigenous ancestors.

Therefore, understanding the experiences of Indigenous students across different levels of the educational system through their stories is of great relevance. This approach shifts the focus towards a more humanistic perspective, distancing itself from calculations and trends, to concentrate on concrete achievements and challenges faced by real people. Therefore, we present some of the narratives collected using life stories, in order to understand how doctoral students in the fields of exact and natural sciences in Chile, through a reflexive process, express their voices of reclamation in relation to their ethnic identity in institutional educational spaces.

The Voices of Ethnic Assertion from Indigenous Postgraduate Students

The research, conducted between 2017 and 2020 and funded by the National Agency for Research and Development in Chile (ANID), focused on the experiences of Chilean Indigenous students pursuing doctoral studies in scientific disciplines, exploring their life experiences from childhood to adulthood and the motivations that led them to pursue postgraduate scientific studies. In this chapter, our focus is on how their ethnic identities intertwine with scientific knowledge in the context of higher education. We explore how this interaction translates into voices of assertion directed both towards university institutions and from these institutions. Two significant aspects we will examine are (1) the role of the family in developing ethnic identity in a context of discrimination and struggle; and (2) the university and the study of exact and natural sciences as spaces where Indigenous knowledge and scientific knowledge interlace to advocate for culture, identity, and territory.

The Narratives

Most of the narratives shared by the 24 indigenous students who participated in the study indicated that they never lived in an Indigenous community. This was because their parents belonged to a generation that had migrated from rural areas to cities and, in many cases, their history and culture were not transmitted to them. In other words, their parents chose not to instill Mapuche identity in their children in order to protect them from the discrimination and racism they had experienced. For example, they did not teach them their mother tongues. However, the life stories of Indigenous students revealed an early curiosity that later turned into a compelling need to discover their ethnic origins. In this sense, many of our interviewees' grandparents decided to share their culture and knowledge with their grandchildren when they asked and requested to be taught about who they were and where they came from. Thus, the teaching they received, mainly from their grandparents, was crucial in nurturing and strengthening their ethnic identity, especially in relation to their respect for nature, balance with the environment, and appreciation of their history and culture. This act of reconnecting with the past and their roots allowed many to feel that they could co-exist with the knowledge of Mapuche culture, which influenced their decision to study science. Carolina expressed it this way:

> I feel that my origin is Mapuche, not just because of my last name but because of the love for nature, the desire to protect it, and even more, to do science to achieve it. I don't know if this is in my blood, but I am one of those people who get excited when they see a sunrise because there is a connection with the earth... Mapuche people are of the earth; I feel part of it. That's why I realized that my motivation to continue in science is to protect the environment; I think it's inside me, in my genes.

In the same vein, Francisca remembered her paternal grandfather and shared her longing to live in the countryside with him. She associated this experience with her ethnic identity because the way of life in her Mapuche community is characterized by being disconnected from technology and centered on nature. She emphasized that her grandfather and ancestors had a different appreciation for things, not driven by monetary interest but by a worldview that valued living in harmony with the environment.

Several narratives expressed criticism of excessive capitalism and a society centered on money, which has had an impact on the traditional way of life of the Mapuche, including land usurpation and exploitation, which has altered the landscape. Fabiola shared:

> During vacations, we used to walk a lot in the countryside with my grandmother. I remember that when I was younger, we used to go to a river where I used to swim, and I used to ask her about what that place was like in the past. She told me that there used to be a variety of trees there, such as mallines, boldos, arrayanes, and peumos, as well as springs that dried up with the arrival of pine and eucalyptus trees due to forest plantations. I believe that's where my identification with my ethnicity comes from and, on the other hand, with my scientific interest, in search of something that allows us to protect and restore the ecosystem.

Octavio shared how his grandmother taught him the Mapuche view of being humble with nature, of 'taking only what is needed'. He also highlighted the belief that nature is alive and, therefore, deserves respect. Gabriela recounted her close relationship with her Aymara grandfather, who played a crucial role in her upbringing by teaching her about her ethnicity, including ceremonies and beliefs. She emphasized the importance of gratitude and reciprocity in her culture and how this influenced her choice to study marine biology and pursue a doctoral program in the same field, as an act of reciprocity and respect for nature by combining scientific knowledge and ancestral wisdom to protect, conserve, and restore the natural environment.

Despite experiencing discrimination in school, including taunts related to their surnames, phenotypic traits and humble rural family backgrounds, several of the interviewees, as an act of resistance, were raised with a strong sense of pride in their indigenous identity. Javiera recalled how her mother instilled this pride in her from a young age by sharing stories of Mapuche resistance against the Spanish, highlighting both the suffering and dispossession as well as the strength and ongoing struggle to defend their customs, lands, and nature:

> I feel very happy and proud of my roots, of where I come from. I never miss an opportunity to highlight it. I feel like a rather unique person. I like being Mapuche because identifying with an ethnicity gives you characteristics. Knowing where you come from, what your origins are. For example, I know where my Antullanca surname comes from, but I can't trace my origins through my Spanish surname; besides, Mapuche history is fascinating regarding the resistance they had against the Spanish, how they

lived, and how they organized. But I also realize that we've been a very suffering people, violated many times, so I like being Mapuche because it represents a struggle; we are a fairly admirable people in that sense.

As they transitioned from childhood to adulthood, the university experience is narrated as another significant stage in the process of claiming their indigenous identity, even though several faced situations of discrimination and racism, such as Antonio, who a teacher would 'jokingly' tell: 'Don't go around burning forests'. The diversity of people, ideas and socioeconomic levels in the university allowed them to emphasize their sense of ethnic belonging. In this regard, Pablo expressed concern about the lack of Indigenous knowledge in classrooms, curricula and scientific research. He argued:

> In Chilean universities, Indigenous culture should always be present, taught, disseminated, and studied to promote the appreciation and respect for native cultures and to foster a more inclusive society aware of its diversity.

Thus, the connection between indigenous knowledge and science emerges as a conducive space for the defense of their human rights, the preservation of their cultural heritage, self-determination, social justice, and equal opportunities. In the same vein, and more critically, Gonzalo, who is Aymara, challenges universities as spaces that train professionals who reproduce extractive and exclusionary logics for indigenous communities:

> In fact, I believe that universities, in general, need to mix a bit with the real world; I think universities are selfish in that regard. They're very selfish because there are people who know everything and will teach you how to do things, but when you get to the real world, you encounter a different world, a different perspective, other people who won't like you to intervene in a totally disrespectful way; I don't know if you understand me. So, what happens... and I saw that in Arica, I saw it in Temuco, I worked in many communities, so what happens is, you arrive there, and you arrive with the thought, in the case of the Mapuches, or it doesn't even have to be ethnic [that people who have lived all their lives in a rural area and have done things the same way for years and years], so you arrive there, you get off your high horse with your big boots, and you say, 'You know what? You've got everything wrong here because they taught me in university that it should be this way, and this way it works well,' so what they've been doing for years and years [they see it as] wrong, and that's actually a lack of respect because... and I think there's a very strong issue here, first, at university, they teach you that you know [everything]; that you, with magical products, will solve a problem, ... it's not like that. You arrive at a place, and in the end, you realize that if you don't lower your head, if you don't humble yourself with them

[the peasants, the indigenous people], you won't get anywhere. So, I think sometimes it's necessary for agronomy, medicine, and other areas that don't necessarily have to be mine, to have a blend of knowledge [scientific and indigenous].

Considering universities as potential spaces for the empowerment of Indigenous communities invites us to think about a new kind of teaching, where educators – in this case – teach science with cultural and ethnic relevance. Regina's narrative, also of Aymara descent, illustrates this idea. She shared with us that when she entered university, she didn't feel very connected to her Aymara identity, but that changed when she met a teacher who helped her to reconnect with her roots and to feel proud of them, as shown in the following dialogue:

> **Regina:** Thanks to this teacher, she helped me rediscover my roots and feel proud of them, and understand that I can combine both. That I can do science within my indigenous context, and as an Aymara, I feel it's important to understand how our land or sea functions, because it's part of our community. If I had been just a regular citizen without that 'background,' it would have been harder for me to realize that. It would have been in the context of 'Oh, they are messing things up, let's just leave.' But it's something that also comes from your worldview, from a social role, of someone who realizes the harm that humans are causing to the environment.
>
> **Marta:** Indeed, it's something much deeper, so to speak.
>
> **Regina:** Yes, indeed, they are harming my mother.

This last sentence alludes to the fact that environmental damage ultimately harms her people and, therefore, her mother.

Even from the perspective of scientific knowledge, Alejandro, a member of the Mapuche ethnicity, uses the concept of co-existence as a critique of the capitalist way of life, especially in contrast to the concept of competition. From an ecological perspective, Alejandro explained that co-existence refers to when organisms avoid competition to avoid depleting available resources. This contrasts with the traditional model that posits that species organize based on competition. Rodrigo emphasizes that the co-existence and interrelationship of organisms are a millennia-old worldview of his people. He explained:

> If we look at the forest from an ecological perspective, we know that beneath it, there are interconnected networks, such as mycorrhizae, which are fungi that connect one plant to another, and through that network, they communicate, sharing food and water. Essentially, a forest resembles a supra-neural network, something that is just starting to be studied, but it is known to function this way. So, we can say that this is part of the Mapuche worldview because they view the forest and the

ecosystem as a large organism, a place where energy constantly flows and connects everything through it. It's a network that can't be seen with the naked eye. Elders used to say that there's an energy that flows among the trees, a network in the forest, and the ancients used to send messages through it, using the trees as connection points.

In this sense, the Mapuche worldview predates science and other Indigenous cultures, and they already understood nature holistically. Alejandro concluded:

It doesn't make sense to separate phenomena for study since you can't understand one element outside the whole, which is nature.

The narratives of Indigenous students in Chilean graduate science programs that we shared underscore the profound connection between cultural identity and academic pursuits. These stories reveal the critical need for universities to not only acknowledge but to actively integrate Indigenous knowledge systems into their curricula. By doing so, higher education institutions can become more inclusive spaces that respect and celebrate cultural diversity, rather than perpetuating colonial and extractive practices.

The experiences shared by students like Gonzalo, Regina and Alejandro highlight the potential of blending scientific and Indigenous worldviews, offering a path forward where education serves not only as a tool for personal advancement but also as a means of cultural preservation and environmental stewardship (Figure 10.1). As universities evolve, embracing this intercultural approach will be essential for fostering a more just and equitable academic environment – one that empowers Indigenous communities and acknowledges their invaluable contributions to both local and global knowledge systems. This shift is not merely an academic exercise: it is a necessary step towards rectifying historical injustices and ensuring that Indigenous students can thrive in spaces that honor their identities and perspectives.

Final Reflections

The narratives presented speak to us of stories of loss as well as recovery and reclamation. The voices of the Indigenous people who kindly shared their stories with us invited us to re-visit our own biographies, our losses, and our struggles as Latin American women, Amerindians, mothers and educators. Thus, the constant reflexivity to which both parties are subjected in the life-history interview allowed us to question our own Eurocentric views as we delved into the experiences narrated by others.

In accordance with our experience as researchers working with life stories of under-represented groups, we believe that active and attentive

Figure 10.1 *We Just Overlook* by Ale Garín-Fernández, science communicator, Aymara, research participant

listening creates a scenario and an atmosphere that connects us with our own life journeys. In this sense, these encounters become learning spaces for all individuals involved. Therefore, reflexivity emerges as a dimension that allows us to remain aware of our own interpretations and perspectives on what is narrated, in order to maintain a necessary balance between our own being and that of the participants. Reflexivity in the life-story interview process is a fundamental element, as it urges us to be present in both body and soul, one might say, and to constantly reflect, not only as researchers but also as women, mothers, wives, daughters, caregivers and members of our communities.

As Latin American women engaging with the voices of Indigenous students, we are acutely aware of the intersections between our identities and the lived experiences of those we study. This shared cultural and geographical context places a particular responsibility on us to approach our research with humility, empathy, and a commitment to challenging the dominant narratives that have historically marginalized Indigenous knowledge and perspectives. Our work is not just an academic exercise: it is a deeply personal and political act of solidarity with the communities we study, as we seek to amplify their voices and advocate for their rights within the academic and social spheres.

The journey of identity of Indigenous students, from a childhood and adolescence where their caregivers and family played a vital role in the initial cultivation and strengthening of their ethnic identity, to a young adulthood in which they recognize themselves as Indigenous, taught us that we must work to build universities with territorial and identity relevance through dialogue between ethnic knowledge and scientific knowledge. This dialogue could create fertile ground for Indigenous peoples to exercise their rights and preserve their cultures. The narratives presented take us into the educational trajectories of higher education students in science programs, revealing the particularities of their life stories and ancestral cultures. These stories, along with the experiences and lived realities they portray, are a powerful source of knowledge and wisdom to help promote and implement more inclusive universities.

The life stories we studied remind us that the search for our roots is ultimately an act of reclaiming our identity in different under-represented groups. In this claim, we must work to cultivate, with humility and the participation of various actors and institutions, particularly hegemonic ones like scientific institutions, an approach that is less extractive, less neoliberal, and more meaningful in knowledge for under-represented groups and communities. This process has taught us that the university, as a space for learning and academic development, must be a bastion where all voices, especially those historically marginalized, can raise their voices and actively fight for their rights. Academia must be fertile ground for transformation and the construction of a more inclusive and respectful knowledge of ethnic diversity.

As researchers, the voices we heard invited us to take on a continuous commitment to promoting justice, equality, and the preservation of the cultural richness of our Indigenous peoples, ensuring that the university is a space where everyone has the opportunity to claim their place and contribute to the social change we so desperately need. As Latin American women, our involvement in this research is not merely a professional obligation: it is a deeply rooted commitment to our own identities, histories, and the future we envision for our communities – a future where the richness of Indigenous knowledge is fully recognized and integrated into the fabric of academic life and beyond.

References

Arias-Ortega, K., Samacá, J. and Riquelme, L. (2022) Educación Universitaria en Contexto Indígena: El caso Mapuche en Chile. *Educação & Realidade* 47. Available at https://doi.org/10.1590/2175-6236120674vs01.

Council of Education (Consejo Nacional de Educación, CNED) (2017) *Indices Educación Superior.* Available at https://www.cned.cl/indices-educacion-superior.

Ministry of Social Development (Ministerio de Desarrollo Social y Familia, Observatorio Social (2017) *Encuesta de Caracterización Socioeconómica*/CASEN. Available at https://observatorio.ministeriodesarrollosocial.gob.cl/encuesta-casen-2017.

Segovia González, F. and Flanagan-Bórquez, A. (2019) Desafíos de ser un estudiante indígena de primera generación en la universidad chilena de hoy. *Revista mexicana de investigación educativa,* 24 (82), 745–764. Available at http://www.scielo.org.mx/scielo.php?script=sci_arttext&pid=S1405666620190003007 45&lng=es&tlng=s.

Silva, M., Brito, J. and Sanzana, P. (2020) Saberes tradicionales y disciplinas STEM: Repensando concepto de identidad étnica en la educación superior. *Utopía y Praxis Latinoamericana* 25 (9), 177–196. Available at https://produccioncientificaluz.org/index.php/utopia/article/view/34241.

United Nations Development Programme (2017) Desiguales. Orígenes, cambios y desafíos de la brecha social en Chile/El PNUD en Chile. Available at https://www.cl.undp.org/content/chile/es/home/library/poverty/desiguales--origenes--cambios-y-desafios-de-la-brecha-social-en-.html.

Webb, A., Canales, A. and Becerra, R. (2017) Las desigualdades invisibilizadas: Población Indígena y segregación escolar. *Propuestas para Chile,* 279–305.

11 Reflections and Actions on Linguistic Resistance in Formal and Informal Spaces as a Proposal for Decolonization in Wallmapu/Wajmapu

Carolina Kürüf Poblete, Silvia Calfuqueo and Kelly Baur

This chapter is a reflection on three unique experiences linked to the struggle to maintain and revitalize the Indigenous Mapuche culture and language. The discourses of the three authors combine elements of research, linguistic revitalization, and political activism. From both Chile and the United States, these experiences are narrated by references in orality, contextual reality and its intersection with the fields of research and theoretical frameworks that dialogue with the epistemological and philosophical perspectives of the South. These experiences include a critical analysis of anti-Mapuche discourse in Chilean mass media, the endogenous experience of language revitalization in Mapuche territory and, lastly, the embodiment of the Mapuche language through ancestral games as a meaningful pedagogy. These three experiences highlight elements of the Mapuche struggle and offer a reflective critique about the processes of linguistic revitalization in the Mapuche context.

Positionality

In a certain light, this chapter is a culmination of several years of collaboration and friendship between three rebellious women. We met through our own paths intersecting, leading us to meet each other in spaces dedicated to the fight for the revitalization of the Mapuche language: Mapuzugun. We are, perhaps, an unexpected alliance when you look superficially at our positionalities: a documentary filmmaker from the United States, a professor at the University of Santiago de Chile, and a mother raising her children within her Mapuche community in Llaguepulli. However, this grocery-list approach to positionalities does not go deep enough to address 'how every aspect of research is dynamically impacted by the durable yet impermanent social positions of those involved' (Ríos & Patel, 2023: 6). Our identities are much more than a profession and a place of birth.

In 2015 we found ourselves at the first Mapuche language-immersion summer camp, organized by the Mapuche Federation of Students. It took place in the territory of Llaguepulli, where Silvia lives with her extended family and community (or 'lof' in Mapuzugun). Carolina arrived from Santiago as a participant interested in learning her ancestral language, last spoken in her family by her great-grandmother. Kelly was invited by the organizers to document this immersive language revitalization strategy, as a documentary filmmaker already working with Mapuche communities to document their land reclamation. During the language camp, the three of us connected over our common interest in elevating women's knowledge and we began to weave a tapestry of friendship and collaboration. After several years building our relationships, we felt the urge to speak up internationally in support of the Mapuche struggle and to seek resources to continue fighting. In collaboration with Kelly's community of political organizers and academic colleagues, we organized a speaking tour in March 2023 in the United States. We drove from Portland, Oregon, to Tempe, Arizona, visiting universities, Indigenous communities, and community centers, sharing our experiences and expanding/deepening our network of support and struggle. This chapter, in part, is a summary of that journey and a time to reflect on everything we have created together so far. Our fight will continue: amulepe taiñ weichan!

Context and Background

Indigenous languages have been marginalized through historical processes of genocide, displacement and contemporary linguistic discrimination (Skutnabb-Kangas & Dunbar, 2010). From the ontological point of view, we feel/think[1] that those who exercise economic power within a system of neoliberal capitalism, particularly in Chile, have created a hegemonic monopoly and a persistent control of life and existence through the imposition of a single validated system of monocultural linguistic and social practices. In this chapter, we reflect on our personal and professional work, which we recognize as contextualized in neocolonialism, since we can identify a lack of critical reflection on the legacies of colonial life and subsequent independent life as the nation-state called Chile. One of the essential reflections that is not often made about Chile is that the language revitalization policies that began at the end of the 20th century were only needed due to the initial prohibition of the Mapuche language during the installation of the Chilean nation-state at the end of the 19th century until, at least, the middle of the 20th. Certainly, it requires more sociocultural and linguistic analysis about the consequences of this history. The nominative reparations to certain sectors of Mapuche society, as is the case of state scholarships for secondary and university studies in cases where Indigenous quality is accredited to people through government documents known as the 'certificate of indigeneity', is not enough to ameliorate the current marginalized status of the Mapuche language and culture.

We understand language as an act of communication. Ontologically speaking, it is an act of creation and constant re-creation of the human being in society; it is, 'very frequently sharing similar assumptions and sensitivities' (Echeverría, 2017: 30). The Mapuche language, Mapuzugun, is considered 'definitely endangered' by UNESCO (Moseley, 2010) and, therefore, our culture and a way of understanding human existence from the perspective of these territories (southern Chile, Mapuche territory, Wallmapu) is also in danger. On this first idea we want to motivate reflections around the questions: Where is the existence of the Mapuche language in danger? By whom and how is the existence of a culture transmitted? In this case, everything that is Mapuche? Are autonomous cultural practices a form of linguistic resistance that unmasks hegemonic languages in their monocultural plan?

There is no standardized process to revitalize an Indigenous language, which might otherwise be an expected strategy in the positioning of languages as hegemonic or otherwise compared to those dominant languages. Cultural, geographical and historical contexts determine and define strategies for language reclamation. These are all factors that inform the multitude of strategies for peoples to resist the linguicide exerted by linguistic imperialism (Phillipson, 2018). However, our strategies are subjected to practices of marginalization by arguing that they are inconsistent, and thus, diminish the value of our ancestral language and our strategies of resistance. It is therefore crucial to listen to the experiences of Mapuche language reclamation on the ground, so that we can create and re-create a diversity of tactics, while we strategize for the future in which our Indigenous languages are no longer marginalized.

All Indigenous language revitalization strategies are acts of resistance. However, in conversations with Mapuche language activists, we have come across the questioning of whether we are truly revitalizing the language or whether we are merely reacting to a state of cultural emergency, guided by the logic proposed by Ortiz (1997). Meaning that, to initiate a revitalization process, the Mapuche language requires a minimum number of constituents to make decisions on crucial issues such as a standardized writing system or pursuing official status, which implies an allocation of state funding for its development. Because these minimum actions have not been completed by the institutional structure of the state, it urges us to think that calling these processes a 'revitalization' is more of a political act than a reflection of current reality. Understanding cultural emergencies from the perspective of the philosophy of the south (Dussel, 2015), we are not only in a state of linguistic emergencies but also in a process of linguistic re-creations, from the possibilities of the monocultural structure itself. According to Naguil (2020: 140), 'we see that in this field, Mapudungun, as well as many other languages in America, is far from being able to claim to have the minimum conditions for revitalization'. For example, Mapuzugun is not recognized as an official language by the Chilean state in the regions that form Wallmapu (Mapuche territory), which means that the consequent use in all spheres of society and daily life are also lacking. These basic conditions do not exist, as we have mentioned, due to the obtuse idea of the linguistic monoculture of Spanish in all spheres of life in Chile, leaving the Mapuche language relegated to spaces of folklorism in schools. Students may learn about being Mapuche for certain holidays, anniversaries, and workshops in school, but not as a way of life. Mapuche subjects and our language are decontextualized from the daily life of teaching for Mapuzugun. The status (low or null) of the language in the curricular model of teaching in Chilean education is a clear example of the lack of political will on the part of the Chilean state.

Consequently, when Mapuche children enter Chilean public-school education, they learn exclusively from and about Chilean culture, denying all possibilities of strengthening and understanding their own living culture. This situation is exacerbated by monocultural teaching and learning processes, contents and objectives, alien to the Mapuche sociocultural and linguistic context (Quintriqueo & Mcginity, 2009).

Mapuzugun has been in constant resistance since the occupation of Wallmapu by the Chilean nation-state no more than 140 years ago. Strategic political groups and Mapuche activists in all social spheres have given presence–resistance to Mapuzugun. Despite this persistent and widespread struggle, schools, universities, and other educational spaces have heightened the cultural emergency. As Hornberger (2008) makes clear, linguistic ideologies impact revitalization efforts in schools. From the field of psychology, Myers (2006) argues that people who learn a language are capable of learning culture; along with this, he affirms that 'language determines the way we think' (2006: 409). This is why reflections and actions in diverse cultural and educational spaces are essential to allow us to move from resistance–emergency to true revitalization. But we are far from the revitalization of Indigenous pedagogies and educational sovereignty proposed by McCarty and Lee (2014).

As we have mentioned, the use of Spanish dominates the ways we have of explaining and communicating in Chilean daily and intellectual life. But it also extends to traditional Mapuche areas, where the breakdown of intergenerational transmission reaches critical levels (Wittig, 2009). According to what was exposed by Wittig (2009), the phenomenon of disuse of Mapuzugun is a fact that is increasingly affecting Mapuche communities, even reaching intra-community levels, such as the most intimate traditional spheres. For example, the disuse of Mapuzugun in ancestral ceremonies such as the ngillatun.[2] This is critical, because in the communicative sense of traditional Mapuche ceremonies there are codes of ontological and epistemological existence that are different from the hegemonic culture of the Spanish language and which are, therefore, not authentically or fully communicated in Spanish.

We are aware that colonization and post-colonization have left their mark on Mapuche families, especially in those who choose not to transmit the language because of their deep-seated fear of discrimination. The great majority of Mapuche people are affected by this reality, even though there are also many families who have opted for different strategies of language preservation. Today, it is their descendants who have taken the initiative of resistance–emergency–revitalization. It is the Mapuche youth and adults, many of them professionals, who have started a process of linguistic resistance based on concrete actions. Despite this progress, there are still 'many Mapuches who are monolingual in Spanish [who] possibly know some greetings and some vocabulary, but they cannot communicate even in a basic or elemental way with Mapuzugun' (Gundermann et al., 2011: 116). This should be one of the greatest concerns for anyone involved in the revitalization of Mapuzugun. However, to initiate revitalization processes in a monocultural, capitalist-neoliberal, patriarchal, and racist context,[3] the necessary spaces must still be ensured and protected. Because the Mapuche people have no official sovereignty or recognition as a nation, we do not have the autonomy needed to make our own decisions on the distribution of human and material resources for this process. Without our own autonomy and territory, it is not possible to allocate the necessary resources to the project of language revitalization due to the centralism[4] in which Chilean public policies are grounded.

The current Mapuche sociocultural context is diverse,[5] as are the ways of existing as Mapuche, despite our existence within the very monocultural Chilean context. However, there is a socializing element that is transversal in the life of every Mapuche person born in Chile. That is the monocultural schooling experience that synthesizes both the difficulties of existing as a Mapuche and speaking Mapuzugun into a single experience. Cassany (2008) affirms that one of the ways to achieve effective learning in school is by responding to the needs and linguistic characteristics present in the sociocultural context. This would mean that the school would be capable of, and permitted to develop, its own teaching and learning strategies. In this sense, those of us who work to revitalize Mapuzugun do so by looking for spaces of cultural significance to awaken both the need and the desire to speak Mapuzugun again, both at school and in all spheres of daily life.

According to Díaz (2017), the teaching of Mapuzugun is directly related to the social and cultural practices of Mapuche communities, which explains why, with more widespread Mapuche sociocultural practices in place, more language learning also takes place. Searching for these social and cultural practices in or through which to position Mapuzugun is a constant challenge for new generations. This is due in large part to the fact that our language does not have the necessary status and use in the public and political spheres, let alone daily life, to highlight the need for linguistic revitalization and the inclusion of Mapuzugun at all educational levels. It is an incredible challenge to fight for the existence of the Mapuche language when it is maintained in such unequal conditions compared to the hegemonic language of Spanish.

In this chapter, we will present three reflections based on our own experiences, research, and language revitalization efforts. These three experiences highlight elements of the Mapuche struggle for a reflective critique about the processes of linguistic revitalization in the Mapuche context. The three authors, through their experiences in Chile and the United States, narrate through references of orality, the contextual reality and its intersection with the fields of research and theoretical references that dialogue from the epistemological and philosophical perspectives of the south (Dussel, 2015).

Discursive Context of the Chilean Press as an Accomplice in the Criminalization of the Mapuche People

The information conveyed by the mass media is influenced by many other pre-existing contexts that are created reciprocally between different forms of human communication. Thus, Diaz (2017) points out that context is an essential element in any communicative process, affecting verbal and linguistic aspects. Mass media, such as the journalistic media of the written press and television, configure contexts that go through editorial filters that respond to a way of interpreting those contexts. In this sense, Diaz points out that 'the media transmission and dissemination of an informative event – in any of its written or audiovisual, analog or digital supports – is, first and foremost, a fact of specifically human systemic communication' (2017: 248). Understanding the systemic complexity of society, and also understanding the responsibilities of the news media, I will follow the reflective logic of Chomsky and Herman (1990: 193), to say that 'the mass media act as a system of transmission of messages and symbols for the average citizen'. Therefore, analyzing the framing or meaning given by these means of communication through the linguistic choices made when referring to the Mapuche people, provides us with the opportunity to understand the difficulties that Mapuche people face when resisting a state that maintains a centralist, monocultural policy and defines its actions based on a neoliberal capitalist economic system.

One example of the biased linguistic choices made by the Chilean press is the prevalence of the term 'Mapuche conflict' rather than 'land conflict' or 'capitalist state conflict'. While both may be possible choices to describe the same events, the preferred term of the Chilean press assigns agency to the Mapuche, which is clearly the party perceived as the aggressor in this context. The proliferation of this term, 'Mapuche conflict', is one of the many strategies of the Chilean state, by way of the press, to describe the Mapuche people as terrorists, making invisible their legitimate right as a Native people to continue living in their territory. Using critical discourse analysis and the data from a Spanish linguistic corpus, we see in Figure 11.1 how the word 'conflict' is among the most common collocations with the word 'Mapuche'. Along the same lines, the more neutral options of 'Mapuche movement', 'Mapuche cause' and 'Mapuche issue' are used less frequently than 'Mapuche conflict'.

Despite several institutional initiatives from the Chilean state, such as the creation of the National Corporation for Indigenous Development

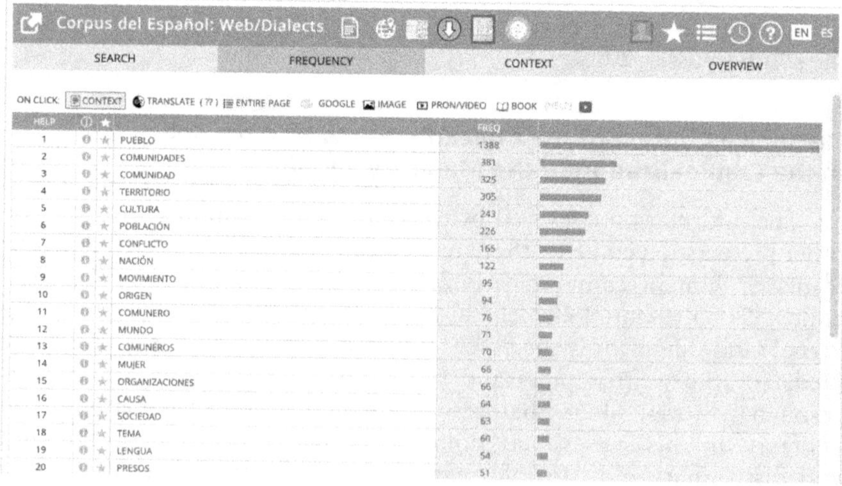
Corpus del Español: Web/Dialects

SEARCH | FREQUENCY | CONTEXT | OVERVIEW

ON CLICK: CONTEXT | TRANSLATE (??) | ENTIRE PAGE | GOOGLE | IMAGE | PRON/VIDEO | BOOK

HELP		FREQ
1	PUEBLO	1388
2	COMUNIDADES	381
3	COMUNIDAD	325
4	TERRITORIO	305
5	CULTURA	243
6	POBLACIÓN	226
7	CONFLICTO	165
8	NACIÓN	122
9	MOVIMIENTO	95
10	ORIGEN	94
11	COMUNERO	76
12	MUNDO	71
13	COMUNEROS	70
14	MUJER	66
15	ORGANIZACIONES	66
16	CAUSA	64
17	SOCIEDAD	63
18	TEMA	60
19	LENGUA	54
20	PRESOS	51

Figure 11.1 Table of Spanish Corpus data showing the top 20 most common nouns that appear immediately before or after the word Mapuche

(CONADI) in 1993 and joining the International Labor Organization's Convention 169 on Indigenous peoples' rights in 2008 (despite it being written in 1989), the greatest concern of the Chilean state continues to be the protection of national economic interests. Evidence of these economic interests taking precedence over human rights is seen through the widespread criminalization of the Mapuche struggle through the application of the anti-terrorist law. This law, created during the Pinochet dictatorship, is often discussed publicly through television media and the written press when direct actions on behalf of the Mapuche people negatively affect the forestry industry that dominates the local economy while impoverishing and degrading the lands adjacent to the Mapuche communities. Despite the Inter-American Court of Human Rights declaring Pinochet's anti-terrorist law a violation of the Mapuche people's fundamental human rights, Chile continues to implement the anti-terrorist law. This practice intensifies anti-Mapuche sentiment by conflating Mapuche resistance with terrorism. By painting the Mapuche people as terrorists, the press reinforces and justifies the state's use of the anti-terrorist law to repress and undermine the Mapuche struggle.

This configuration of the imaginary Mapuche terrorism that is generated through the language of mass communication is noteworthy because, as Van Dijk (1991: 44) points out, 'we may expect that any group or proposal that advocates weakening of white group control, and especially of political and corporate control (for example, political organization of minorities, serious forms of affirmative action or energetic measures against discrimination), will be attacked with the media's own, symbolic strategies'. Critical discourse analysis can be used to understand how the press functions as an accomplice to the Chilean state in this criminalization. Kosiner and Aruguete (2020) have also recently proposed a conceptual and thematic framework to analyze precisely this polarized description by the Chilean press of the Mapuche conflict, helping us understand why the Mapuche struggle is defined as a problem. This is also in line with a study from Del Valle (2005), which identified that the Chilean press associated Mapuche issues with conflict, intolerance and police presence.

This study focuses on the media portrayal of an emblematic case of property damage and police misconduct, known as Operation Hurricane, which took place in August and September of 2017 in the Biobío, Araucanía, and Los Ríos regions of Chile. Operation Hurricane was one of the largest arson attacks allegedly carried out by Mapuche groups known as Coordinadora Arauco-Malleco and Weichan Auka Mapu, which resulted in 29 logging trucks being burned. However, it was ultimately discovered that the police had fabricated evidence in order to frame the Mapuche groups. Despite these revelations, the media continued to implement linguistic strategies to deepen the image of the Mapuche as terrorists and their struggle as a criminal act, rather than waiting for a trial or questioning the veracity of the public declarations made by police. One of the strategies used was synechdochization (Toft, 2014), where the press categorized burning logging trucks as terrorism, which was then used as a synonym for the Mapuche struggle for liberation.

This critical discourse analysis included 64 news articles published between August 28 and September 27 from the international English-language media (3 articles), Argentine media (7 articles) and Chilean media (54 articles) to compare how the Chilean press and the international press chose to represent the Mapuche people regarding this incident. Five lexical items were analyzed, following the logic of Lazar and Lazar, who explain how

> the characterization of the Other as 'criminal' is achieved through rhetorical strategies that represent both the transgressive acts and the perverse state of mind of the transgressor: overlexicalization and enumeration of criminal acts, characterization of the victims, concretization of criminal acts, and highlighting the intentionality and perversity of the actors. (Lazar & Lazar, 2007: 49)

The case of Operation Hurricane was selected for this study due to the great impact it caused in the media, further incriminating Mapuche groups through the repetition of statements made by right-wing politicians calling the arson an 'act of terrorism' and by publishing other falsified evidence provided by the police without questioning its veracity.

The clearest example of prejudice in the Chilean press was in how the event was described. While the least biased way to describe the event might be to call it a fire or say 29 trucks were burned. The words 'fire' and 'burn' (in all their possible forms) appeared 124 times in the Chilean press. Within those 124 times, the word 'burn' was used 6 times to describe other events, including previous accusations against the Mapuche people, such as burning churches or burning people alive in their homes, thus linking this event to acts of an even more extreme character. Despite having neutral options to describe the act, the word ataque appears 85 times and the word atentado 127 times. However, there is an interesting subtlety between these two words. In English, these two words could be translated as just one word: 'attack'. However, in the *Royal Spanish Academic Dictionary*, atentado is defined as an 'aggression or serious contempt for authority or offense against a principle or order that is considered right', while ataque is defined as the 'action of attacking, rushing or undertaking an offensive'. Looking at the official definitions of these words, atentado is a more severe type of violence that is specifically against authority, which in this case would be the Chilean state.

In addition to these different definitions, the word atentado is almost always associated with terrorism at a sociocultural level. Using

	WORD	W1	W2	W1/W2	SCORE		WORD	W2	W1	W2/W1	SCORE
1	QUIMICO	1931	6	655.2	110.7	1	TERRORISTA	916	1205	0.8	4.5
2	MILITAR	3394	2	1,697.0	286.8	2	GRAVE	227	102	2.2	12.8
3	SUPUESTO	2081	0	4,162.0	703.5	3	CRIMINAL	102	57	1.9	11.0
4	POSIBLE	1479	104	14.2	2.4	4	SUICIDA	132	136	1.0	5.7
5	CARDIACO	1426	0	2,852.0	482.1	5	MAYOR	127	226	0.6	3.3
6	TERRORISTA	1205	916	1.3	0.2	6	NUEVO	110	659	0.2	1.0
7	PRESUNTO	1105	27	40.9	6.9	7	POSIBLE	104	1479	0.1	0.4

Figure 11.2 Table of Spanish Corpus data showing the top 7 most frequently appearing collocations with the words ataque and atentado

the Spanish Corpus tool (Figure 11.2), we can compare the frequency with which these word combinations of 'terrorist ataque' vs. 'terrorist atentado' appear in the media. There is a much stronger association between atentado and terrorist than between ataque and terrorist. Despite having the word ataque as an option, the Chilean press strongly preferred the word atentado. Perhaps atentado is preferred because they don't have to say 'terrorist' explicitly, due to the sociocultural conflation of the words atentado and terrorist. Thus, the press can imply terrorism without having to say it explicitly: the connection between these two words is so strong that people can finish the phrase in their own subconscious.

This is just one example of how the press uses linguistic strategies that contribute to a national anti-Mapuche narrative that ultimately functions as an unofficial collaboration with the state in its extrajudicial project to criminalize the Mapuche people. Despite the fact that in 2014 'the UN Human Rights Committee requested the reform of the [anti-terrorism] law, and the Inter-American Court of Human Rights ordered the revocation of eight sentences applied in 2003 against seven Mapuches and an activist under this legal figure' (Molina, 2014), the state, together with the press, continue to justify the application of this law against the Mapuche people through the deeply biased narrative disseminated through the mass media. The portrayal of the Mapuche people as criminal terrorists exacerbates an already hostile environment for the development and maintenance of Mapuche society. This context also affects the possibilities of revitalizing the Mapuche language, Mapuzugun. The work of maintaining and teaching Mapuzugun is a key component of Mapuche resistance and serves to combat racism and discrimination by the state. However, despite this hostile environment and limiting conditions, language revitalization continues to expand its reach through the creation of autonomous spaces and by being strategic within non-Mapuche institutions. The following experiences narrate examples of two educational projects of Mapuche women and Mapuche communities in resistance that show how important it is not only to resist but also to form their own Mapuche-centered narratives to change the discourse at the local and national level.

The Mapuzugun Language Strengthened from the Internal Context of the Mapuce Bafkehce Communities of Lake Budi[6]

Like many other Wajmapu territories, the Bafkehce territory surrounding Budi Lake has been dramatically reduced due to widespread usurpation of Mapuce territory and the people have suffered from assimilation processes imposed mainly through the arrival of religious and educational institutions. These issues have continued since the beginning of the occupation of the Araucanía Region from 1883 onwards. This is why, year after year, the loss of the Mapuzugun language has occurred. Today, our language is maintained mostly by the elderly and its use has been reduced primarily to ceremonies.

International conventions, signed by Chile, such as the ILO Convention 169 mentioned earlier, recognize the right of Indigenous peoples to have 'control over their own institutions, ways of life and economic development, and to maintain and develop their identities, languages and religions, in the framework of the States in which they live' (Art. 28, p. 57). However, Mapuce people have limited possibilities to exercise this right, given the precarious tools the state has offered us in our struggle to autonomously revitalize our language. Tired of living in a country that does not recognize the rights of the Mapuce people, the Budi territory has chosen to make its own decisions, including the revitalization of Mapuzugun and the strengthening of our cultural practices. We see this as a challenge that we engage with from our own contexts to achieve a territorial development based on values and principles from the thought and wisdom of our Mapuce way of life.

Kom Pu Lof Ñi Kimeltuwe (The School for All Communities) was born in 2006 through a process of land reclamation and toma (takeover)[7] of a school that had been run by a Catholic organization. The Llaguepulli community took charge of the school, as part of a process of cultural vindication within the territory. This powerful act, in terms of its significance for autonomy, promoted the re-design of Plans and Self-designed Programs, with an Emerging Critical Curriculum, something totally opposed to the evangelizing and hegemonic methods of the Catholic institution that had administered the school for years.

With the purpose of strengthening the Mapuce cultural identity, the mission of this educational space is

> to be the model School, which forms Mapuce and non-Mapuce children, through an Emerging-critical Curriculum Design with Mapuce identity, favoring an intellectual development with sociocultural roots, relevant to

today's society, from the solid principles of an ancient people. (Esc. Kom pu lof ñi kimeltuwe, 2016: 12–13)

The vision of the school is:

> to form children who are speakers, proud, and committed to their Mapuce cultural identity, with a high sense of community and belonging to a unique ancestral people, with solid life principles, in harmony and balance with all tangible and intangible beings. (Esc. Kom pu lof ñi kimeltuwe, 2016: 12)

This process – the recovery of the school and the implementation of strategies for the revitalization of the language through formal education – has been a constant challenge. However, it has also been a source of inspiration, which has allowed for moments of reflection and dialogue that strengthen children's self-esteem, identity and knowledge. The Kom Pu Lof School works on different strategic–pedagogical elements (described in Table 11.1), which have been allowing children, young people, and adults to feel like they are a part of a territory despite their Wajmapu being claimed legally as Chilean territory. The most significant example of this cultural shift is the active participation of our elders in conversations with school students.

The central elements implemented in this educational space are summarized in Table 11.1, which is based on key Mapuce kimvn (knowledge) concepts.

There is also another form of creative resistance in the Lake Budi community that gives children and young people from our school an opportunity to continue learning during the summers. It is called the Mapuce Ayja Rewe Budi Film and Communication School.

This initiative comes from the need to make visible and denounce the environmental conflicts that threatened our territory in 2010. Young people needed opportunities to get to know and value the places they inhabited. We did this through the generation of spaces that allowed our youth to verbalize their feelings as Mapuce, creating spaces to talk about our people from our own perspective and incorporating the Mapuzugun language to show that our territory contains knowledge and has a voice. We use the tools of documentary film and other audiovisual techniques.

The exercise of communicating in Mapuzugun about the current environmental problems in Mapuce Bafkehce territory, as well as sharing our knowledge or Mapuce kimvn, has been a door for children and young people to reconnect with being Mapuce. By listening to their own voice in their own language, they are able to speak more fluently and more securely of their territorial belonging as Bafkehce Mapuce, which strengthens their knowledge and self-esteem. This is reinforced in every instance where conversation with our elders is generated, which can later be observed in the documentaries made at the film school.

Table 11.1 Explanations based on the interpretation of the concepts in Mapuzugun

Element	Description (These descriptions try to interpret the meaning of the element as understood in Mapuzugun)
kimeltucefe	Person who shares knowledge, ways of knowing, wisdom, and experience. Mainly used to refer to our elders and traditional authorities.
kimeltuwun	Process of acquisition of teaching and learning, which the elders contribute to together with the children.
kimkantu	Learning by doing, children and young people appropriate spaces to create.
ashgejutun	Play-learning, playing leads to incredible moments for children, therefore it is an element that cannot be left out.
kimkonvn	Acquired learning: since children are part of the creation process, this component is absolutely necessary.
kim komkvley	Learning in progress: as long as we see each child with enthusiasm, we can verify that learning is happening.
kim konpuay	It will be learned: since not everything is learned immediately, there is the possibility of doing an activity again until you achieve it.
kim ajkvtuael	Knowing how to listen is a very present skill in the process of learning a language and understanding its significance. This can be seen when an adult communicates with children and they pay full attention.
kim nentual ñi rakizuam	Knowing how to express your thoughts is part of the development of self-esteem. It is necessary to strengthen self-esteem to eradicate shame.
kim ñi azumuael	Knowing how to make decisions; someone with strengthened self-esteem will not hesitate to make this component their own.

Experience has taught us that when a person is clear and sure of their origin, in addition to daily management of their language, they begin to assume greater responsibilities, collaborate actively in the space where they live, and are committed to the cause of their people from a place of deep spirituality. We have experienced that by understanding the connection between the material and immaterial world, we can better maintain a balance in our lives, thus strengthening a growing territorial identity. This identity is formed by our thoughts and knowledge, accompanied by our language that emerges with each sound that nature emits: the lake, the sea, the forest, the rain, the wind, lightning, thunder, etc. That's why we call it Mapuzugun. 'Mapu' means land and 'zugun' means language: that is, the language of the land.

When Playing Awakens the Ability to Re-create Culture and Language: The Case of the Mapuche kimün aukantun

The Mapuche culture contains knowledge and ways of knowing as deep and diverse as its existence and history of more than 13,000 years since the arrival of people from Asia through the South Pacific (Dillehay, 1990). In the Mapuche language, Mapuche wisdom and ways of knowing are known as 'kimün' and from that place emanate the explanations and meanings of our existence of life on earth, known as 'azmapu' (Loncon, 2023).

Games and playing are an essential part of being human by embodying our existence through pleasure (Maturana & Verden, 2016), which allows us to connect our culture and learn in a fluid and natural way. Like any culture, Mapuche society has developed its own games, adapted to give meaning and existence to the ways we transmit our culture. These practices are developed in childhood and accompany the Mapuche people throughout our lives. This is why it is possible to understand the Mapuche game as a pathway to understanding Mapuche kimün. As a Mapuche woman, teacher and researcher committed to the revitalization of Mapuche culture through bodily practices, this is the path I have traveled.

Mapuche society is inserted within a political structure of two nation-states: Chile and Argentina. From this zone of 'not being' an autonomous culture and society, as Fanon (2021 [1961]) would say, we have had to resist the dominant culture and maintain our language of origin in order to reveal our untold history despite the official history taught in Chilean classrooms. Being a Mapuche person in Chile today means reframing the present, observing the knowledge of the past, and reconsidering everything that hegemonic communication in Spanish implies, not only in the classroom but also in the media. We know that the ubiquitous nature of the Spanish language delays us in developing a deep understanding of our language. However, we also know that we can resist and make our language flourish through Mapuche cultural practices. There are often speculations about how to understand or how to teach Mapuche knowledge in traditional education classrooms and even in so-called intercultural classrooms. Not all classrooms have the same possibilities for language revitalization as the Kom Pu Lof School described in the previous section. Rather than following the path of Kom Pu Lof, we often fall back into accommodating the official normative structure of official bodily practices, with all that it implies, imbuing ourselves with a competitive and success-driven logic of contemporary Western sports systems. A concrete example of this is the very undervalued initiatives to incorporate ancestral sports in the school through the public policy of the ministries tasked with these issues. However, these programs lack an understanding of how to teach a Mapuche game in the complex context of the public school system (Poblete, 2021). They simply reiterate what is already taught in any school sports education: compete, discriminate, and receive trophies.

Things would look very different if we tried to respect cultural principles of teaching and the sociocultural development of Mapuche bodily practices. That is to say, to understand its historical existence, to develop Mapuche values of existence such as the 'azche',[8] to enjoy and understand the 'azmongen' from the Mapuche or azmapu philosophy, would mean Mapuche games would also be taught by incorporating these elements. These Mapuche cultural aspects correspond to the action of teaching or 'kimeltuwün', developed by Mapuche families and mostly carried out by our elders. This reality is greatly diminished because the formal school setting has become the primary teaching benchmark for Mapuche children, thus forgetting the important work of our elders and vice versa in terms of transmitting the culture and language to the next generations. How we teach Mapuzugun has been a key component to generating language and cultural revitalization processes. This is how learning to play games through Mapuzugun becomes a component of linguistic and cultural revitalization that pushes us to work through actions of kimeltuwün. Figure 11.3 shows six aspects of kimeltuwün that were developed to teach six Mapuche games in rural schools in the Araucanía region of Chile. The logic of its foundation consists of what is framed in the circle of progression in the image.

Mapuche 'aukantun' or games, should be taught using the logic of kimeltuwün; only in this way could the transmission of Mapuche kimün or Mapuche wisdom and ways of knowing be promoted, including our language as well. This logic is not exclusive to the Mapuche people; it is a logic that contributes to the understanding of our environmental context and biodiversity in all its possible manifestations. Thus, a sociocultural impact is generated that is significant enough to develop lifelong lessons that show us that not only can cultures of different people (Chilean, Mapuche or others) co-exist, but also that the diversity of all living beings can be respected. For a culture so ancient and rich in knowledge to contribute to newer cultures and society in general, it must continue

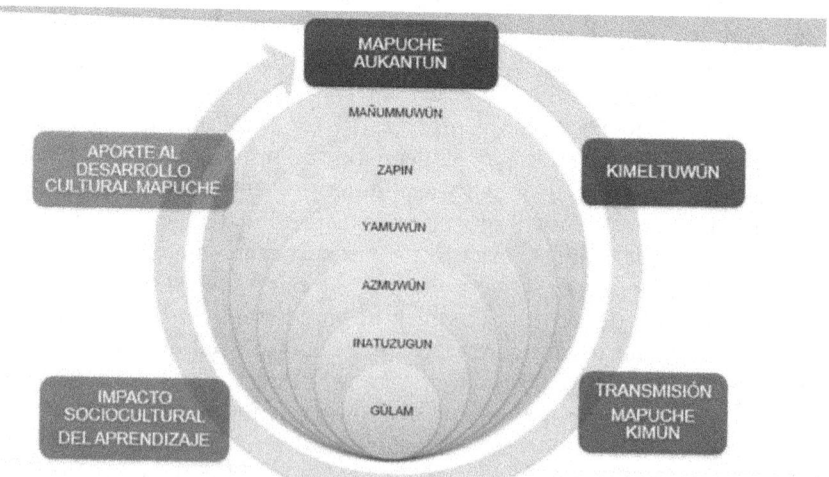

Figure 11.3 Contributions of kimeltuwün for Mapuche cultural development through the learning of aukantun. Research carried out in 2017 with the contribution of FONDART (National Fund for Arts and Culture in Chile)

to develop in such a way that spaces of resistance are transformed every day into spaces of revitalization and interculturality, no longer simply 'functional' as Walsh would say (2009) but an interculturality where cultures can be strengthened without vilifying the other.

To exemplify the scope of kimeltuwün, I will present the meaning of the concepts used in the research and described in Figure 11.3. 'Gülam' is a counseling protocol which corresponds to the action of giving advice but that implies both learning to listen to advice and to give it. 'Inatuzugun' is about learning to know your origin, your history, and that of your community, to strengthen your identity. 'Azümuwün' recognizes the characteristics and diversity in all spheres of life. 'Yamuwün' means learning to respect people, especially our elders. 'Zapin' is the act of walking carefully and knowing how to take care of yourself. And finally, 'mañummuwün' is learning to be grateful and to give thanks for our existence and everything that makes up our lives.

Collective Conclusions and Reflections

At the beginning of writing this triad of intertwined experiences, we set out to reflect on three questions that motivated the reading of this chapter from a critical and sentimental perspective based on the stories analyzed from our work, which we carry out from different platforms in favor of the revitalization of Mapuzugun.

Where does this 'endangered' language circulate? Mapuzugun continues to circulate in various spheres of Mapuche life, but mainly in the spaces of resistance and feeling–thinking consciousness that address the explanatory importance of being Mapuche in current times. Thus, despite the hegemony of the Spanish language in the mainstream media that tries to paint a one-dimensional and homogeneous image of the Mapuche as a conflictive people and even as terrorists, spaces for self-education based on Mapuche ancestral wisdom continue to arise to instill in our youth an understanding of how to be a Mapuche person. Additionally, we see institutional spaces that are reinvented to communicate the Mapuche way of learning and our values that have determined our existence throughout different periods of history. Therefore, we could say that the Mapuche language circulates among tensions and dispositions, which try, on the one hand, to resist the linguistic monoculture in order to continue existing and, on the other hand, to cling to the idea that everything that is Mapuche is a conflict for the Chilean nation-state and, thus, needs to be analyzed.

A second question was, by whom and how is the existence of a culture transmitted? For those who maintain the idea that Chile should be monocultural and monolingual, the press is their best ally. Through the mass media, they are teaching Chileans to fear the mere existence of the Mapuche people. On the other hand, Mapuche people, who are aware of the importance of cultural transmission through language, create and re-create in formal and non-formal spaces, opportunities to learn Mapuzugun through an essential principle that is kimeltuwün.

And finally, do these autonomous cultural practices serve as a form of resistance for the language, unmasking hegemonic languages in their monocultural plan? Undoubtedly, the Mapuche spaces of resistance, creation and re-creation are seen as conflictive spaces for those who do not understand the value of true interculturality. We think that, in the case of Mapuzugun in Chile, there are still historical–cultural wounds that have not healed and therefore create and maintain barriers to the intercultural circulation necessary for the Spanish and Mapuche languages to co-exist. However, we believe that the path of involving Mapuche and non-Mapuche people in learning Mapuzugun is a necessary path to heal wounds and move towards a soulful understanding of Mapuzugun and Mapuche history in these territories.

Notes

(1) The feel/thinking (*sentipensar*) in words and reflections of Eduardo Galeano is the act of feeling and regret in an indissoluble and necessary way for the critical reflection of sociocultural processes of the truth. For more details see: https://youtu.be/wUGVz8wATls
(2) Ngillatun: Mapuche ceremony of gratitude and request to the energies of the territory from their own feyentun (spirituality/beliefs).
(3) For more context of Chile and its racist gaze, see *Palabra Pública* 9, 2018, Universidad de Chile (uchile.cl).
(4) Chile has a hierarchical and centralist administrative policy. The decisions about and distributions of the country's resources are made in the capital, Santiago, as well as major political authorizations and decisions.
(5) Being a Mapuche in Chile today implies knowing and understanding the sociocultural reality in which families have developed, whether in the countryside or the city, and where, from this, the Mapuche identity has been transformed and updated like any living culture.
(6) We wish to highlight for the reader that the spelling of Mapuzugun words in this section follows the Raguileo writing system. This is a political act of linguistic diversity, which is why we have chosen to respect the norms of the community in which the author lives. Mapuzugun has no official spelling system but, rather, multiple proposals for writing systems. For more information about the spelling systems, see Álvarez-Santullano Busch *et al.* (2015).
(7) The act of reclamation (recuperación) refers to the historical possession of the Bafkehce territory of the Budi Lake Region, and the action of takeover (toma) refers to the realization of that recovery based on the pressure to request the devolution of the school to the communities of the Budi communities for its administration, effectively returning the school to the community from the Catholic Church, who were the previous administrators.
(8) Azche: aspirational characteristics of the Mapuche to truly become a person. This contemplates being Nor che (correct and consistent person), Küme che (person who works in a good, sincere and responsible manner), Kim che (person who cultivates wisdom, is instructed and communicates wisdom/knowledges) and Newen che (person who is strong, proactive, and enthusiastic with energy).

References

Álvarez-Santullano Busch, Forno Sparosvich, A. and Risco del Valle, E. (2015) Propuestas de grafemarios para la lengua mapuche: Desde los fonemas a las representaciones político-identitarias. *Alpha* 40, 113–130.

Cassany, D., Luna, M. and Sanz, G. (1994) *Enseñar lengua*. Grao.

Del Valle, C. (2005) Interculturalidad e intraculturalidad en el discurso de la prensa: cobertura y tratamiento del discurso de las fuentes en el 'conflicto indígena mapuche' desde el discurso político. *Revista de Estudios para el Desarrollo Social de la Comunicación* 2, 83–111.

Diaz, Y. (2017) Los medios de comunicación masiva: una lengua nueva. *Cuadernos de Información y Comunicación* 22, 247–258.

Dillehay, Tom (1990) El Formativo del Extremo Sur de Chile. *Gaceta Arqueológica Andina* 17, 101–114.

Dussel, E. (2015) Descolonizacion, Y & Transmodernidad. *Filosofia Del Sur Descolonización y Transmodernidad*.

Echeverría, R. (2017) *Ontología del Lenguaje*. Ediciones Granica.

Esc. Kom pu lof ñi kimeltuwe (2016) *Proyecto Educativo Institucional* (pp. 12–13). Available at https://wwwfs.mineduc.cl/Archivos/infoescuelas/documentos/6443/ProyectoEducativo6443.pdf.

Fanon, F. (2021) *The Wretched of the Earth* (trans. R. Philcox; 60th anniversary edition). Grove Press.

Gomez, V.N. (2020) Lengua y territorio: relación estratégica para la revitalización del mapuzugun. *Caracol* 20, 134–165. https://www.revistas.usp.br/caracol/article/view/173722.

Gundermann H., Canihuan J., Clavería A. and Faúndez, C. (2011) El mapuzugun, una lengua en retroceso. *Atenea* 503, 111–131.

Herman, E.S. and Chomsky, N. (2002) *Manufacturing Consent: The Political Economy of the Mass Media*. Pantheon Books.

Hornberger, N.H. (2008) Introduction: Can schools save Indigenous languages? Policy and practice on four continents. In N.H. Hornberger (ed.) *Can Schools Save Indigenous Languages?* Palgrave Macmillan. https://doi.org/10.1057/9780230582491_1.

International Labor Organization (1989) *C169 – Indigenous and Tribal Peoples Convention, 1989*. Available at https://www.ilo.org/dyn/normlex/en/f?p=NORMLEXPUB:12100:0::NO::P12100_ILO_CODE:C169.

Kosiner, N. and Aruguete, N. (2020) El conflicto mapuche en la prensa chilena. anotaciones teórico-metodológicas para el análisis de los encuadres mediáticos. *Perspectivas de la Comunicación* 13 (1), 203–217.

Lazar, M.M. and Lazar, A. (2007) Enforcing justice, justifying force: America's justification of violence in the New World Order. In A. Hodges and C. Nilep (eds) *Discourse, War and Terrorism* (pp. 46–65). John Benjamins.

Loncon, E. (2023) *Azmapu: Aportes de la filosofía mapuche para el cuidado del Lof y la Madre Tierra*. Editorial Ariel.

Maturana, M. and Verden, G. (2016) *Amor y Juego: Fundamentos Olvidados de lo Humano*. Editorial JC, Saez.

McCarty, T.L. and Lee, T.S. (2014) Critical Culturally Sustaining/Revitalizing Pedagogy and Indigenous Education Sovereignty. *Harvard Educational Review* 84 (1), 101–124. https://doi.org/10.17763/haer.84.1.q83746nl5pj34216.

Molina, P. (2014, August 1) Los Problemas de Chile y su ley antiterrorista. BBC News. Available at https://www.bbc.com/mundo/noticias/2014/08/140801_chile_ley_antiterrorista_nc.

Moseley, C. (2010) *The UNESCO Atlas of the World's Languages in Danger*. UNESCO.

Myers, D.G. (2006) *Psicología Social* (7th edn). McGraw-Hill Interamericana.

Naqill Gomez, V. (2020) Lengua y territorio: relación estratégica para la revitalización del mapuzugun, Caracol (São Paulo, Brazil), 20, 134–164.

Ortiz, R. (1997) *Mundialización y cultura*. Alianza.
Phillipson, R. (2018) Linguistic imperialism. In C.A. Chapelle (ed.) *The Encyclopedia of Applied Linguistics*. Wiley. https://doi.org/10.1002/9781405198431.
Poblete, C. (2021) El Palin mapuche como práctica corporal enseñable en la educación física chilena: Reflexiones para un pensamiento crítico en educación [The Mapuche Palin as a teachable bodily practice in Chilean physical education: Rreflections for critical thinking in education]. Ágora para la Educación Física y el Deporte 23, 218–240.
Quintriqueo, S. and Mcginity, M. (2009) Implicancias de un modelo curricular monocultural en la construcción de la identidad sociocultural de alumnos/as mapuches de la IX región de la Araucanía, Chile. *Estudios Pedagógicos* 35 (2), 173–188.
Ríos, C. de los and Patel, L. (2023) Positions, positionality, and relationality in educational research. *International Journal of Qualitative Studies in Education* 1–12. https://doi.org/10.1080/09518398.2023.2268036.
Skutnabb-Kangas, T. and Dunbar, R. (2010) Indigenous Children's Education as Linguistic Genocide and a Crime Against Humanity? A Global View. *Resource Centre for the Rights of Indigenous Peoples*. https://doi.org/https://www.researchgate.net/publication/278033737_Indigenous_Children's_Education_as_Linguistic_Genocide_and_a_Crime_Against_Humanity_A_Global_View.
Toft, A. (2014) Contesting the deviant other: Discursive strategies for the production of homeless subjectivities. *Discourse & Society* 25 (6), 783–809. http://www.jstor.org/stable/24441567.
Van Dijk, T. (1991) *Racism and the Press*. Routledge.
Walsh, C. (2009) Interculturalidad Crítica y educación intercultural. Ponencia presentada en Seminario Interculturalidad y Educación Intercultural, La Paz: Instituto Internacional de Integración del Convenio Andrés Bello. https://sermixe.org/wp-content/uploads/2020/08/Lectura10.pdf (accessed March. 2025).
Wittig, F. (2009) Desplazamiento y vigencia del Mapudungún en Chile: Un análisis desde el discurso reflexivo de los hablantes. *Revista de Lingüística Teórica y Aplicada* 47 (2), 135–155.

Poem: Kuú teku/Ser de colores/Being of Colors

Author: Celerina Patricia Sánchez Santiago
Language: Tu'un ñuu savi (Mixtec)
From: San Juan Mixtepec, Distrito de Santiago Juxtlahuaca, Oaxaca, México
English Translation: by Lori DiPrete Brown

kuú teku

níí kuí kuâ'á
rii nika'í naáyu tsi nuni kuâ'á
raa kue ikiche'é
nikutsi ñaáyu tsi nuni yàà

kue ixixini tsi kue nduchinuú
nika'í ñaayu tsi nuni ncháí

raa ɨɨn
kuí sa'ma ñaá ndakasí naá nûú tsi nuni kuàán
ñaá ndaka'í nditu'uso mee
raa nikutsíayu vìì nchuaso
tono se'e si'i xínàá ñu'ún

Being of Colors

I am part of the earth, made of the colors of corn.

my blood is red
dyed from *nuni* corn that was red
my bones
were sculpted from *nuni* with each kernel white

my hair and eyes of black
were dyed from *nuni* of black

my skin
was blanketed with *nuni* of yellow
every part of me was painted this way
I was sculpted with such fineness
as if I were the ruling daughter of all the earth

Epilogue

Julieta Briseño-Roa, Paulina Griñó,
Vanessa Anthony-Stevens and José Antonio Flores Farfán

To close this book, we would like to revisit some of the reflections resonating from the process. In our role as editors, we recognize we have gained considerable insight from our diverse collaborators. At its core, this book aims to contribute to the critical questioning of academia and knowledge, and to propose actionable ways to build an anti-colonial academy that listens to diverse voices. Spaces for Indigenous people, their epistemologies, ontologies, experiences and their situated knowledges must be considered essential to academic endeavors. We believe this to be vital for Indigenous and global futurity. A turn toward embracing multiple epistemologies is critical for planetary well-being. As we prepare to close our time in intimate relationships with the people, places, and languages shared across so many pages, we note a few insights We note a few valuable insigths to take with us.

One significant insight we continue to contemplate from this process relates to the tension between different time- and sociocultural frames. Colonial efficiency-driven academia dictates a rapid pace for knowledge production, often with the goal of maximizing efficiency and productivity within a constrained timeline, praising individualism and individual expertise. This model of academic productivity faces significant critique from various decolonial, Indigenous, feminist, ableist and other critical perspectives. It is from these critiques and alternative viewpoints that this book in fact was shaped. Different ways of conceiving time, or different formats appropriate for representing an important idea, are at times incommensurable.

Writing text for academic publication across diverse time- and sociocultural frames is challenging. Asking those on the frontlines of Indigenous community education to contribute written pieces about their experiences and theories of change adds a layer of constraint to already busy lives. Each author involved in this project juggles professional responsibilities with community engagements, caregiving, family obligations, and numerous other daily activities. For many, being one of few knowledge keepers or a leader of a community-based movement demands accountability to the community beyond oneself.

This is very different from a standardized institutional work week. As editors, we choose to navigate and negotiate deadlines, schedule in-person, phone, and videoconference progress updates, and hold collective meetings to support authors in the development of their chapters. Though we engaged in this process with care, we did not overcome the tensions between the rigid timelines standardized by academia and the contextually different dependent schedules of the authors. We tried to the best of our abilities to live and work within those tensions.

To engage in a decolonial practice means acknowledging diverse temporalities and making intentional decisions to validate, even privilege, sociocultural frames marginalized by coloniality. It requires us to rethink traditional academic structures and timelines that may not align with or respect the varied rhythms of different contributors. Recognizing and valuing other-than-colonial timeframes is essential for creating a space where multiple epistemologies can exist and thrive. By doing so, we purposefully seek to undo the power relations of the colonial episteme so ingrained in our academic expectations and institutions. Indigenous sociocultural timeframes challenge anthropocentric and decontextualized norms of the nation-state. Accountability to seasonal change and ceremonial cycles constitutes a lived time in relationship with the land, including past and future relations. The practices of reclamation beautifully narrated across each chapter live in relationship with being primary providers for families and sustaining food, shelter, and safety in communal settings constrained by centuries of capitalist interests. The legacy of settler oppression over Indigenous lands and peoples in the Americas translates to contexts where most authors persist to breathe life into their language reclamation work, pervading the constrictions of colonial capitalism. Attending the production of a book within diversities and inequities reinforces our commitment to creating an anti-colonial academic practice that challenges existing power structures and builds new frameworks that are more inclusive, responsive and representative of diverse voices and experiences.

As a second insight, we started from the understanding that language functions as cognitive territories and as a means of collective and counter-hegemonic reclamation. Thus, even when the editorial language of the proposal is English, it was essential to create spaces for minoritized languages within the book. Living with these tensions was also not easy. How could we propose a book in English while also endeavoring to ensure that other languages were heard? As a small but intentional practice, the book includes paragraphs in Indigenous languages without translation, proposing a multilingual space of many voices. We acknowledge that this approach is not sufficient on its own of course, and we would have to imagine new paths for linguistic vindication, such as elevating oral means of communication and creating innovative academic spaces in the digital era.

We realized that we still have a long way to go, too. Linguistic and territorial community claims continue to face barriers that, despite our efforts, remain challenging. In a globally connected planet, listening through the experiences of this book has made it clear that while we have made strides, ongoing work is needed to address decolonial issues more effectively and to work toward inclusive spaces for diverse languages and knowledge systems. To ensure diversity, these spaces of multilingualism and local knowledge production may indeed need to be conceptualized simultaneously, rather than all in one. Respect for local histories, local representation, and multiple perspectives makes space for multicentric knowledge: that is, the full acknowledgement that there are multiple perspectives, multiple manifestations of well-being, and multiple histories that influence our contemporary experiences. Multicentricity allows us to reject the pervasive universality of a single way of knowing or speaking, to make space for local experiences and diversities to have a seat in the teaching and learning circle (Anthony-Stevens & Liou, 2023).

Crises – such as the ones we are living on a global scale – unravel the potential of 'hidden' territorial and linguistic knowledge systems that still prevail, despite systematic oppressive constraints such as school system timeframes nationally driven by a monolingual curriculum. For instance, as Damian (Chapter 5) reminds us, due to forced confinement during the pandemic, the Ngigua's own educational systems re-surfaced to treat COVID-19. These Indigenous knowledges are inextricably linked to the earth and associated with local plants management in their sociocultural environment. Interrogating cartographic representations of author locations while envisioning a map to locate peoples' territories as defined by local community members themselves is another eloquent illustration of the need to decenter and deconstruct universalist colonial heritages. Together with self-naming the locations and communities in the authors' own terms, blurring and erasing imposed borders became an important practice during the process of making this book. Further, grappling with the limitations imposed by writing this book in English, or even Spanish, despite the rich linguistic diversity living beyond the written and academic words and worlds, demanded the enactment of sensitivity and relationships of trust to honor the integrity of epistemologies and ontologies uncontainable in the colonial tongues.

Our extended reflection re-surfaces the critical calls with which we opened this volume: that is, to transform the colonial gaze, it is important to engage with deeper criticism regarding received normalized neocolonial academia, criticism that when appropriated and developed by present and next generations of students will hopefully allow scholars to reject mainstream neocolonial structures that sustain epistemic violence and racism. Powerful hegemonic ideologies should be dismantled, such as common predominant trends in language documentation, which constitute disciplinary, privileged comfort zones, at least implicitly denying speakers agency to reclaim and revitalize their Indigenous languages on their own terms. Indigenous language documentation has long been molded by the colonizing Christian salvation narrative. Whether a goal or the effect, anthropological and documentary linguistics 'preserve' or 'save' minoritized languages for the sake of the advancement of (linguistic) science, what has even been labeled 'salvage linguistics', which constitutes an ideology entailing subtle forms of what has been called 'covert racism' (Kroskity, 2021). We are witness to too many narratives where the anthropologist is credited with creating an 'ethnography of speaking', also a stand-in metaphor for 'saving' a language (Perley, 2012).

Such ideologies imply a systemic conception of homogeneous, ideal languages, which can be detached from their communities of speakers, objectifying and commodifying tongues and their semiotic knowledge systems, so-called 'natural' languages, or 'material culture', away from peoples' own epistemologies, including their so-called cultural 'artifacts', 'crafts', 'garments', and the like, to be exhibited in a museum or held in an archive, no matter how 'digital' or 'sustainable' it is. The disembodiment of language from people, land, water, other-than-human relations, is quintessential to colonial dispossession. While authors described and reflected ways they breathe life back into their heritage languages, the statement 'We are our languages' came into clear relief as an anecdote to neoliberal language documentation. The words of First Nations linguistic anthropologist Bernard Perly (2012: 134), resonated: 'the confusion between the living language and the documentary artifacts has misplaced expert attention on the language as a code rather than language as the conduit and catalyst for social relationships'. Reviewing each chapter of this book brought to mind the power of re-connecting people, language, lands and waters.

Academic programs that reproduce covertly racist ideologies and practices are unfortunately far from being memories, and some are highly sophisticated in the ways they indoctrinate and coerce their students in such ideologies, instilling in them ideas such as the 'real' – of course monolingual – 'one and only way', of practicing linguistics or anthropology. Along the alluded lines in which not only Indigenous languages do not belong to their speakers but are, rather, submitted to normalized biases such as the 'correct', 'pure', even 'legitimate', language, such ideologies function as 'natural' ways of social control and exclusion. Such practices even instill forms of inverse racism, favoring individualism over communitarianism.

Reproducing similar long-standing ideologies perpetuates psycho-social traumas and stigmas defined by the colonial gaze, which, after all, constitute the institutional politics of representation. Even when extremely powerful resources, the colonial gaze is still interrupted and contested within the hegemonic educational system itself by members of the communities themselves. As seen across the chapters, appropriating the diverse tools of linguistics or anthropology can constitute powerful means for emancipation; likewise sustaining and revitalizing local knowledges and their accompanying tools does the same.

The Pathways that Have Been Revealed for Us to Follow in this Collaborative Journey

In a return to the concept of Indigenous language reclamation (Leonard, 2017), we ask ourselves what does it mean to be in good relationship with efforts of Indigenous communities to claim, enact, and expand their rights to speak and live in their languages holistically? As partners, collaborators, and allies to reclamation, we acknowledge that our roles, too, are never independent of the environment in which speakers live. Much of the reclamation work offered in this volume articulates the importance of 'non-linguistic' forms of community knowledge transmission and meaning-making, in place, with humans and other-than-humans, and across generations. As collaborators in Indigenous-led reclamation work, it was (and is) essential for us to remain humble and to be guided by situated spaces of diverse linguistic and sociocultural contexts that were not often our own.

Finally, our approach involved acknowledging the importance of allowing authors to present their own perspectives on their own cultural, cognitive, and physical territories, rather than imposing an external, one-sided viewpoint. This approach aligns with the principles of decoloniality, which emphasize the importance of local knowledge and self-representation. However, rethinking and reflecting on these territorial issues is complex and challenging. It is not merely an academic exercise: it is also a necessary and ongoing task that requires sustained effort and engagement beyond publishing an isolated academic book. We recognize that there are still many gaps for further development: outstandingly, the need to recast the profound meanings and diverse conceptualizations encapsulated in languages themselves, reclaiming their own cognitive processes. The task of addressing these issues is ongoing, and we are committed to continuing this work to deepen our understanding and to foster more inclusive and representative discussions collectively. We aim to build on the reflections from diverse territorial positions and ensure that future efforts address concerns of localisms and multicentricity more comprehensively. And yet, we hope that this book will inspire others – as it has inspired us – to continue rethinking ways of actively decolonizing academia, becoming much more open to other ways of speaking, thinking and doing, from which we have so much to learn.

Acknowledgements

We are profoundly grateful to all those who accepted our invitation and engaged in this collaborative process over the past two years. Their contributions to the texts, along with the support from those who assisted with translations from Spanish to English, have been invaluable: Eulalia Gallegos Buitron, Miguel Cervantes Aguilar, Pamela Velázquez Camacho Velázquez, Kelly Strachan, Ernesto Colín and Leah Reicheck. We also extend our sincere thanks to Elizabeth Sumida Huaman for her thoughtful and impactful words that provide a meaningful framing for this book.

References

Anthony-Stevens, V. and Liou, D.D. (2023) Covid and the liberatory potentials of local knowledge: Disrupting school expectations for knowledge production. *The Forum of American Journal of Education*. Available at https://www.ajeforum.com/covid-and-the-liberatory-potentials-of-local-knowledge-disrupting-schoolexpectations-for-knowledge-production-by-vanessa-anthony-stevens-and-daniel-d-liou/.

Kroskity, P. (2021) Covert linguistic racisms and the (re-)production of white supremacy. *Linguistic Anthropology* 31 (1), 180–193.

Leonard, W.Y. (2017) Producing language reclamation by decolonising 'language'. *Language Documentation and Description 14*. (Special Issue on Reclaiming Languages) https://doi.org/10.25894/ldd146.

Perley, B.C. (2012, July) Zombie linguistics: Experts, endangered languages and the curse of undead voices. *Anthropological Forum* 22 (2), 133–149.

Index

Note: *f* denotes an in-text figure

ableism 197
Abya Yala 11; colonization and 11–12
academics and the academy 1, 9, 38, 48, 109, 113, 130, 152, 174, 197, 201–202; bias, cultural 129; colonialism and 2, 128, 197–98; Eurocentric ideologies and 144, 152; extractive/exploitative practices and 39, 45, 48, 157, 173–74; hegemony and 12, 17; Mesoamerican studies and 129; neocolonialism and 199; racism and 200; resources, distribution of 48–49; spirituality and 130; *see also* Anawakalmekak; Autonomous Communal University of Oaxaca (UACO); decolonization; education, higher
Acatlan 128, 132
activism 8–9, 24; meaning of term 25; *see also* climate change and crisis, global; communities; language activism; teachers
adaptation xviii, 7, 17
addiction and substance abuse 16, 143–44; *see also* San Carlos Apache Reservation
aggression 60
Aguilar, Marcos 130–33, 136
AILDI *see* American Indian Language Development Institute (AILDI)
AIUPNA *see* Anawakalmekak
Alaska 38–39, 46, 48; Barrow 49n2; Brevig Mission 40; Diomede Islands 40, 42; Eagle River 40; King Island 40; Kotzebue 49n2; Native languages in 38; Native peoples and 39–40, 49n3; non-Native peoples and 39, 41; Point Hope 49n2; Rocky Point 40; Seward Peninsula 39–40, 45–47; Shishmaref 40; Teller 40; *see also* Wales (Kingigin)

Alaska Native Language Center 49n1
Aleut 40
American Indian Language Development Institute (AILDI) 24
Americas 10–11, 40, 198; *see also* Abya Yala
amnesia, colonial 27
Anahuac 136
Anahuacalmecac International University Preparatory of North America (AIUPNA) *see* Anawakalmekak
Anawakalmekak 124–27, 127*f*, 128–36; Cantares Project at 126–36; character of 126; Chicomecoatl Icuic, study of 131; collaboration at 129; corn-planting project at 132; decolonization and 136; graduation expectations at 126–27; guiding documents of 127–28; IndigeNations program at 126; as International Baccalaureate (IB) World School 126; Mexican communities, collaboration with 126–28, 133; music at 129, 131–36; Nahuatl teaching at 126, 128; text-painting at 132; trilingual nature of 125; xinachtli (seed), metaphor for 126; *see also* Xinachcalco Center
ancestry, Indigenous xviii, 3, 38, 40
Anchorage 39, 47
Andes xvii–xviii
ANID *see* National Agency for Research and Development in Chile (ANID)
animals xvii, 31, 96–97, 110, 119, 124, 133, 139, 148, 164; biodiversity and 190; birds 110, 119; dló łitsogé 150; elk 153; insects 110; lions 133; lizards 102; muskrats 159; mussels 154; quails 148; salmon 159; snakes 120, 145–46; texcal 89; turtle doves 133; wolf-dogs 156*f*; wolves 159
Aotearoa 136
Anthony-Stevens, Vanessa xx, 2, 13

203

anthropocentrism 11, 153, 198
anthropology 11–12, 33, 78, 94, 101, 200–201; extractivist anthropology 11
anticolonialism 37
Apache 2, 6, 30–31, 143–47; coming-of-age ceremonies and 28; culture and 145–51; epistemology and 143; European definitions of 143–44; federally recognized tribes and 144; góshdii 148; gozhooné 16, 144–45, 147; hunting and 28; knowledge and 146, 148; KYAY radio station and 150; love and 147; methodology and 146; Na'i'ess ceremony and 144; n'daa 16, 143–45, 147; Ndee 16, 144; Ndee Bini Bidaa Ilzaah (pictures of Apache Land) project 26, 33; as Nnee 6, 16, 143–45; ontology and 143–45, 150, 151n2; shiatii shiloozho and 151; shiwohe shiłi'oozhé (phrase) 146–47; Spanish rule and 143; spirituality and 147; Sunrise Dance 25; Western Apache 65; White Mountain Apache 13, 25, 28; youth and 16; see also Apache language; Apache Youth Mentorship (AYM); pedagogy; San Carlos Apache; San Carlos Apache Reservation; women
Apache language 25–26, 29, 31, 34, 36, 145–51; teaching of 29–31, 33–35, 146–48; translation of 145; verbs and 33, 146
Apache Youth Mentorship (AYM) 16, 144–49, 149f, 150–51; lessons and teaching at 146–49; San Carlos Wellness Center and 144; Substance Abuse and Mental Health Services Administration Native Connections Grant and 144; see also Lorenzo, Louie; San Carlos Apache Reservation
APPO see Popular Assembly of the Peoples of Oaxaca (APPO)
Apu xvii, xxin3
Aragón, Erika Candelaria Hernández 14, 81
Archibald, Jo-ann 53
Arica 170
Arizona 24–26, 34, 177
Armstrong, Skip 159
arts 7, 12, 15, 96; see also dance; language reclamation; music; songs; stories; storytelling
assimilation 11–12, 64, 113, 144; see also San Carlos Apache Reservation
Atuk, Jane 48

Atuk, Richard xix, 13, 38–49; biography of 40
autobiography 8
Autonomous Communal University of Oaxaca (UACO) 14, 75, 77, 79–84; autonomy and 84; Community Learning Units and 81; Communal University Assembly and 82; Community University Centers and 81; governance of 81, 84; Organic Law and 83
autonomy 11, 14, 73, 81, 83–85, 106, 125–26, 145, 186; as communal principle 83–84; decision making and 180; individual 145; language 126; pedagogical 84; political 84 schools and 125; see also Autonomous Communal University of Oaxaca (UACO)
axiology, Indigenous 57, 60, 63; trust and 57; see also law, Indigenous
AYM see Apache Youth Mentorship (AYM)
Aymara xviii, 169–71, 172f
Ayuuk 80
Aztecs 92, 126; see also Mexica

Basso, Keith: Wisdom Sits in Places (1996) 33
Baur, Kelly 17, 177
Benito Juárez Autonomous University of Oaxaca 80; Master's degree in Communal Education at 80–81
Bering Straits School District 44
Berlin–Kay color theory 146
bilingualism 93, 98, 113, 131; see also education, elementary
biolinguistics 5, 9
biology 94
boarding schools, list of: Carlisle Indian Industrial School (Carlisle, Pennsylvania) 53; Catholic Mission School (Slickpoo Mission, Culdesac, Idaho) 53; Chemawa Boarding School (Oregon; Forest Grove Indian Boarding School) 53; Chilocco Indian Industrial School (Newkirk, Oklahoma) 53; Spalding Indian Boarding School (Spalding, Idaho) 53
Borrows, John 60
Bowdler, Thomas 54
Bowhead whales 42
Brayboy, Bryan M.J. 153
Briseño-Roa, Julieta 2
British Columbia 51

Budi Lake 186–87; Mapuce Ayja Rewe Budi Film and Communication School and 187
Burns, Ashley 26
Burns, Jennie xx, 26, 28–32, 35–37; biography of 26–27; children of 26–29; Cumusi story and 32; language education and 27–37
Burns, Jordan 26
Burns, Kendallgapu 26–27
Burns, Ralph 26–28, 37; language education and 26–29
Burns, Wesleygapu 26–27
Burns, William 26

Cajete, Greg 4–5
Calderón, Arnulfo 133
Calfuqueo, Silvia 17, 177
California 26, 125; California State Board of Education 126; Common Core State Standards and 126; Southern California 133; University of California A-G high school graduation requirements and 126; *see also* Los Angeles
Canada 35, 49n2, 53
Cantares Mexicanos 8, 15–16, 125, 128–29, 133; content of 128; translation of (Miguel León Portilla) 128; *see also* Anawakalmekak
capitalism xviii, 74, 169, 174; neoliberal capitalism 177, 180; *see also* violence
Capulálpam de Méndez 81
Carhuamaca Huaman, Acisclo xxin2
Carhuamaca Huaman, Flora xxin2
Carhuamaca Huaman, Marina xxin2
Carhuancho, Huallallo (Waytapallana) xxin3
Cascade Mountains 51
CASEN *see* Socioeconomic Characterization Survey of Chile (CASEN)
Cayuse 51
CEDES *see* Center for Educational Studies and Development (CEDES)
censorship 14
Center for Educational Studies and Development (CEDES) 78, 80
ceremony 56, 60–62; Crying Ceremony 61; Na'i'ess ceremony 144–45; Ngillatun 192n2; puberty and 25; research and 130; *see also* ritual
Chang, Curt 162
cheqchiy xviii
Chicagoland 2, 27

Chicano 15
Chief Tahgee Elementary Academy 163
children and youth xix–xx, 6, 9, 13, 15–16, 26–35, 39, 46, 103, 105–107, 110, 128, 130, 145–47, 152, 154–56, 158–62, 168, 170, 174, 180, 187; boarding schools (residential schools) and 53, 147; childcare 36; daycare 31–32; English, forced learning of 42–43, 46; Head Start and 31–32, 37n2; punishment, for using Indigenous languages and 42–43, 118; self-esteem and 106; Western educational structures and 42; youth marriage and 114; *see also* Apache Youth Mentorship (AYM); boarding schools, list of; communities; Nez Perce; *Nunayaaġviŋmi itut Uvlumini (A Day at Camp)*
Chile 17, 165, 176–78, 181–83, 187, 189–92, 192nn3–5; anti-terrorist law and 183–84; Araucanía 183, 186; Biobío 183; culture and 179; education in 179–81, 189; Los Ríos 183; media in 182–85; Ministry of Social Development and Family and 165; monoculture and 180–81, 191–92; Pinochet dictatorship and 183; universities in 166–74; *see also* education, Indigenous; Mapuche; Socioeconomic Characterization Survey of Chile (CASEN)
ch'ixi xviii; *see also* cheqchiy; world, ch'ixi
Christianity: Apostles and 120; baptism and 53; churches 124, 139, 192n7; church leaders and 43; conversion and 12; Euro–Christian values and 32; evangelization and 12, 107, 129, 186, 200; Jesus and 120; salvation and 200; values and 53; *see also* god, European; missionaries
Cibecue 26, 30, 33, 36
Clark, William 53, 160
Clarkston 54
Clearwater River Casino 56, 62, 64; Héetwey Plaza and 64
climate change and crisis, global 2, 8–10, 110; activism and 130; *see also* Ngigua
CMPIO *see* Coalition of Indigenous Teachers and Promoters (CMPIO)
CNED *see* National Council of Education (CNED)
CNTE *see* National Coordinating Committee of State Workers (CNTE)

Coalition of Indigenous Teachers and Promoters (CMPIO) 113
de los Cobos, Maurice Pico 102
Coeur d'Alene 51
co-existence xviii
cognitive dissonance 155
Coixtlahuaca 86
Colín, Ernesto 15
Collao Quechua xviii, xxin1
collectives 6, 84; educational collectives 126; Indigenous collectives 10
colonialism and colonization xvii–xviii, 4, 11, 16, 31, 53, 155, 160, 180, 197, 199; books, destruction of 129; ideology and 31; institutions and 3; post-colonization and 180; settler colonialism 13, 34, 36, 50, 128, 157–58, 198; settler colonial migration trail and 27; violence and 51; *see also* boarding schools, list of; imperialism, European; missionaries; neocolonialism
coloniality xviii, xx, 198
Colorado 144
communities xvii–xviii, 7–9, 13, 23, 25–26, 28, 30, 33, 35–38, 40–43, 79–82, 94–96, 104–109, 118f, 126, 157, 174, 177, 186, 201; activism and 1, 10, 81; childcare and 36; collaborations/shared decision-making and 12, 14, 45–46, 48, 104, 107–108, 117; economic resources and 15; education and 2, 9, 15–17, 24, 27, 29, 44, 97; empowerment and 155, 171; family and xx, 2, 13, 16, 28–30, 34–35, 53, 97, 99, 105–106, 108–109, 151n1, 157, 161, 174, 177; Indigenous xx, 1, 3, 7–9, 14–15, 23, 39, 127, 139, 171, 177, 197, 201; knowledge and 2–3, 15, 77, 82f, 114, 116–17, 122–23, 127, 136, 201; leaders and xviii, 127; minoritized 34; Native 39–40; power and 105, 157; social action and 1; teachers/scholars and 76, 106, 114, 121, 153; tribal communities xx, 32; values of 117; *see also comunalidad* (communality)
comunalidad (communality) 14, 74, 78–84, 113, 122–23; Academia de la Comunalidad and 80; definition of 14, 74; education and 80; festa/celebrations and 74, 80–81; language and 74, 80–81, 84; tequio and 74, 80; self-government/assembly and 74, 80–81; territory and 74, 79–81

CONADI *see* National Corporation for Indigenous Development (CONADI)
conviviality xviii
Coronel-Molina, Serafín 10
Corps of Discovery 53
cosmology 35, 117–18, 128, 136
creators, Indigenous 7
critical discourse analysis 182
Cuentepec 128–29, 132–33
Cuicateco 87
cuisine xx, 124, 154
culture: identity and 131; Indigenous 107, 122, 170; revitalization of 16, 125, 190; survival of 131
Cusicanquim, Silvia Rivera xviii; *see also* world, ch'ixi
Cuthá 86

Dakota Access Pipeline 11
dance 39–40, 43, 45–46, 96, 107, 129; Aztecs and 126; colonial oppression of 46; reclamation of 47; Tecuane dancers and 132; *see also* Inupiat; Kingikmiut Dancers and Singers of Anchorage
decolonization 1, 3, 9–10, 17, 51, 53–55, 66, 131, 136, 197–202; decolonial possibility and xx–xxi; indigenization and 53, 66
Dehose, Francis 25
Dehose, Judy 25
Dehose, Julee xx, 13, 23–26, 28–31, 33–37; biography of 25–26; Butterfly clan (doolé) and 25; language education and 29–37; Row of White Cane People (Tło'ką̄ą̄ dogain) and 25
Dehose, Sarah 25
Dehose, Virgil Sr 25
Delgado, Amanda Galván 102
Democratic Movement of Education Workers of Oaxaca (MDTEO) 76
Dena'ina 40
devil, European xviii
DGEI *see* General Directorate of Indigenous Education (DGEI)
DGEIIB *see* General Directorate of Intercultural and Bilingual Indigenous Education (DGEIIB)
Díaz, Floriberto 80, 114
Dibaku 87
Diixazá (Zapotec) 7, 11, 87
discrimination 16–17, 89, 125, 167–70, 177, 180, 185
dreaming and dreams 34–36

Earth 139, 196; destruction of xix; Mother Earth 9, 11, 139
education: adult 5; communal 74–84; multilingual 4; state 1, 14; *see also comunalidad* (communality); education curricula; education, elementary; education, higher; education, Indigenous; education, land-based; education, middle/secondary; education, reform of; pedagogy
education, elementary 2, 33, 80, 83, 87–88, 91–94, 102, 115; bilingualism and 113; communal education and 80; Indigenous students and 14, 36, 48, 106, 113; *see also* Octavio Paz Indigenous Primary School (San Marcos Tlacoyalco); Plan para la Transformación de la Educación en Oaxaca (PTEO)
education, higher 74, 83–84, 114, 158; communal education and 80–81, 84; Indigenous students in 166–74; scholarships and 166, 178; Western Eurocentric perspectives and 166; *see also* Autonomous Communal University of Oaxaca (UACO)
education, Indigenous 1, 4, 6, 17, 28, 81, 87–100, 110, 186–88; Catholic schools, appropriation of 186, 192n7; Chile and 165–75; micro-teaching and 98; policies and 113–17; self-determination and 158, 170; *see also* education, land-based
education, land-based 2, 6–7, 9, 16, 34, 36, 62, 91, 109, 163; river-based activities and 6
education, middle/secondary 113–23, 126, 131; scholarships and 178
education, reform of 76, 83–84, 89, 115; *see also* Mexico
education curricula 10, 15, 17, 31, 89, 90, 98, 113, 125, 132–33, 170, 186; basic grades (Indigenous language education) and 106; decolonization and 136; Eurocentric 167; history teaching and 41; Indigenized curricula and 126–27; institutionalized curricula and 32; New Mexican School and 89, 91
elders 2, 6, 8, 26, 36, 38, 41, 54, 62, 100, 102–105, 110, 120, 139, 147, 152, 161, 168–69, 172; education and 41, 43–44, 94–95, 187; grandmothers 8, 26, 32, 64, 66, 96, 103, 139, 146, 151n1, 169, 177; grandfathers 8, 26, 42, 66, 103, 168–69; grandparents xx, 25–26, 30, 40–41, 43–45, 90, 94, 96, 99, 101–102, 105, 108, 116, 119–20, 147, 168
emergencies, cultural 179
English xviii, 26, 29, 32, 34–35, 40, 42–43, 46, 56, 124, 126, 129, 146–48, 198; alphabet of 43; standardization of 41, 49n2; teaching of xix, 44; *see also* Los Angeles
epistemologies, Indigenous 10, 12, 15–16, 55, 60, 62, 78, 136, 180–81, 197, 199–200; *see also* Apache
ethics 78, 96
ethnography 101, 200
etymology, Eurocentric 147

Facebook 94
Fairbanks 47
Federal Preventive Police (PFP) 76
Ferguson, Minnie 130
Fernández, Marta Silva 17
First Nations 36, 53, 200
Flathead 51
Florentine Codex 125, 128–29; *see also* Anawakalmekak
Flores Farfán, José Antonio 3, 102
Flores, Haydée Morales 14
FONCA *see* National Fund for Culture and the Arts (FONCA)
forests 755, 139, 169, 170–72, 183, 188
Fort Apache Reservation 26
Fort Bidwell 26
Fort Hall Indian Reservation 16, 155
Frank Church River of No Return Wilderness 159
Fraser R. 51

Gabrielino Shoshone 126
Galeano, Eduardo 91, 192n1
Garcia, Karen Eben 46
García, Rigoberto Vásquez 81
gaze, colonial 9–10, 200–201
gender 14, 32, 51, 63, 147; equity 114; fluidity 32; language and 147; roles 32; *see also* violence
General Directorate of Indigenous Education (DGEI) 93
General Directorate of Intercultural and Bilingual Indigenous Education (DGEIIB) 96, 110
genocide 8–9, 11, 41
god, European xviii
gods 69, 105
González, Beatriz 15

good, common 74, 78, 80
Google Earth 56
Grande, Sandy 153
grandparents *see* elders
gratitude 169, 192n2
Great Basin 26, 51
Greenland 49n2
Griñó, Paulina 2, 17
Guerrero 128, 132

healers and healing xvii, xix, 7, 9, 28–29, 44, 60–63, 103, 110, 128, 136, 153, 155
herbalists xvii
Hernández, Cornelio 15
Herrera Borja, Yolanda xxin2
Hñahñu/Otomi 87
Hñahtr/Mazahua 87
Ho-Chunk 2, 27
Hohepa, Margie Kahukura 35
horizontality 84
Huaman, Herminia Salazar xxin2
human rights 51, 170, 183; *see also* United Nations Human Rights Committee; Inter-American Court of Human Rights
hunting and fishing xix, 28, 40, 58, 153, 159–60; night fishing and 160; *see also* Apache; Inupiat

IB *see* International Baccalaureate (IB)
IBE *see* Intercultural Bilingual Education (IBE)
Idaho 16, 50–51, 158
Ikoots 116
imperialism, European xvii; linguistic 178
INALI *see* National Institute for Indigenous Languages (INALI)
India 11
Indigeneity 10–11
Indigenous Community Middle School (model) 113
Indigenous Community Middle Schools of Oaxaca 15
Indigenous Community Middle Schools (SECOIN) 15, 113–23, 123n1; achievements of 122–23; culture reclamation and 114; learning projects and 115–117, 122; media and 121–22; Parents' Representative Council and 122; research programs in 115–22; resources for 115; statistics for 114–15
individualism 122, 152, 197, 200
inequities and inequality 10, 162, 198; digital 1; economic 1, 10; power, asymmetrical 10, 13; power dynamics and 5; social 1; *see also* peoples, Indigenous

Institutional Revolutionary Party (PRI) 76
Instituto Superior Intercultural Ayuuk (ISIA) 80
intellectualism 158
Inter-American Court of Human Rights 183, 185
Intercultural Bilingual Education (IBE) 113, 122; Castilianization and 122
interculturalism 78, 173
interdisciplinarity 130–31
International Baccalaureate (IB) 126; Middle Years Program (MYP) (6–10) 126; Primary Years Program (PYP) (K-5) 126
International Labor Organization 183, 186; Convention 169 and 183
intersectionality 3
Inuit 10
Inupiaq 13, 38–42, 45–46, 49n2; educational materials and 46; English alphabet and 43; Kingikmiut dialect of 38–43, 45–48; Kingikmiut people 46–47; non-Native people and 41; *North Slope Inupiaq to English Dictionary* 43; North Slope region and 41; standardization, Western attempts at 39, 41; structure of 43; teaching of 41–44; teaching resources and 42, 45, 48; Utqiaġvik and 41; *see also Nunayaaġviŋmi itut Uvlumini* (*A Day at Camp*)
Inupiat xix, 38, 40–41, 44; culture and 46–47; dancing and 46–47; English language, unsuitability for 44; history of 40–41, 44; hunting and 40; *see also* Inupiaq
ISIA *see* Instituto Superior Intercultural Ayuuk (ISIA)
Ixcatec 87

Jara, Teresa Damian xix, 8, 14
justice 60–61, 165, 174; environmental 154; social justice 9, 157–58, 170; tribal justice 2

Kansas 144
karma 60
Kay Pacha xx
Kenzie, Early 25
Kenzie, Ida 25
Kidman, Joanna xx
Kingikmiut Dancers and Singers of Anchorage 39, 46; Aluii aniaq and 46; Float Coat Dance and 46; Kizhuq and 46; Tipsizuklui and 46

knowledge: forms of 78; hierarchies and 2, 4, 31; knowledge bearers 44, 121–22; place-based 6; scientific 17; sharing 24; suppression of 3; systems 32; transmission of 3, 118; *see also* communities; knowledge, Indigenous; land; languages, Indigenous; Ngigua; Niimíipuu; teachers; women
knowledge, Indigenous 5, 12, 31, 33–34, 36, 56, 107–108, 131, 156, 159–60, 167–74, 201; cemíitx (huckleberries) and 57, 57f, 61–63, 66; knowledge reclamation and 53; knowledge transfer and 31, 36; land and 66; scientific knowledge and 17; *see also* land; languages, Indigenous; Ngigua; Niimíipuu; teachers; women
Kopenawa, Davi 2
Korean 30
Kotzebue 49n2

land: dispossession and 17, 200; exploitation of 4; homelands and 6; knowledge co-production and 6; living beings and 6; reclamation 186; relationality and 6; rematriation 2, 37; removal 16; restoration 26; self-in-relationship with 6, 37; *see also* education, land-based
language activism 5, 7, 24, 31
language reclamation 1, 3–9, 12–13, 15, 23–25, 27, 31, 33, 35, 44, 51, 125, 157, 178, 201; arts and 7; colonial healing and 7; planetary well-being and 7; resources for 13
language restrictionism xviii; *see also* schools
languages: culture and 50–51; education of 5; language shift 5, 10, 13; commodification of 13; documentation of 5, 15, 41, 100–106, 108–109, 200; global xviii; hierarchies of 4; homogeneous/ideal 200; identity and 25, 39, 100; languages, dormant 9; minoritized 3–4, 7–8, 200; oral 46; relationships and 28–29, 31, 36; teaching of 24–37; values and 35; *see also* language activism; language reclamation; language restrictionism; languages, Indigenous; languages, revitalization of; languages, threatened/endangered
languages, Indigenous 3–4, 7, 10–11, 14, 17, 24–25, 35, 38, 74, 79, 89–90, 96–100, 114–23, 126, 131, 139, 177–81, 198; alphabets and 118–19; cinema production and 7; knowledge, transmission and 118; linguistic discrimination and 177; marginalization and 35, 177–78; speakers and 3, 44, 89, 146, 150; teaching of 27–37, 41–42, 88–97, 102, 106–110, 113–23, 133; uses for 118–19; *see also* language reclamation
languages, revitalization of 5, 16, 38, 45, 88, 92, 100–102, 107–108, 119, 125, 130, 176, 178–80, 185–90; resources and 38, 45; *see also* Mapuzugun; Ngigua language
languages, threatened/endangered xviii, 4, 9, 46–47, 88, 108; 'Verbal Arts of National Indigenous Languages at Risk of Disappearing' (registry) 100
Lapwai 51
LAUSD *see* Los Angeles Unified School District (LAUSD)
law, Indigenous 13–14, 50, 60; Niimíipuum tamáalwit and 62, 66; tamáalwit and 60–63
Leaders in Environment, Access, and Diversity (LEAD) 162
leadership, Indigenous 14, 126–27
Leonard, Wesley 3–4
Lewis, Meriwether 53, 160
Lieberman, Nicolás García 133
linguicide 9, 178
linguistics 94, 200–201; documentary linguistics 9, 101, 105–109; extractivist linguistics 11; hierarchies and 146; monolingualism and 200; salvage linguistics 200; translanguaging practices and 131
linguists 101, 105
listening and hearers 9, 37, 46, 55, 58, 95, 109, 116, 145, 152, 173, 187, 199
Llaguepulli 177; Kom Pu Lof Ñi Kimeltuwe (The School for All Communities) and 186–89
Lorenzo, Louie 9, 16, 145–48
Los Angeles 15, 124, 128, 132; Griffith Park 133; Indigenous language/cultures and 124–26; racism/discrimination and 125; Spanish/English, use of 124; *see also* Los Angeles Unified School District (LAUSD); Tongva; Tovangaar
Los Angeles Unified School District (LAUSD) 124, 126; Office of Civil Rights complaint and 125
Lott, Sam 66

Māori xx, 35
Mapuche 11, 17, 171–72, 176–92, 192n5; ancestral games and 176, 188–90, 190f, 191; anti-Mapuche discourse (Chile) and 176–85; azche philosophy and 189, 192n8; azmapu philosophy and 189–90; Argentina and 189; Bafkehce 186–87, 192n7; certificate of indigeneity and 178; Coordinadora Arauco-Malleco and 183; culture and cultural identity 17, 168–72, 176, 178, 180–81, 186, 188–89; denigration of, by Chilean media 182, 182f, 183–85; kimeltuwün and 190, 190f, 191–92; kimvn (knowledge) and 187–88; nature and 169; ngillatun ceremony and 180, 192n2; ontology/epistemology and 180; repression of, by Chilean government 183; society and 178; Spanish, resistance to 169–71; terrorists, designation as 183–85, 185f, 191; toma (takeover) and 186, 192n7; Weichan Auka Mapu and 183; *see also* Budi Lake; Llaguepulli; Mapudungun; Mapuzugun; Operation Hurricane; pedagogy; Wallmapu

Mapuche Federation of Students 177
Mapudungun 179
Mapuzugun 17, 177–81, 185–88, 188f, 192; endangered status of 178, 186, 191; marginalization of 177–78; non-official language status of 179; Raguileo writing system and 192n6; revitalization of 178–81, 185–90; Spanish, threat of 179–81; spirituality and 188; summer language camp for 177
Mariachi 129
Martin, Nathan 9
Martínez Luna, Jaime 74, 80–81, 114
Martínez, Xiuhtezcatl 130, 133
Matsaw, Abrianna 154f
Matsaw, Jessica xix, 8, 16, 154f
Matsaw, Luzahan 153
Matsaw, Malia 159
Matsaw, Sammy xix, 8, 16
Maya 3
Maya language 3
Maya Zapatista movement 11
Mazatec 87
MDTEO *see* Democratic Movement of Education Workers of Oaxaca (MDTEO)

meaning-making 3–4, 201
media 95, 100, 117, 120–22, 130; Argentine 184; films and 159, 177, 187; international media 184; mass media 176, 181–85; social media/networks 7, 120; Tik Tok 7; *see also* Chile; Indigenous Community Middle Schools (SECOIN); Mapuche; Operation Hurricane
medicines, Indigenous xvii, xix, 60, 67, 102–104, 107, 109, 153, 171; plants and 102–104
memory 69, 74, 76–77, 94, 119, 160
Menomenni 27
Me'phaa/Tlapanec 87
methodologies, Indigenous 55–57, 130
Mexica 87, 92
Mexico 3, 7, 10–11, 14, 36, 53, 73, 75, 88, 100, 102, 106–107, 113, 126, 129, 132, 144, 150; educational system and reform in 83–84, 89–91, 110, 113, 115; Ministry of Culture and 100; revolution of 105
Mexico City 133
Miami 27
Middle Fork (Salmon River) 16, 152, 154f, 155–56, 158, 161, 161f, 162–63, 163f
Ministry of Public Education (SEP) 96, 102, 110, 123n1
missionaries 53; bowdlerization and 54; North American 37n1; Presbyterian 53; Spanish 12; *see also* boarding schools, list of
Mixtec *see* Ñu Savi ('Mixtec'); Tu'un Savi/Mixtec
modernity xviii
Molala 51
monolingualism 96, 180, 200
Montana 51, 54
Monzón, Juan José Rendón 80
Morelos 128–29, 132–33
multicentricity 199
multiculturalism 78
multilingualism 7, 10, 28, 135, 199
music 7, 13, 45, 129–33; hip-hop 7; Indigenous 126; pre-Columbian 133; rap 7, 126; *see also* Anawakalmekak; dance; Natsiká, 'Travesía/Journey'; pop stars, Indigenous; songs
Myaamia 2–3

ñaa kuú 69–70
Nahua 128; culture of 129

Nahuatl 12, 15, 103, 125–32; classical 128, 133; modern 126, 129, 132–33; poetry and 125, 129; standardization of 129; *see also* Anawakalmekak; Cantares Mexicanos; Florentine Codex
Na'qáac 64, 66; *see also* Ramsey, Rena Katherine
Naranjo-Morse, Eliza xxi
Naranjo, Tessie xxin4
National Action Party (PAN) 76
National Agency for Research and Development in Chile (ANID) 167
National Coordinating Committee of State Workers (CNTE) 75–76
National Corporation for Indigenous Development (CONADI) 166, 183
National Council of Education (CNED) 166
National Fund for Culture and the Arts (FONCA) 100
National Institute for Indigenous Languages (INALI) 89, 100
National Science Foundation 39; Arctic Social Sciences Program 45
National Union of State Workers (SNTE) 75
Nation-building, Tribal 2
Nations, Native 34
Nations, Tribal 35
nation states 35, 178–79, 189, 191, 198
Native American Heritage Month 153
Natsiká, 'Travesía/Journey' 7
Nava, Farías 133
Nava, Victorino Torres 129, 133, 135
Ne'íic 64; *see also* Yearout, Rosa Mae Spencer
neocolonialism 17, 177; exploitation and 2
Nevada 26–27
Newene 16, 153, 157; colonial policies and 16
Newe (Shoshone) 27, 152
Newe (Western Shoshone) 26
New Zealand 36
Nez Perce 50, 50f, 51, 52f, 54, 64; boarding schools and 53; Nez Perce Reservation (North Central Idaho) 55; *see also* boarding schools, list of; Niimíipuu
Ngigua xix, 11, 14–15, 86–110, 199; biographies and 105; culture and 89, 91–92, 104, 107; Chochos/Chocholtecos, pejorative term for 87; climate change, impact on 110; evangelization and 107; health/public education policies and 107; identity and 100, 108; knowledge and 91, 96, 99–100, 103–105, 108–109; legends and 102; nchianchea (temazcal steam bath) and 97, 102–104, 109; plants/crops and 96–97, 97f, 101f, 102–105, 107, 110; PROSPERA and 107; rituals and 103–105; rural communities and 97; Spanish conquest and 105; spirits of 103; *Toriteros* dance and 107; *see also* Ngigua language; Octavio Paz Indigenous Primary School (San Marcos Tlacoyalco); pedagogy; Puebla; songs; women

Ngigua language 87–110; archive/register of 105–110; craft books and 99; documentation projects and 100–102, 105–109; endangered status of 88, 100, 108; Experiencias pedagógicas de docentes Nġiguas poblanos and 92; linguistic family of 87; oral proficiency, strategies for 98; Popoloca, pejorative name for 87, 92; resources and 94, 110; revitalization of 94–95; script of 94; strategies regarding 93; teaching of 87, 89–95, 95f, 96–99, 99f, 102, 104–110; Tsjen ku tangi (sing and learn) 98; Tsuntaaun ku tangi (play and learn) 98; verbal arts and 102–105; Verbal Arts of National Indigenous Languages at Risk of Disappearing (registry) 100

Nigeria 11
Niimíipuu 13, 50–51, 53, 57, 60, 62; bowdlerization and 53–54; Chief Joseph and Warriors powwow 64; Chief Timothy and 54; Christianity and 53; colonization, impact on 53; Crying Ceremony and 61; knowledge and 51, 54, 56, 58, 60, 66; Nimipuunéewit and 62; Nimipuuwíitki and 54, 60, 62; re-indigenization and 54; runners and 51; Teecukwenéewit and 54; territory of 51–53, 55, 67; waláhsat and 61; Wet ew éet and 63–64; *see also* law, Indigenous; Niimíipuu Female Educators; Niimíipuu Female Educators' Talking Circles; Nimipuutímt; titwáatit (story)
Niimíipuu Female Educators 14, 51, 55, 57–58, 66
Niimíipuu Female Educators' Talking Circles 51, 54–59, 61, 66; píiten'wet cíilpcilp, name for 55–57; trust/friendship and 55
Nimipuutímt 56, 64–65
Nome 47
Northwest River Supply 162

Nixon 26
Numic 160
Numu (Paiute) 25–26; Kedu Tuka'a band and 26; Kooyooe Tukadu band and 26
nunashimi xviii
Nunayaagviŋmi itut Uvlumini (*A Day at Camp*) 46, 47f
Ñu Savi ('Mixtec') 7

OARS–Idaho 162
Oaxaca 14–15, 73–83, 86–87, 113, 117; Afro–Mexicans and 113; Asunción Nochixtlan massacre 76–77; Cañada 114; characteristics of 75, 78, 80; education in 77–83; history of 75; Indigenous peoples and 79–81; Ixtlán de Juárez 120; languages of 75; laws in 115; Mixteca 76, 114; Papaloapan 114; pedagogical movement and 77, 81; San Pedro Yaneri 119–21; Santa María Zoogochí 120; Sierra Norte 81, 114, 119–20; Sierra Sur 81, 114; teachers' movement and 77, 79, 115; teachers' struggle and 75–77, 80, 83; Zócalo 76; *see also* Democratic Movement of Education Workers of Oaxaca (MDTEO); Indigenous Community Middle Schools of Oaxaca; Indigenous Community Middle Schools (SECOIN); National Coordinating Committee of State Workers (CNTE); Plan para la Transformación de la Educación en Oaxaca; Popular Assembly of the Peoples of Oaxaca (APPO); teachers
Octavio Paz Indigenous Primary School (San Marcos Tlacoyalco) 87, 90
Operation Hurricane 183–84; media and 184
oppression 8, 12
orality 176, 181
oral traditions 41, 53, 89, 94, 98, 100–106; oral history and 101
Oregon 51, 177

Pacheco, Jennifer Brito 17
Paiute 13, 27–29, 31; language, teaching of 27, 31–32; lifeways and 36; values of 32; Wycliffe alphabet and 29, 37n1; *see also* Numu (Paiute)
Palouse 51
PAN *see* National Action Party (PAN)
pandemic (Covid-19) 1, 3, 10, 13, 24–25, 31, 34–35, 55–56, 79, 97, 102–104, 108–109, 121–22, 199; education and 1–2, 13, 97, 102–104, 108, 127; language education and 25
Papua New Guinea 11
Patel, Leigh 1
patriarchy 180; hegemony and 13, 51
peace pipe 56
pedagogy 78, 109–23, 130; American 41–42; ancestral games and 176, 188–90, 190f, 191; Apache 147; ethnocentric policy and 113; Euro-Western 31, 110, 147; Indigenous 16, 113, 156; intercultural 166; monocultural 166, 178–81, 191–92; Ngigua 90, 92–100, 110; Red Pedagogy 157; revitalizing 131; Shoshone–Bannock 154, 156–60, 163
Peña, Felipe 105
Peñaloza, María Marisol 129, 131–32
Peña Nieto, Enrique 76
Penutian languages 51, 52f
peoples, Indigenous 1, 4–6, 12, 50, 54; agentivity and 3, 5; Andean xvii–xviii; collective work and 113; health care services and 2; inequities and inequality 1–2, 117; as informants 3; rural isolation and 2; *see also* elders; Oaxaca
Peoria (people) 2
Pérez, Tomasa Gómez 105
Perly, Bernard 200
perseverance 14
Peru xviii–xix, 11; population of xviii; Quechua speakers in xviii
Pete-Sanchez, Katherine 26
PFP *see* Federal Preventive Police (PFP)
philosophy 6, 17, 74, 78, 106, 109, 179, 189
Phoenix 34; Apache name for 34
pictographs 155, 161, 163
Picunche 2
Pinkham, Josiah 54
Plan para la Transformación de la Educación en Oaxaca (PTEO) 14, 74, 77–79, 83–84, 115; action areas of 77–78; funding and 79; resources and 79
plants and crops 96–97, 97f, 101f, 102–105, 107, 110, 119, 132, 150, 153, 169; cemíitx (huckleberries) and 57, 57f, 61–63, 66; corn and 93, 96, 105, 110, 119, 132, 195; maternal spirit and 132; sage and 55, 161; sweetgrass and 55; tobacco and 161; trees and 34, 97, 107, 119, 169, 172; wild carrots and 153; *see also* Anawakalmekak; knowledge, Indigenous; medicines, Indigenous; Ngigua

Plateau cultural area 51
plurality 78
Poblete, Carolina Kürüf 17
poetry xx, 7, 15, 125, 128–32; *Los cantos religiosos de los antiguos mexicanos* 131; *see also* Nahuatl
pop stars, Indigenous xviii
Popular Assembly of the Peoples of Oaxaca (APPO) 76
Portland 177
Potawatomi 2, 27
PowerPoint 93
powwows 64
prayer xxi, 25, 35, 105, 107
PRI *see* Institutional Revolutionary Party (PRI)
PTEO *see* Plan para la Transformación de la Educación en Oaxaca (PTEO)
Puebla 86–87, 92–94, 97, 106, 109; Cuayuca 87; San Gabriel Chilac 87; San Jose Buenavista 109; San Juan Ixcaquistla 87; San Marcos Tlacoyalco 87, 90, 94, 109; Santa Inés Ahuatempan 87; school zone 408 and 89, 92–93; Tepanco de López 87; Tepexi de Rodríguez 87; Tlacotepec de Benito Juárez 87, 89; Zapotitlán Salinas 87; *see also* Octavio Paz Indigenous Primary School (San Marcos Tlacoyalco)
Putnam Mt. 156*f*
Pyramid Lake Jr/Sr High School 26
Pyramid Lake Paiute Tribe 26
Pyramid Lake Reservation 26–27, 36

Quechua xvii–xviii, 10, 12; spoken xxin1; symbolic presence of xviii; varieties of xviii; written xxin1; *see also* Collao Quechua; Peru; Wanka Quechua; Yanantin
Quetzalcoatl 105

racism xviii, 5, 89, 125, 158, 168, 170, 180, 185, 200; policies and 34; racist gaze 192n3; systemic xviii; *see also* academics and the academy; discrimination; Los Angeles
Ramsey, Rena Katherine 64, 66
reciprocity 11, 24, 55, 84, 95, 108, 155, 160, 162, 169
reclamation 1, 3, 23; community histories and 3; cultural 2; definition of 3; ecological approach to 3–5; *see also* dance; knowledge, Indigenous; land; language reclamation

Reed High School 27
Reese River 26
relationality 1, 6, 55, 157, 160
religion 11–12, 44, 53, 121, 186, 128; *see also* Christianity; prayer; rituals
Reno 26
Reno–Sparks Indian Colony 26–27, 36; daycare at 31–32; Head Start at 31–32
Reno–Sparks Tribal Health Clinic 26
research, Indigenous xx, 62, 115–22; *see also* methodologies, Indigenous
research, reciprocal 38–39, 45
resilience 12, 131
resistance xix, 11–12, 14, 17, 23, 77, 80, 83–84, 107–108, 143, 155, 183–86, 191–92; collective 8; colonialism and 160, 169; educational 77; Indigenous 23; linguistic 178–80
revenge 58–61
ritual 6, 60–62, 96, 103, 105, 128–29, 180
River Newe 16, 152–58, 161–63, 163*f*, 164; community-based learning and 156; Isha (wolf) teachings and 159; relationship-building 156; *River of Return* 159; salmon camp and 159
Rocky Mountains 51
Rodeo–Chediski fires 33
Ruiz, Felipe 7
Ruiz, Ulises 76
runakuna xix
runasimi xviii–xix

Sahaptian 51
Saint Mary's Hospital 26
Salish 51
Salmon River 159, 161; *see also* Middle Fork (Salmon River)
San Carlos Apache 16, 27–28, 35; Chiricahua and 144; Eastern White Mountain and 144; Eurocentric definition of 144; Tonto and 144; Western White Mountain and 144; *see also* San Carlos Apache Reservation
San Carlos Apache Reservation 144; assimilation and 144; poverty/suicide and 144; substance abuse and 144
Sanchez, Anita 26
Sánchez, Celerina Patricia 7
Sanchez, Tony Sr. 26
Santa María Yaviche 81
Santiago 2, 192n4
Santiago, Gustavo Ramírez 81

schools 5, 7–8, 12, 16, 105–106, 124, 131, 139, 179–81, 186–88; charter schools 125–26, 130; Euro–Western school formats and 5, 33; language restrictionism in xviii; resources and 36; reterritorialization and 125; schooling paradox 3; sport in 189; timeframes and 199; *see also* boarding schools, list of; children and youth
sciences, natural 166–68
SCJN *see* Supreme Court of Justice of the Nation (SCJN)
SECOIN *see* Indigenous Community Middle Schools (SECOIN)
Seis, Vicente 132
self, concept of 11
self determination 14, 51, 92, 155, 157–58, 170
self-in-relation 6, 24; *see also* land
SEP *see* Ministry of Public Education (SEP)
Shoshone 26, 32, 157–58; language diversity and 160; Western Shoshone 26; *see also* Newe (Western Shoshone); Shoshone–Bannock
Shoshone–Bannock xx, 16, 152–53, 155–59, 162–63, 163f, 164; tygi and 153, 156, 160; *see also* Newene; pedagogy
Siberia 40
Simpson, Leanne Betasamosake 62
slaves and slavery 41–42
Smith, David E.K. xix, 13, 38–49; biography of 40
Smith, Linda T. 153, 160
Smokey Valley 26
smoking 56
sociology 78, 94
SNTE *see* National Union of State Workers (SNTE)
Socioeconomic Characterization Survey of Chile (CASEN) 165–66
songs 39–40, 56, 92, 107, 133–36; bird songs and 133; chants 56; Tsjen ku tangi (Sing and learn) 98; *see also* Kingikmiut Dancers and Singers of Anchorage
South Korea 30
sovereignty, Indigenous 2, 11, 157, 180
space-making, practice of 1
Spain xviii
Spalding, Henry Harmon 53–54; bowdlerization and 54
Spanish 2, 14–15, 74, 80, 93, 96, 107, 119, 126, 129, 133, 179–82, 189, 199; hegemony of 119, 189, 191; inadequacy of, for Indigenous ceremonies 180; monoculture and 179; *Royal Spanish Academic Dictionary* 184; *see also* Los Angeles
Sparks 27
speakers xix, 7, 44, 101, 146, 150, 200; commodification of 13; as informants 5; Kingikmiut and 44–45; neo-speakers 9; *see also* languages, Indigenous
spirits 55, 103; anthropomorphic spirits 145
Spokane 51
State Public Universities (UPE) 83
STEAM (Science, Technology, Engineering, Art, and Mathematics) 16, 162
STEM (Science, Technology, Engineering, and Mathematics) 158–59
Stevens, Philip 6, 16, 27
Stevens, Vanessa 27–28, 35; biography of 27–28
stories 51, 93, 98; Indigenous stories 53–54, 66; oral stories and 96; sexual content and 54–55; Western worldview and 53; *see also* storytelling; storywork; titwáatit (story); women
storytelling 14, 51, 145; *see also* storywork; titwáatit (story); women
storywork 16, 55, 58, 60, 66
Sumida Huaman, Elizabeth 6, 9
Summer Institute of Linguistics 37n1
sun 58, 139
Supreme Court of Justice of the Nation (SCJN) 83
survivance 131

Talaltlílpt, Angel Sobotta 8, 13–14
talking circles 51, 55; spiritual connections and 55; *see also* Niimíipuu Female Educators' Talking Circles
Tawantinsuyu xvii–xviii, 136
teachers 1–2, 4, 6, 10, 15, 27–37, 41–44, 47, 76–79, 87, 92, 101–123, 131, 133; activism and 23; Euro-Western ideas of 24; ghettoization of 14; Indigenous elementary school educator (title) 89, 95; as knowledge managers 106, 118; learner-teachers and 127, 135; as mediators 106; as policymakers 10; resources for 105–107; training of 88; *see also* communities; Democratic Movement of Education Workers of Oaxaca (MDTEO); education, Indigenous; Niimíipuu Female Educators; Oaxaca

Tecamachalco 86
Tehuacán Viejo 86
Tempe 177
Temuco 170
Tepexi el Viejo 86
Teqsimuyu xvii, xxin1
Terraciano, Kevin 129
Tewa xxi, 4
thought, Indigenous xviii, 4, 24
titwáatit (story) 14, 51, 54, 56–66; Animal People 55, 65–66; Hayóoxchacwal kaa Paqáxpaqax (Cottontail Boy and Small Rattlesnake) 58, 65; K'assaynóomy'ac (Elbow Child/baby) and 58–59, 59f, 60–62, 65, 65f; land, links to 51, 64; Netíitelwit and 57, 66; Niimíipuu and 54; Titwatiyaw'áat/co-Titwatiyaw'áat (storyteller/co-storyteller) 55–66; Titwatityáaya (story people) 55, 57, 66; Tukeyúutpe (Laying Down Place) 58; Weх̱wéqt and 65; *see also* titwáatit (themes)
titwáatit (themes); boundaries and responsibility 60–61, 63; epistemology 60; ceremony and ritual 60–62; grief/mourning and 62; healing and 61; hostile aggression/violence/unhealthy coping 60; justice/karma 60; protection/caring 60–61; revenge, forgiveness, and healing 60–63, 66
Tlacopan 133
Tongva 124, 132–33
Tovangaar 124
trauma, colonial/historical 8, 131, 155
treaty rights 157–58
trilingualism 125, 131
Tucson 24
Tu'un Savi/Mixtec 87
Turtle Island 159

UACO *see* Autonomous Communal University of Oaxaca (UACO)
Umatilla 51
UNICEM *see* Universidad Intercultural de Cempoaltépetl (UNICEM)
unions 75–76
United Nations Declaration on the Rights of Indigenous Peoples 125
United Nations Educational, Scientific, and Cultural Organization (UNESCO) 88, 178
United Nations Human Rights Committee 185
United States Army 40; Corps of Engineers and 54

United States Navy 42
United States of America 35–36, 40–41, 50, 53, 176–77, 181; Federal Indian Self-Education policy in 10
Universidad Intercultural de Cempoaltépetl (UNICEM) 80–81
University of Arizona 24
University of California, Los Angeles 129
University of Fairbanks 49
University of Idaho 51
University of Nevada–Reno 27
University of New Mexico 30
University of Santiago de Chile 177
UPE *see* State Public Universities (UPE)
Uto-Aztecan (linguistic branch) 133, 160

Veil Falls 163f
Vietnam 40
violence 60, 76–77, 158; capitalism and 74; gender-based xvii

Wadsworth 27
Wajmapu 186–87
Wales (Kingigin) 39–40, 42, 46–47, 49n2
Wallawalla 51
Wallmapu 10–11, 17, 178–79; occupation of 179, 186–87
Wanka Quechua xvii–xviii, 9
Washington (state) 50–51, 54
Washiw (Washoe) 27
Washoe County School District 27
Wasu 32
water 4, 30, 34–35, 54, 75, 103, 105, 120, 127, 139, 154–55, 161, 171, 200; rain and 69, 104–105, 139, 188; water resources 26, 30; water safety 46, 49n3; *see also* Middle Fork (Salmon River); River Newe
Watters, Samuel 56
wealth distribution 34
wellness and well-being 2, 4, 7, 12, 16, 23, 31–32, 35, 62, 197, 199
Wheel of Fortune (tv show) 29
White, Vanna 29
Wilson, Elizabeth Penney 56
Wilson, Shawn 55
Winnemucca, Bernita 26
wisdom 57, 66–67, 100, 110; in-between spaces/liminality and 3; Indigenous 127, 135; salmon wisdom 16
Wiitmíipn'ime 66
world, ch'ixi xviii
world, natural xviii
worlds, Indigenous xvii, xix

worldviews, Indigenous 54, 171–73; language and 60
women xvii, 25–26, 28, 75, 103, 105, 147, 173–74, 176–77, 185, 189; Apache Sunrise Dance and 25; aunts 28, 63; daughters xxin2, 2, 25, 27–28, 54, 58–59, 61, 66, 154, 159, 162, 196; feminism and 75, 197; gendered responsibility and 63; human rights and 51; knowledge and 51, 177; menstruation and 32; mothers 2, 26–28, 30, 34, 64, 74, 103, 146, 154, 169, 171, 173, 177; Na'i'ess ceremony and 144–45; patriarchy and 51; as storytellers 14, 51; *see also* elders; Niimíipuu Female Educators
writing, collective 98
Wycliffe Bible Translators 37n1
Wyoming 51

Xidza' Didza' (Zapotec) 15, 119–20
Xidza' *see* Xidza' Didza' (Zapotec)
Xinachcalco Center 133

Yakamas 51
Yanantin xvii–xviii
Yanomami 2
yarning 23–24, 36–37
Yearout, Rosa Mae Spencer 64
Yucatan 3
Yupe naap, Diana 152
Yupik 40

Zapotec 118–20; alphabet of 120; *see also* Diixazá (Zapotec); Xidza' Didza' (Zapotec)
Zoom 24–25, 55

For Product Safety Concerns and Information please contact our EU Authorised Representative:

Easy Access System Europe

Mustamäe tee 50

10621 Tallinn

Estonia

gpsr.requests@easproject.com